Cooking Light.

fresh food superfast

Cooking Light®

fresh
food
superfast

Oxmoor House®

ISBN-13: 978-0-8487-3433-6
ISBN-10: 0-8487-3433-5
Library of Congress Control Number: 2010933262
Printed in the United States of America
First Printing 2011

Be sure to check with your health-care provider before making any changes in your diet.

Oxmoor House

VP, Publishing Director: Jim Childs
Editorial Director: Susan Payne Dobbs
Brand Manager: Michelle Turner Aycock
Managing Editor: Laurie S. Herr

Cooking Light® Fresh Food Superfast

Senior Editor: Heather Averett
Project Editor: Holly D. Smith
Senior Designer: Emily Albright Parrish
Director, Test Kitchens: Elizabeth Tyler Austin
Assistant Director, Test Kitchens: Julie Christopher
Test Kitchens Professionals: Wendy Ball, Allison E. Cox, Torie Cox, Julie Gunter, Alyson M. Haynes, Kathleen Royal Phillips, Catherine Crowell Steele
Photography Director: Jim Bathie
Senior Photo Stylist: Kay E. Clarke
Associate Photo Stylist: Katherine Eckert Coyne
Production Manager: Theresa Beste-Farley

Contributors:

Copy Editor: Dolores Hydock
Proofreader: Norma Butterworth-McKittrick
Indexer: Mary Ann Laurens
Nutritional Analyses: Lauren Page, RD
Interns: Sarah Bélanger, Christine T. Boatwright, Mary Britton Sensenney, Allison Sperando, Caitlin Watzke
Photographer: Lee Harrelson
Photo Stylist: Mindi Shapiro

Cooking Light®

Editor: Scott Mowbray
Creative Director: Carla Frank
Deputy Editor: Phillip Rhodes
Food Editor: Ann Taylor Pittman
Special Publications Editor: Mary Simpson Creel, MS, RD
Nutrition Editor: Kathy Kitchens Downie, RD
Associate Food Editors: Timothy Q. Cebula, Julianna Grimes
Associate Editors: Cindy Hatcher, Brandy Rushing
Test Kitchens Director: Vanessa T. Pruett
Assistant Test Kitchens Director: Tiffany Vickers Davis
Chief Food Stylist: Charlotte Autry
Senior Food Stylist: Kellie Gerber Kelley
Recipe Testers and Developers: Robin Bashinsky, Adam Hickman, Deb Wise
Art Director: Fernande Bondarenko
Junior Deputy Art Director: Alexander Spacher
Associate Art Director: Rachel Lasserre
Designer: Chase Turberville
Photo Director: Kristen Schaefer
Senior Photographer: Randy Mayor
Senior Photo Stylist: Cindy Barr
Photo Stylist: Leigh Ann Ross
Copy Chief: Maria Parker Hopkins
Assistant Copy Chief: Susan Roberts
Research Editor: Michelle Gibson Daniels
Editorial Production Director: Liz Rhoades
Production Editor: Hazel R. Eddins
Art/Production Assistant: Josh Rutledge
Administrative Coordinator: Carol D. Johnson
CookingLight.com Editor: Allison Long Lowery
Production Assistant: Mallory Daugherty

To order additional publications, call 1-800-765-6400.

For more books to enrich your life, visit **oxmoorhouse.com**

To search, savor, and share thousands of recipes, visit **myrecipes.com**

Cover: Apricot-Glazed Grilled Chicken Thighs, page 292
Front flap: Chili-Lime Flank Steak, page 228
Back cover: Coconut Corn Chowder with Chicken, page 48; Beef and Bok Choy Stir-Fry, page 227; Mahimahi with Grilled Pineapple, page 183

welcome

On the heels of our best-selling Fresh Food Fast series, including *Cooking Light Fresh Food Fast* and *Cooking Light Fresh Food Fast: Weeknight Meals,* comes our latest, greatest quick-meal cookbook: *Cooking Light Fresh Food Superfast.* This book is jam-packed with more than 280 delicious 5-ingredient, 15-minute recipes—more than 100 of which boast 4 ingredients or can be prepared in 10 minutes or less! Now that's superfast!

With high-flavor ingredients and ease of preparation, each tried-and-true recipe meets at least one of these two criteria: It calls for five ingredients or less (excluding water, flour, cooking spray, oil, salt, pepper, and optional ingredients) or it can be prepared in 15 minutes or less. And many even fill the bill for both!

Cooking Light Fresh Food Superfast resembles its popular predecessors but is updated with even more exciting features such as:
- "Fix It Faster" tip boxes offering ways to speed things up
- "Ingredient Spotlights" focusing on fresh ingredients
- "Quick Flips" providing substitution ideas to completely transform a recipe into a new one

And if all that is not enough, we've even added a Seasonal Produce Guide offering guidelines for buying the freshest produce for optimal flavor and cost savings, as well as a section devoted to our Test Kitchens experts' favorite kitchen tools and gadgets.

For busy cooks who want to maintain a healthy lifestyle without sacrificing time and flavor, this book is a must-have. Here's to making healthy taste great superfast!

The *Cooking Light* Editors

contents

66

28

141

welcome, 5

soups, 8
These one-dish meals fill the bill for any occasion and are always in season.

sandwiches, 50
Turn the usual grab-and-go fare into memorable meals with these inspired variations.

salads, 92
Seasonal fruits and vegetables star in colorful combinations for simple suppers.

meatless main dishes, 134
Only minutes in the making, these tasty meals creatively marry fresh ingredients.

237

216

337

fish and shellfish, 176
Versatile, fast-cooking fish offers a light, healthy option for easy weeknight dinners.

meats, 218
Serve one of these hearty, satisfying entrées when you're short on time.

poultry, 260
Savor a variety of classic to contemporary recipes that will please everyone.

desserts, 302
Indulge in any of these delectable sweet treats from home-style puddings to elegant delights.

seasonal produce guide, 354
time-saving tools & gadgets, 358
nutritional analysis, 360
metric equivalents, 361
index, 362

soups

Gazpacho with Smoky Shrimp, 10
Quick Shrimp Gumbo, 12
Borscht, 15
Garbanzo-Carrot Soup, 16
Greek Lentil Soup with Mint-Yogurt Sauce, 19
Minestrone, 21
Roasted Tomato–Basil Soup, 22
Creamy Roasted Red Bell Pepper Soup, 25
Curried Vegetable Soup, 26
Baked Potato Soup, 28
Broccoli-Cheese Soup, 31
Easy Vegetable-Beef Soup, 33
Beef and Barley Soup, 34
Beer-Braised Beef Stew, 37
White Bean and Lamb Soup with Gremolata, 39
Chorizo Rice and Bean Soup, 40
Chicken Pot Sticker Soup, 43
Chicken Posole Chili, 44
Chicken Tortilla Soup, 46
Coconut Corn Chowder with Chicken, 48

Gazpacho with Smoky Shrimp

Prep: 5 minutes • Cook: 4 minutes

1 (14.5-ounce) can fire-roasted diced
  tomatoes with garlic
1½ cups chopped cucumber
1 (8-ounce) container refrigerated prechopped
  tomato, onion, and bell pepper mix

1 cup water
2 tablespoons red wine vinegar
¼ teaspoon salt
¼ teaspoon freshly ground black pepper
Smoky Shrimp

1. Place diced tomatoes in a food processor; process until smooth. Pour tomato puree into a bowl. Place cucumber and tomato, onion, and bell pepper mix in processor; pulse 5 times or just until chunky. Add cucumber mixture to tomato puree. Stir in 1 cup water and next 3 ingredients.
2. Prepare Smoky Shrimp.
3. Ladle soup into 4 bowls; top evenly with shrimp. Yield: 4 servings (serving size: about 1 cup soup and 7 to 8 shrimp).

CALORIES 171; FAT 2.2g (sat 0.5g, mono 0.5g, poly 1.1g); PROTEIN 24.8g; CARB 11.1g; FIBER 2.3g; CHOL 172mg; IRON 3.1mg; SODIUM 475mg; CALC 78mg

Smoky Shrimp

Prep: 2 minutes • Cook: 4 minutes

1 pound peeled and deveined large shrimp
1 large garlic clove, minced
1 teaspoon smoked paprika

¼ teaspoon salt
¼ teaspoon crushed red pepper
Cooking spray

1. Combine all ingredients except cooking spray in a bowl; toss well.
2. Heat a large nonstick skillet over medium-high heat. Coat pan with cooking spray. Add shrimp mixture; sauté 3 to 5 minutes or until shrimp reach desired degree of doneness. Yield: 4 servings (serving size: about 7 to 8 shrimp).

CALORIES 124; FAT 2g (sat 0.5g, mono 0.4g, poly 1g); PROTEIN 23.2g; CARB 1.6g; FIBER 0.2g; CHOL 172mg; IRON 2.8mg; SODIUM 314mg; CALC 62mg

fix it faster

Take a tip from savvy shoppers to get dinner on the table fast: Buy shrimp already peeled and deveined. It's a clever shortcut and time-saver.

Chilling this refreshing summer soup makes it a little more special and is worth the extra time if you have it. The fire-roasted tomatoes and paprika add a smoky zing.

Quick Shrimp Gumbo
Prep: 1 minute • Cook: 14 minutes

Cooking spray
4 ounces reduced-fat smoked turkey sausage (such as Oscar Mayer), chopped
1 (16-ounce) package frozen gumbo vegetables (such as McKenzie's)
1 (14.5-ounce) can diced tomatoes with zesty mild green chiles, undrained
1½ cups water
2 teaspoons salt-free Cajun seasoning (such as Frontier)
¼ teaspoon freshly ground black pepper
1 bay leaf
2 tablespoons all-purpose flour
1 tablespoon canola oil
1 pound peeled and deveined medium shrimp
Hot sauce (optional)

1. Heat a Dutch oven over medium-high heat. Coat pan with cooking spray. Add sausage; cook 2 minutes or until browned, stirring occasionally. Add frozen vegetables; cook 2 minutes or until vegetables thaw, stirring occasionally. Stir in tomatoes and next 4 ingredients. Bring to a boil.

2. While soup comes to a boil, combine flour and oil in a small microwave-safe bowl, stirring until smooth. Microwave at HIGH 2 minutes to 2 minutes and 30 seconds, stirring after 30 seconds and then every 15 seconds. Stir flour mixture and shrimp into soup; cover, reduce heat, and simmer 4 minutes or until shrimp turn pink and soup is slightly thick. Remove bay leaf. Serve soup with hot sauce, if desired. Yield: 6 servings (serving size: 1½ cups).

CALORIES 191; FAT 5.4g (sat 1g, mono 2.4g, poly 1.9g); PROTEIN 19.8g; CARB 14.2g; FIBER 2.5g; CHOL 127mg; IRON 2.5mg; SODIUM 644mg; CALC 93mg

serve with
Cajun Rice
Prep: 1 minute • Cook: 5 minutes

1 (8.8-ounce) package ready-to-serve whole-grain brown rice (such as Uncle Ben's)
Cooking spray
1 cup refrigerated prechopped celery, onion, and bell pepper mix
¼ cup fat-free, lower-sodium chicken broth
1 teaspoon salt-free Cajun seasoning (such as Frontier)
2 teaspoons chopped fresh oregano (optional)

1. Microwave rice according to package directions.

2. While rice cooks, heat a medium saucepan over medium-high heat. Coat pan with cooking spray. Add celery mix; cook 2 minutes or until tender, stirring occasionally. Stir in rice, chicken broth, Cajun seasoning, and, if desired, oregano. Cook 2 minutes or until liquid evaporates. Yield: 6 servings (serving size: about ⅓ cup).

CALORIES 73; FAT 1.3g (sat 0.2g, mono 0.5g, poly 0.5g); PROTEIN 1.8g; CARB 13.8g; FIBER 1g; CHOL 0mg; IRON 0.3mg; SODIUM 30mg; CALC 5mg

Gumbo in 15 minutes? You bet! The secret is to prepare the roux in the microwave. It can even be made ahead, cooled completely, covered, and chilled. Just reheat over low heat before using.

This richly colored, hearty soup doesn't miss a beat. Accompany the Russian-inspired dish with meat pierogi or a main-dish salad.

Borscht

Prep: 10 minutes • Cook: 18 minutes

Dill Sour Cream
- 1 tablespoon olive oil
- 5 cups coarsely chopped peeled beets (about 3 large)
- 2 cups chopped onion
- 2 cups chopped peeled celeriac (celery root)

- 1 (32-ounce) carton fat-free, lower-sodium beef broth
- ¼ teaspoon salt
- ¼ teaspoon freshly ground black pepper
- Fresh dill sprigs (optional)

1. Prepare Dill Sour Cream.
2. Heat oil in a Dutch oven over medium-high heat. Add beets, onion, and celeriac. Sauté 8 minutes or until vegetables are golden brown. Add broth, salt, and pepper. Bring to a boil; cover, reduce heat, and simmer 7 minutes or until beets are tender.
3. Place one-third of beet mixture in a blender. Remove center piece of blender lid (to allow steam to escape); secure blender lid on blender. Place a clean towel over opening in blender lid (to avoid splatters). Blend until smooth. Pour into a bowl. Repeat procedure twice with remaining beet mixture.
4. Ladle soup into bowls. Top each serving with a dollop of Dill Sour Cream, and, if desired, garnish with fresh dill sprigs. Yield: 6 servings (serving size: 1⅓ cups soup and about 1 tablespoon sour cream).

CALORIES 108; FAT 4.9g (sat 1.9g, mono 2.4g, poly 0.4g); PROTEIN 3.7g; CARB 13.2g; FIBER 2.4g; CHOL 8mg; IRON 0.7mg; SODIUM 569mg; CALC 61mg

Dill Sour Cream

Prep: 2 minutes

- ½ cup reduced-fat sour cream
- 2 tablespoons chopped fresh dill

- 1 teaspoon grated lemon rind
- ¼ teaspoon salt

1. Combine all ingredients in a small bowl; cover and chill until ready to serve. Yield: 6 servings (serving size: about 1 tablespoon).

CALORIES 27; FAT 2.4g (sat 1.5g, mono 0.7g, poly 0.1g); PROTEIN 0.6g; CARB 0.9g; FIBER 0.04g; CHOL 8mg; IRON 0mg; SODIUM 105mg; CALC 22mg

Stir-ins make soups fun, and hummus is the secret to the creamy texture of this savory one. Because there are so many flavored varieties of hummus, there's no reason to use a plain-Jane version. Experiment with different options until you find your favorite.

Garbanzo-Carrot Soup
Prep: 3 minutes • Cook: 18 minutes

1 tablespoon olive oil
½ cup diced carrot
1 (16-ounce) can reduced-sodium chickpeas (garbanzo beans; such as Bush's), rinsed and drained
3 cups organic vegetable broth
¼ teaspoon freshly ground black pepper
½ cup refrigerated spicy hummus (such as Sabra)
Sliced green onions (optional)

1. Heat oil in a Dutch oven over medium-high heat. Add carrot and chickpeas; sauté 4 minutes or until lightly browned. Add half of broth and pepper, scraping pan to loosen browned bits. Mash chickpeas slightly with a potato masher. Stir in remaining broth. Bring to a boil; cover, reduce heat, and simmer 5 minutes. Uncover, and simmer 5 minutes or until carrot is tender.
2. Add hummus to soup, stirring until blended. Ladle soup into bowls, and top with green onions, if desired. Yield: 4 servings (serving size: 1 cup).

CALORIES 178; FAT 10.6g (sat 1.5g, mono 5.6g, poly 3.4g); PROTEIN 5.6g; CARB 19.3g; FIBER 4.2g; CHOL 0mg; IRON 1.5mg; SODIUM 647mg; CALC 33mg

serve with
Feta-Olive Sandwiches
Prep: 10 minutes

⅔ cup (5.2 ounces) tub-style fat-free cream cheese
3 tablespoons crumbled feta cheese with basil and sun-dried tomatoes
4 teaspoons chopped pitted kalamata olives
¼ teaspoon freshly ground black pepper
4 (1½-ounce) whole-grain white sandwich thins (such as Pepperidge Farm), split and toasted
2 cups loosely packed arugula

1. Combine first 4 ingredients in a small bowl, stirring until smooth. Spread cheese mixture evenly on bottoms of sandwich thins; top each with ½ cup arugula and tops of sandwich thins. Yield: 4 servings (serving size: 1 sandwich).

CALORIES 168; FAT 3.6g (sat 0.8g, mono 1.2g, poly 1.4g); PROTEIN 14.4g; CARB 23.8g; FIBER 5.4g; CHOL 12mg; IRON 1.2mg; SODIUM 560mg; CALC 284mg

4-ingredient

A minty yogurt sauce energizes this bold lentil soup and adds traditional Mediterranean flavor.

Greek Lentil Soup with Mint-Yogurt Sauce

Prep: 9 minutes • Cook: 19 minutes

2 teaspoons olive oil
1 cup refrigerated prechopped onion
½ cup chopped carrot
2 cups organic vegetable broth
¼ teaspoon pepper

⅛ teaspoon salt
2 (15-ounce) cans organic lentils
Mint-Yogurt Sauce
Fresh mint or cilantro sprigs (optional)

1. Heat oil in a Dutch oven over medium-high heat. Add onion and carrot. Cook 4 minutes or until vegetables are lightly browned, stirring occasionally. Stir in broth and next 3 ingredients. Bring to a boil; reduce heat, and simmer, uncovered, 10 minutes or until carrot is tender. While soup simmers, prepare Mint-Yogurt Sauce. Ladle soup into bowls. Top with Mint-Yogurt Sauce and, if desired, fresh mint or cilantro. Yield: 4 servings (serving size: 1½ cups soup and 2 tablespoons sauce).

CALORIES 234; FAT 2.5g (sat 0.3g, mono 1.8g, poly 0.3g); PROTEIN 16.4g; CARB 36.6g; FIBER 16.2g; CHOL 0mg; IRON 0.4mg; SODIUM 628mg; CALC 43mg

Mint-Yogurt Sauce

Prep: 6 minutes

½ cup plain fat-free Greek yogurt
1 tablespoon chopped fresh mint
1 tablespoon chopped fresh cilantro

1 teaspoon ground cumin
1 teaspoon grated lemon rind
2 garlic cloves, minced

1. Combine all ingredients in a small bowl. Yield: 4 servings (serving size: 2 tablespoons).

CALORIES 20; FAT 0.1g (sat 0g, mono 0.1g, poly 0g); PROTEIN 2.7g; CARB 2g; FIBER 0.3g; CHOL 0mg; IRON 0.2mg; SODIUM 12mg; CALC 28mg

quick flip

Turn the Mint-Yogurt Sauce into Dill-Yogurt Sauce by substituting dill, parsley, and green onions for the mint, cilantro, and cumin. Fresh, wispy dill adds a sweet, citrusy hint to this Mediterranean-inspired sauce.

Healthy greens and sautéed pancetta add a contemporary flavor to this Italian mainstay. The Basil-Asiago Grissini, an update on crisp breadsticks, help kick off the fun. Cook the pasta separately to make the soup even faster.

Minestrone
Prep: 3 minutes • Cook: 15 minutes

¼ cup uncooked ditalini (very short tube-shaped macaroni)
2 ounces pancetta, chopped
1 cup refrigerated prechopped celery, onion, and bell pepper mix
½ cup chopped carrot
2 cups chopped Swiss chard
1 cup water

1 (15-ounce) can no-salt-added cannellini beans, rinsed and drained (such as Eden Organic)
1 (14.5-ounce) can no-salt-added diced tomatoes, undrained
1 (14-ounce) can fat-free, lower-sodium chicken broth

1. Cook pasta according to package directions, omitting salt and fat. Drain.
2. While pasta cooks, cook pancetta in a Dutch oven over medium-high heat 3 minutes or until browned, stirring frequently. Add celery mix and carrot; cook 3 minutes or until vegetables are tender and browned. Stir in chard and next 4 ingredients. Bring mixture to a boil; cover, reduce heat, and simmer 6 minutes. Stir in pasta. Yield: 4 servings (serving size: 1½ cups).

CALORIES 176; FAT 5.5g (sat 2.1g, mono 2.4g, poly 1g); PROTEIN 8.1g; CARB 24.1g; FIBER 5.6g; CHOL 10mg; IRON 1.9mg; SODIUM 619mg; CALC 62mg

serve with
Basil-Asiago Grissini
Prep: 3 minutes • Cook: 12 minutes

½ sheet frozen puff pastry dough, thawed
Cooking spray
1 large egg white, lightly beaten
⅓ cup (1.3 ounces) shredded Asiago cheese

½ teaspoon dried basil
¼ teaspoon garlic powder
¼ teaspoon freshly ground black pepper

1. Preheat oven to 400°.
2. Place pastry dough on a baking sheet coated with cooking spray. Press pastry into a 9½ x 5–inch rectangle. Brush egg white over pastry. Sprinkle evenly with cheese and remaining ingredients. Cut pastry into 8 thin strips. Carefully twist each strip into a curly breadstick about 10 inches long.
3. Bake at 400° for 12 to 13 minutes or until browned. Yield: 4 servings (serving size: 2 grissini).

CALORIES 62; FAT 3.9g (sat 2g, mono 0.9g, poly 0.9g); PROTEIN 4g; CARB 2.5g; FIBER 0.2g; CHOL 9mg; IRON 0.3mg; SODIUM 63mg; CALC 94mg

fix it faster

Short on time? You can save a step by substituting quick-fix refrigerated tortelloni stuffed with chicken and prosciutto for the ditalini and pancetta. The choice ingredients for the soup will still deliver the Italian flavor you desire.

Oven-roasted tomatoes and fragrant basil perk up boxed soup—no one will ever know it's not made completely from scratch.

Roasted Tomato–Basil Soup

Prep: 2 minutes • Cook: 23 minutes

5 plum tomatoes, halved lengthwise (about 1 pound)
6 (¼-inch-thick) slices Vidalia or other sweet onion (about 9 ounces)
1 tablespoon olive oil
½ teaspoon freshly ground black pepper
¼ teaspoon kosher salt
2 tablespoons chopped fresh basil
2 (18.3-ounce) containers tomato-herb soup (such as Campbell's V8)
¼ cup (1 ounce) grated fresh Parmigiano-Reggiano cheese

1. Preheat oven to 475°.
2. Place tomato and onion on a large rimmed baking sheet; drizzle with oil, and sprinkle with pepper and salt. Bake at 475° for 18 minutes or until charred (do not stir).
3. Transfer roasted vegetables and any accumulated juices to a Dutch oven. Process mixture with a hand-held blender (immersion blender) until almost smooth. Stir in basil and tomato-herb soup. Cover and cook over medium-high heat 5 minutes or until thoroughly heated. Top each serving with 1 tablespoon cheese. Yield: 4 servings (serving size: 1½ cups soup and 1 tablespoon cheese).

CALORIES 195; FAT 5.9g (sat 1.9g, mono 3.2g, poly 0.6g); PROTEIN 7.4g; CARB 29.6g; FIBER 5g; CHOL 7mg; IRON 1.5mg; SODIUM 740mg; CALC 155mg

serve with
Fontina-Pesto Toasts

Prep: 3 minutes • Cook: 6 minutes

12 (¼-inch-thick) slices French bread baguette
Olive oil-flavored cooking spray
3 tablespoons commercial reduced-fat pesto with basil (such as Buitoni)
½ cup (2 ounces) shredded fontina cheese

1. Preheat oven to 400°.
2. Place baguette slices on a baking sheet. Coat slices with cooking spray; spread evenly with pesto.
3. Bake at 400° for 3 minutes. Top evenly with shredded cheese. Bake an additional 3 minutes or until cheese melts. Yield: 4 servings (serving size: 3 toasts).

CALORIES 297; FAT 9.7g (sat 3.8g, mono 3.6g, poly 2.2g); PROTEIN 12.4g; CARB 40.9g; FIBER 1.9g; CHOL 19mg; IRON 2.2mg; SODIUM 650mg; CALC 235mg

4-ingredient

10-minute

Clever shortcut: Use chive-flavored cream cheese in place of multiple ingredients. Prefer another flavor? Try sun-dried tomato–basil or garden vegetable–flavored cream cheese.

Creamy Roasted Red Bell Pepper Soup
Prep: 1 minute • Cook: 5 minutes

2 cups drained bottled roasted red bell peppers
1 cup organic vegetable broth
¼ teaspoon freshly ground black pepper
1 (15-ounce) can no-salt-added cannellini beans, drained

½ cup (4 ounces) tub-style light cream cheese with chives and onion
Freshly ground black pepper (optional)

1. Place first 4 ingredients in a blender or food processor; process until smooth. Pour into a medium saucepan. Bring to a simmer over medium-high heat, stirring occasionally. Add cream cheese, stirring just until melted and smooth. Remove from heat. Serve immediately. Garnish with black pepper, if desired. Yield: 4 servings (serving size: 1 cup).

CALORIES 128; FAT 5g (sat 3g, mono 1.3g, poly 0.6g); PROTEIN 5.8g; CARB 14.3g; FIBER 2.4g; CHOL 15mg; IRON 0.8mg; SODIUM 625mg; CALC 59mg

serve with
Goat Cheese and Olive Pitas
Prep: 5 minutes • Cook: 10 minutes

1 (6-inch) whole-wheat pita
Olive oil-flavored cooking spray
½ teaspoon dried Greek seasoning (such as Cavender's)

2 tablespoons bottled olive tapenade
½ cup (2 ounces) crumbled garlic-and-herb goat cheese

1. Preheat oven to 400°.
2. Cut pita into 8 wedges. Separate each wedge into 2 triangles. Place triangles, rough sides up, in a single layer on a large baking sheet. Coat triangles with cooking spray; sprinkle evenly with seasoning. Top triangles evenly with tapenade and goat cheese.
3. Bake at 400° for 10 minutes or until cheese melts. Serve warm or at room temperature. Yield: 4 servings (serving size: 4 triangles).

CALORIES 108; FAT 6.4g (sat 2.9g, mono 2.7g, poly 0.6g); PROTEIN 4.4g; CARB 9.9g; FIBER 1.7g; CHOL 6mg; IRON 0.9mg; SODIUM 357mg; CALC 27mg

Lemongrass paste is a clever find. It keeps in the fridge for a long time and adds tangy, fresh lemon flavor to scores of dishes. Find it in the herb section of the produce department of your supermarket.

Curried Vegetable Soup
Prep: 2 minutes • Cook: 13 minutes

2 teaspoons olive oil
1 tablespoon minced peeled fresh ginger
2 garlic cloves, minced
1 tablespoon curry powder
1 tablespoon lemongrass paste (such as Gourmet Garden)
1 (16-ounce) bag frozen broccoli stir-fry (such as Birds Eye)

1½ cups organic vegetable broth
¼ teaspoon salt
¼ teaspoon freshly ground black pepper
1 (13.5-ounce) can light coconut milk
4 lime wedges
Chopped fresh cilantro (optional)

1. Heat oil in a Dutch oven over medium-high heat. Add ginger and garlic; sauté 1 minute or until tender. Stir in curry powder, lemongrass paste, and frozen stir-fry. **2.** Cook, stirring frequently, 2 minutes or until vegetables thaw. Add broth and next 3 ingredients. Bring to a boil; cover, reduce heat, and simmer 4 minutes or until vegetables are tender. Ladle soup evenly into bowls. Serve with lime wedges and, if desired, garnish with cilantro. Yield: 4 servings (serving size: 1⅓ cups).

CALORIES 148; FAT 8.6g (sat 5.3g, mono 2.7g, poly 0.5g); PROTEIN 2.8g; CARB 16.5g; FIBER 3.5g; CHOL 0mg; IRON 1.4mg; SODIUM 521mg; CALC 39mg

serve with
Chickpea Salad
Prep: 6 minutes

⅓ cup plain fat-free yogurt
2 teaspoons chopped fresh mint
2 teaspoons chopped fresh cilantro
2 teaspoons fresh lemon juice
1 teaspoon extra-virgin olive oil
¼ teaspoon salt

¼ teaspoon freshly ground black pepper
2 cups fresh baby spinach
1 (16-ounce) can reduced-sodium chickpeas (garbanzo beans; such as Bush's), rinsed and drained

1. Combine first 7 ingredients in a medium bowl, stirring with a whisk. Stir in spinach and chickpeas, tossing to coat. Yield: 4 servings (serving size: ¾ cup).

CALORIES 85; FAT 2.3g (sat 0.2g, mono 1.3g, poly 0.8g); PROTEIN 4.8g; CARB 13.9g; FIBER 3.3g; CHOL 0.4mg; IRON 1.5mg; SODIUM 250mg; CALC 78mg

This heart-friendly soup starts with light products and ends with a hit of bacon. It's always ok to splurge if it's done in moderation. Perch the rosemary-infused bacon slice on the rim of your soup mug for dipping, or simply crumble the candied slice on top.

Baked Potato Soup
Prep: 6 minutes • Cook: 13 minutes

1 (24-ounce) package steam-and-mash frozen potatoes (such as Ore-Ida Steam n' Mash Cut Russet Potatoes)
2½ cups evaporated fat-free milk, divided
1½ cups (6 ounces) reduced-fat shredded extrasharp cheddar cheese, divided
1 cup reduced-fat sour cream
½ teaspoon salt
½ cup thinly sliced green onion tops (5 onions)
Freshly ground black pepper (optional)
Peppered Rosemary Bacon (optional)

1. Microwave potatoes according to package directions.
2. Combine hot potatoes and 2 cups milk in a large microwave-safe bowl; mash until smooth. Add 1 cup cheese; stir until cheese melts. Stir in remaining ½ cup milk, sour cream, and salt. Cover and microwave at HIGH 2 to 3 minutes or until thoroughly heated.
3. Ladle soup into bowls; sprinkle evenly with remaining ½ cup cheese, green onions, and, if desired, black pepper and bacon. Serve immediately. Yield: 6 servings (serving size: about 1 cup soup, about 1 tablespoon cheese, and about 1 tablespoon green onions).

CALORIES 325; FAT 10.8g (sat 7g, mono 3.1g, poly 0.5g); PROTEIN 17.4g; CARB 36.8g; FIBER 2.7g; CHOL 36mg; IRON 0.7mg; SODIUM 894mg; CALC 513mg

serve with
Peppered Rosemary Bacon
Prep: 3 minutes • Cook: 18 minutes

2 tablespoons brown sugar
1 teaspoon cracked or freshly ground black pepper
1 teaspoon chopped fresh rosemary
8 center-cut 40%-less-fat bacon slices (such as Gwaltney)

1. Preheat oven to 425°.
2. Combine brown sugar, pepper, and rosemary; press firmly onto 1 side of bacon slices. Place bacon, herb side up, in a single layer on a wire rack in a large foil-lined jelly-roll pan. Bake at 425° for 18 minutes or until crisp. Cool. Yield: 8 servings (serving size: 1 bacon slice).

CALORIES 34; FAT 1.5g (sat 0.5g, mono 0.8g, poly 0.2g); PROTEIN 1.7g; CARB 3.6g; FIBER 0.1g; CHOL 7mg; IRON 0.2mg; SODIUM 91mg; CALC 4mg

If you want to splurge, add a sprinkling of sharp cheddar to each serving. Reserve a few broccoli florets for garnish, if desired, and serve with whole-wheat crackers to round out your meal.

Broccoli-Cheese Soup
Prep: 2 minutes • Cook: 11 minutes

Broccoli Sauté
1½ cups fat-free, lower-sodium chicken broth
1½ cups water
1.5 ounces all-purpose flour (about ⅓ cup)

2½ cups 2% reduced-fat milk
½ (16-ounce) block light processed cheese, cubed (such as Velveeta Light)

1. Prepare Broccoli Sauté.
2. Combine first 3 ingredients in a large saucepan; bring to a boil over medium-high heat.
3. While broccoli mixture comes to a boil, weigh or lightly spoon flour into a dry measuring cup; level with a knife. Combine flour and ½ cup milk, stirring with a whisk until blended. Stir flour mixture into broccoli mixture. Add remaining 2 cups milk; cook, stirring constantly, 5 minutes or until thick. Add cheese to soup mixture, stirring until cheese melts. Remove from heat.
4. Place half of soup mixture in a blender. Remove center piece of blender lid (to allow steam to escape); secure blender lid on blender. Place a clean towel over opening in blender lid (to avoid splatters). Blend until smooth. Stir pureed mixture into remaining soup in pan. Yield: 6 servings (serving size: 1⅓ cups).

CALORIES 213; FAT 7.3g (sat 4.6g, mono 2g, poly 0.5g); PROTEIN 15.5g; CARB 19.8g; FIBER 2.2g; CHOL 27mg; IRON 0.5mg; SODIUM 978mg; CALC 149mg

Broccoli Sauté
Prep: 2 minutes • Cook: 7 minutes

Cooking spray
1 (12-ounce) package broccoli florets, chopped
1 (8-ounce) container refrigerated prechopped celery, onion, and bell pepper mix

¼ cup 50%-less-fat bacon bits
½ teaspoon crushed red pepper
2 garlic cloves, minced

1. Heat a large nonstick skillet over medium-high heat. Heavily coat pan with cooking spray. Add broccoli and celery mix; sauté 5 minutes or until tender. Add bacon bits, crushed red pepper, and garlic; sauté 1 minute. Yield: 6 servings (serving size: ⅔ cup).

CALORIES 48; FAT 1.1g (sat 0.7g, mono 0.1g, poly 0.3g); PROTEIN 3.1g; CARB 5.3g; FIBER 2g; CHOL 3mg; IRON 0.1mg; SODIUM 184mg; CALC 24mg

Italian-style stewed tomatoes and seasoning give this soup an Italian accent. Leftovers, if there are any, freeze beautifully.

Easy Vegetable-Beef Soup
Prep: 1 minute • Cook: 27 minutes

Seasoning Blend
1   pound ground round
2½ cups water
1   (16-ounce) package frozen mixed vegetables

1   (14½-ounce) can Italian-style stewed tomatoes, undrained and chopped
1   (8-ounce) can tomato sauce

1. Prepare Seasoning Blend.
2. Cook beef and Seasoning Blend in a Dutch oven over medium-high heat until browned, stirring to crumble. Drain. Return meat mixture to pan. Stir in 2½ cups water and remaining ingredients. Bring to a boil over medium-high heat; reduce heat, cover, and simmer 20 minutes. Yield: 6 servings (serving size: 1½ cups).

CALORIES 241; FAT 8.1g (sat 3.6g, mono 3.7g, poly 0.7g); PROTEIN 18.4g; CARB 20.9g; FIBER 4.1g; CHOL 49mg; IRON 3.3mg; SODIUM 514mg; CALC 63mg

Seasoning Blend
Prep: 2 minutes

1   (8-ounce) container refrigerated prechopped onion
1½ tablespoons minced garlic

1   teaspoon dried Italian seasoning
½   teaspoon black pepper
¼   teaspoon salt

1. Combine all ingredients in a small bowl. Yield: 1¾ cups (serving size: about ¼ cup).

CALORIES 23; FAT 0.4g (sat 0.1g, mono 0g, poly 0.3g); PROTEIN 0.4g; CARB 3.8g; FIBER 0.6g; CHOL 0mg; IRON 0.1mg; SODIUM 84mg; CALC 8mg

quick flip

Liven up a weekday dinner by transforming this soup into a Tex-Mex rendition. A 24-ounce jar of picante sauce stands in for the Italian-style stewed tomatoes and the tomato sauce, while 2 tablespoons of taco seasoning mix trade places with the Seasoning Blend's minced garlic, Italian seasoning, black pepper, and salt.

This is not your mother's soup. But it's just as good. (Sorry, Mom!) To get that home-cooked taste, use a packaged pot roast as the base for rich flavor. It's ready to simmer in just 3 minutes.

Beef and Barley Soup
Prep: 3 minutes • Cook: 28 minutes

1 (17-ounce) package refrigerated beef roast au jus (such as Hormel)
1 (32-ounce) carton fat-free, lower-sodium beef broth
¾ cup water
¾ cup uncooked quick-cooking barley
1 (16-ounce) package frozen vegetables for soup with tomatoes (such as Pictsweet)

1. Combine first 4 ingredients in a Dutch oven; cover and bring to a boil. Reduce heat and simmer 10 minutes. Add frozen vegetables; return to a boil. Reduce heat and simmer, uncovered, 10 minutes or until vegetables are tender. Yield: 8 servings (serving size: 1 cup).

CALORIES 164; FAT 4g (sat 1.7g, mono 1.8g, poly 0.5g); PROTEIN 15.8g; CARB 17.9g; FIBER 2.8g; CHOL 32mg; IRON 1mg; SODIUM 441mg; CALC 0mg

serve with
Cornmeal-Herb Spirals
Prep: 6 minutes • Cook: 14 minutes

1 (11-ounce) can refrigerated breadstick dough
1 tablespoon olive oil
2 garlic cloves, pressed
2 tablespoons stone-ground yellow cornmeal
1 tablespoon minced fresh rosemary
Cooking spray

1. Preheat oven to 375°.
2. Unroll dough (do not separate dough into strips). Combine oil and garlic; brush evenly over dough. Combine cornmeal and rosemary; sprinkle over dough.
3. Separate and roll up each strip of dough in a spiral pattern with cornmeal mixture on the inside, pinching ends to seal. Place on a baking sheet coated with cooking spray; coat each roll with cooking spray.
4. Bake at 375° for 14 minutes or until lightly browned. Yield: 12 servings (serving size: 1 roll).

CALORIES 89; FAT 2.5g (sat 0.6g, mono 1.7g, poly 0.1g); PROTEIN 2.1g; CARB 13.8g; FIBER 0.6g; CHOL 0mg; IRON 0.8mg; SODIUM 194mg; CALC 2mg

This stew deserves to be on the menu as the perfect after-work Friday night dinner. The dark beer and tomato paste add a deep, rich flavor that belies the short cook time.

Beer-Braised Beef Stew
Prep: 2 minutes • Cook: 13 minutes

2 teaspoons olive oil
1 pound sirloin steak, trimmed and cut into ½-inch pieces
1 cup refrigerated prechopped onion
2 large carrots, cut into ½-inch chunks
1 (8-ounce) package sliced fresh mushrooms
2 tablespoons all-purpose flour

3 tablespoons water
1 tablespoon tomato paste
¾ cup dark beer
½ cup fat-free, lower-sodium beef broth
¼ teaspoon salt
¼ teaspoon freshly ground black pepper
Chopped fresh parsley (optional)

1. Heat oil in a Dutch oven over medium-high heat. Add steak. Cook 5 minutes or until browned, stirring once. Remove steak from pan; keep warm. Add onion, carrot, and mushrooms to drippings in pan. Cook, stirring frequently, 3 minutes or until browned.
2. While vegetables cook, combine flour and 3 tablespoons water in a medium bowl, stirring with a whisk until smooth. Add tomato paste, stirring until smooth. Stir in beer and broth.
3. Add steak, salt, and pepper to mushroom mixture; stir in beer mixture. Bring to a boil; cover, reduce heat, and simmer 2 minutes or until stew is thick.
4. Ladle stew evenly into bowls. Sprinkle each serving with parsley, if desired. Yield: 4 servings (serving size: 1 cup).

CALORIES 247; FAT 7.2g (sat 2.3g, mono 3.9g, poly 0.9g); PROTEIN 27.8g; CARB 14.7g; FIBER 2.6g; CHOL 46mg; IRON 2.4mg; SODIUM 314mg; CALC 41mg

serve with
Chive Cheese Biscuits
Prep: 5 minutes • Cook: 10 minutes

¾ cup low-fat baking mix (such as Bisquick Heart Smart)
⅓ cup (1.3 ounces) reduced-fat shredded sharp cheddar cheese
1 tablespoon chopped fresh chives

¼ teaspoon freshly ground black pepper
¼ cup fat-free milk
2 tablespoons reduced-fat sour cream
Cooking spray

1. Preheat oven to 425°.
2. Combine first 4 ingredients in a medium bowl. Add milk and sour cream, stirring just until moist.
3. Drop dough by heaping spoonfuls onto an ungreased baking sheet to form 8 mounds. Coat tops of mounds with cooking spray.
4. Bake at 425° for 10 minutes or until golden brown. Yield: 4 servings (serving size: 2 biscuits).

CALORIES 124; FAT 4.5g (sat 2g, mono 1.9g, poly 0.5g); PROTEIN 5g; CARB 17g; FIBER 0.3g; CHOL 10mg; IRON 0.9mg; SODIUM 256mg; CALC 181mg

4-ingredient

Gremolata is a treat for the taste buds. This simple, zesty condiment of minced parsley, grated lemon rind, and garlic abounds with flavor. It's often served sprinkled over veal, but it adds a nice fresh flavor to any "meaty" dish.

White Bean and Lamb Soup with Gremolata

Prep: 1 minute • Cook: 20 minutes

2 teaspoons olive oil
1 pound lean boneless leg of lamb, cut into ½-inch pieces
½ cup refrigerated prechopped onion
4½ cups water
½ teaspoon freshly ground black pepper
1 (6-ounce) package dry Tuscan white bean soup mix (such as Alessi)
Gremolata

1. Heat oil in a Dutch oven over medium-high heat. Add lamb and onion; sauté 5 minutes or until lamb is browned and onion is tender. Add 4½ cups water and pepper to lamb mixture. Bring to a boil; add soup mix, stirring for 1 minute. Reduce heat, and simmer, uncovered, 12 minutes or until pasta is done.
2. While soup cooks, prepare Gremolata.
3. Ladle soup into 6 bowls. Top each serving with 2 teaspoons Gremolata. Yield: 6 servings (serving size: ¾ cup soup and 2 teaspoons Gremolata).

CALORIES 169; FAT 3.9g (sat 1.2g, mono 2.1g, poly 0.6g); PROTEIN 11.9g; CARB 20.3g; FIBER 5g; CHOL 23mg; IRON 1.8mg; SODIUM 459mg; CALC 40mg

Gremolata

Prep: 4 minutes

¼ cup minced fresh flat-leaf parsley
1½ teaspoons grated lemon rind
1 garlic clove, minced

1. Combine all ingredients in a small bowl. Yield: ¼ cup (serving size: 2 teaspoons).

CALORIES 1; FAT 0g (sat 0g, mono 0g, poly 0g); PROTEIN 0g; CARB 0.3g; FIBER 0.1g; CHOL 0mg; IRON 0mg; SODIUM 0.2mg; CALC 2mg

Flavor-packed yellow rice and spicy chorizo make this soup a Spanish specialty. Accompany the soup with garlic and tomato–rubbed rustic toasts for a classic staple from the Catalan region of Spain.

Chorizo Rice and Bean Soup
Prep: 2 minutes • Cook: 23 minutes

8   ounces fresh chorizo
4   cups water
2   (15-ounce) cans reduced-sodium pinto beans (such as Bush's), undrained

1   (5-ounce) package yellow rice mix (such as Vigo)
3   tablespoons chopped fresh cilantro

1. Remove casings from chorizo. Cook sausage in a Dutch oven over medium-high heat 5 minutes, stirring to crumble. Add 4 cups water, beans, and rice mix. Bring to a boil, stirring occasionally; reduce heat to low, cover, and simmer 15 minutes or until rice is tender.
2. Ladle soup into bowls; sprinkle evenly with cilantro. Serve immediately. Yield: 8 servings (serving size: 1 cup soup and about 1 teaspoon cilantro).

CALORIES 212; FAT 6.8g (sat 2.5g, mono 3.4g, poly 0.9g); PROTEIN 12.2g; CARB 28.9g; FIBER 5.9g; CHOL 0mg; IRON 2mg; SODIUM 411mg; CALC 40mg

serve with
Rustic Tomato-Garlic Toasts
Prep: 4 minutes • Cook: 2 minutes

8   (½-inch) slices ciabatta
4   garlic cloves, halved
1   (12-ounce) ripe tomato, halved

4   teaspoons extra-virgin olive oil
¼   teaspoon salt

1. Heat a grill pan over medium-high heat. Add ciabatta slices to pan. Cook 1 minute on each side or until toasted.
2. Rub 1 side of each toast with a garlic half, cut side down, until toast is fragrant. Rub tomato halves over toasts to release juice onto toasts. Drizzle each toast with ½ teaspoon olive oil. Sprinkle toasts evenly with salt. Yield: 8 servings (serving size: 1 toast).

CALORIES 109; FAT 3.7g (sat 0.5g, mono 2.6g, poly 0.5g); PROTEIN 3g; CARB 17.6g; FIBER 1g; CHOL 0mg; IRON 1mg; SODIUM 269mg; CALC 7mg

4-ingredient

A coconut-flavored broth is the tie that binds this Thai-inspired soup. It's joined by richly flavored little dumplings.

Chicken Pot Sticker Soup

Prep: 10 minutes • Cook: 10 minutes

1 (24-ounce) package frozen chicken pot stickers (such as Tai Pei; about 21 pot stickers)
2 cups Thai coconut curry broth (such as College Inn)
3 cups water
¾ teaspoon lemongrass paste (such as Gourmet Garden)
2 cups snow peas, trimmed and cut into thin lengthwise strips
Chopped fresh cilantro (optional)

1. Set aside 1 packet soy dipping sauce from pot sticker package, discarding remaining packet or reserving for another use. Place pot stickers in a large microwave-safe bowl; add water to cover. Microwave at HIGH 5 minutes or until tender. Drain.
2. While pot stickers cook, combine reserved dipping sauce, broth, 3 cups water, and lemongrass paste in a Dutch oven. Bring to a boil; cover, reduce heat, and simmer 5 minutes. Stir in pot stickers and snow peas. Cook 1 to 2 minutes or just until thoroughly heated.
3. Ladle soup into bowls. Garnish with cilantro, if desired. Yield: 6 servings (serving size: 1 cup soup and 3 to 4 pot stickers).

CALORIES 215; FAT 4.5g (sat 1.1g, mono 1.6g, poly 1.8g); PROTEIN 9.8g; CARB 33g; FIBER 2.1g; CHOL 25mg; IRON 2.2mg; SODIUM 996mg; CALC 57mg

serve with
Lettuce Wedge with Spicy Miso Dressing

Prep: 3 minutes

1 head iceberg lettuce, cut into 6 wedges
½ cup plain low-fat yogurt
2 tablespoons spicy miso teriyaki sauce (such as Kikkoman)
1½ tablespoons milk
¼ cup matchstick-cut carrots

1. Place lettuce wedges on salad plates. Combine yogurt, teriyaki sauce, and milk, stirring with a whisk until smooth. Spoon dressing evenly over lettuce wedges; sprinkle evenly with carrots. Yield: 6 servings (serving size: 1 lettuce wedge, 2 tablespoons dressing, and 2 teaspoons carrot).

CALORIES 41; FAT 0.6g (sat 0.3g, mono 0.1g, poly 0.1g); PROTEIN 2.2g; CARB 7g; FIBER 1.1g; CHOL 3mg; IRON 0.6mg; SODIUM 168mg; CALC 54mg

Posole is a thick, hearty soup from the Pacific Coast region of Mexico. A Christmas favorite, it traditionally features chicken broth; fluffy white hominy; chopped onions; zesty jalapeño peppers; and tongue-teasing, vibrant green cilantro. Baked tortilla chips are the perfect accompaniment to this flavorful soup.

Chicken Posole Chili

Prep: 1 minute • Cook: 14 minutes

2 cups fat-free, lower-sodium chicken broth	2 cups shredded cooked chicken breast
1 (15.5-ounce) can white hominy, drained	1½ teaspoons ground cumin
¾ cup tomatillo salsa (such as Ortega Salsa Verde)	½ cup chopped fresh cilantro

1. Combine first 3 ingredients in a large saucepan. Bring to a boil.
2. While broth mixture comes to a boil, combine chicken and cumin, tossing to coat; add to broth mixture. Reduce heat, and simmer 10 minutes, stirring occasionally. Remove from heat; stir in cilantro. Yield: 4 servings (serving size: about 1⅓ cups).

CALORIES 186; FAT 3.2g (sat 0.8g, mono 1.4g, poly 1g); PROTEIN 24.3g; CARB 14.2g; FIBER 1.8g; CHOL 60mg; IRON 1.4mg; SODIUM 739mg; CALC 23mg

ingredient spotlight

Hominy is dried corn kernels that have been treated with an alkali of some kind. This process removes the germ and the hard outer hull from the kernels, making them more palatable, easier to digest, and easier to process.

Chicken Tortilla Soup

Prep: 4 minutes • Cook: 11 minutes

1 (14-ounce) can fat-free, lower-sodium chicken broth
1 cup water
1 (10-ounce) can diced tomatoes with green chiles (such as Rotel), undrained

1½ cups frozen whole-kernel corn
2 cups shredded cooked chicken breast
Diced avocado (optional)
Lime wedges (optional)

1. Combine first 4 ingredients in a medium saucepan; bring to a boil. Stir in chicken; reduce heat, and simmer 2 minutes or until thoroughly heated. Top with avocado and lime wedges, if desired. Yield: 4 servings (serving size: 1½ cups).

CALORIES 180; FAT 3.1g (sat 0.9g, mono 1.1g, poly 0.9g); PROTEIN 24g; CARB 13.8g; FIBER 1.8g; CHOL 60mg; IRON 1mg; SODIUM 589mg; CALC 13mg

serve with
Spicy Tortilla Strips

Prep: 3 minutes • Cook: 11 minutes

3 (6-inch) corn tortillas
2 teaspoons canola oil
Cooking spray
½ teaspoon salt-free Southwest chipotle seasoning (such as Mrs. Dash)

¼ teaspoon ground cumin
⅛ teaspoon salt

1. Preheat oven to 350°.
2. Brush 1 side of tortillas evenly with oil. Place tortillas on a large rimmed baking sheet coated with cooking spray. Sprinkle evenly with chipotle seasoning, cumin, and salt. Cut tortillas into 2 x ¼–inch strips.
3. Bake at 350° for 11 minutes or until strips are crisp and golden. Yield: 4 servings (serving size: ¼ cup).

CALORIES 51; FAT 2.7g (sat 0.2g, mono 1.4g, poly 0.9g); PROTEIN 0.8g; CARB 6.8g; FIBER 0.8g; CHOL 0mg; IRON 0mg; SODIUM 77mg; CALC 9mg

quick flip

Want to make this Mexican classic Italian? With just a few tweaks, it can be done. Simply omit the tomatoes with green chiles and frozen corn, and add 1 (14-ounce) can diced tomatoes with green peppers and onions, 1 (9-ounce) package refrigerated cheese-filled tortellini, chopped fresh parsley, and shredded Parmesan cheese.

Start this spicy soup while the oven preheats for the tortilla strips. Then, while the soup comes to a boil, prepare and bake the tortilla strips to sprinkle on top.

4-ingredient

Coconut Corn Chowder with Chicken
Prep: 2 minutes • Cook: 7 minutes

3½ cups (½-inch) cubed medium-sized red
   potatoes (6 potatoes)
2 (14¾-ounce) cans no-salt-added cream-style
   corn
1 (13.5-ounce) can light coconut milk

3 cups pulled rotisserie chicken
¼ teaspoon salt
¼ teaspoon freshly ground black pepper
¼ cup chopped green onions or chopped
   fresh cilantro (optional)

1. Place potato in a large microwave-safe bowl. Cover with plastic wrap; vent.
Microwave at HIGH 3 minutes or until tender.
2. While potato cooks, combine corn and next 4 ingredients in a medium saucepan.
Cook over medium heat 3 minutes or just until bubbly, stirring occasionally.
3. Stir potato into corn mixture. Bring to a boil; reduce heat, and simmer 2 minutes.
Ladle soup into 6 bowls; sprinkle evenly with green onions or cilantro, if desired.
Yield: 6 servings (serving size: 1⅓ cups).

CALORIES 353; FAT 6.7g (sat 4.2g, mono 1.4g, poly 1.1g); PROTEIN 27.6g; CARB 50.2g; FIBER 4.2g; CHOL 60mg; IRON 2.7mg; SODIUM 335mg; CALC 28mg

serve with
Mini Carrot Quiches
Prep: 4 minutes • Cook: 15 minutes • Other: 3 minutes

8 wonton wrappers
Cooking spray
1 large egg
¼ teaspoon salt

¼ teaspoon ground ginger
½ cup shredded carrot
1 tablespoon evaporated fat-free milk

1. Preheat oven to 400°.
2. Press 1 wonton wrapper into each of 8 miniature muffin cups coated with
cooking spray, forming small cups and allowing corners to extend over edges
of cups. Coat wonton cups with cooking spray.
3. Bake at 400° on bottom oven rack for 5 minutes or just until slightly crisp.
4. While wonton cups bake, combine egg, salt, and ginger in a bowl, stirring with
a whisk until foamy. Stir in carrot and milk. Spoon carrot mixture evenly into hot
wonton cups. Bake on bottom rack an additional 10 minutes or until custard is set
and edges of cups are golden. Let quiches cool in pan on a wire rack 3 minutes
before serving. Yield: 8 servings (serving size: 1 quiche).

CALORIES 36; FAT 0.7g (sat 0.2g, mono 0.3g, poly 0.1g); PROTEIN 1.8g; CARB 5.4g; FIBER 0.3g; CHOL 27mg; IRON 0.4mg; SODIUM 130mg; CALC 13mg

Using the microwave is the perfect way to jump-start
this creamy creation.

4-ingredient

10-minute

sandwiches

Grilled Grouper Sandwiches with Chile Mayo, 52
Smoked Paprika Salmon Sliders, 55
Crushed Heirloom Tomato and Shrimp Bruschetta, 56
Havarti-Dill Tuna Melt, 58
Veggie Roll-Ups, 61
Blue Cheeseburger, 63
Flank Steak Sandwiches with Carrot Slaw, 64
Lamb Wraps with Tzatziki Sauce, 66
BLTs with Pimiento Cheese, 69
Waffled Hawaiian Sandwiches, 70
Italian Sausage Calzones, 72
Buffalo Chicken Salad Sandwiches, 75
Greek Chicken Sandwich with Lemon-Feta Spread, 76
Lemongrass Chicken Lettuce Wraps, 79
Mega Crostini Chicken Sandwiches, 81
Shaved Chicken, Apple, and Cheddar Sandwiches with Basil Mayo, 82
California Smoked Chicken Sandwiches, 85
Italian Grilled Cheese Sandwiches, 87
Hot Turkey and Strawberry Sandwiches, 88
Grilled Chicken Sausages with Caraway Slaw, 91

Use any mild-flavored, meaty white fish if grouper isn't available, including sustainable tilapia.

Grilled Grouper Sandwiches with Chile Mayo

Prep: 6 minutes • Cook: 8 minutes • Other: 10 minutes

4 (4-ounce) grouper fillets
2 tablespoons garlic and green onion teriyaki sauce (such as Kikkoman)
Cooking spray
4 green leaf lettuce leaves (optional)

4 (1.8-ounce) white-wheat hamburger buns, toasted
4 (¼-inch-thick) slices tomato (optional)
Chile Mayo

1. Preheat grill.
2. Brush fillets with teriyaki sauce; let stand 10 minutes. Place fillets on grill rack coated with cooking spray. Grill 4 minutes on each side or until desired degree of doneness.
3. Place 1 lettuce leaf, if desired, on bottom half of each bun; top each with 1 tomato slice, if desired, and 1 fillet. Spoon about 1½ tablespoons Chile Mayo over each; top with remaining bun halves. Yield: 4 servings (serving size: 1 sandwich).

CALORIES 249; FAT 4.8g (sat 1g, mono 0.7g, poly 2.9g); PROTEIN 27.6g; CARB 29.1g; FIBER 5.1g; CHOL 42mg; IRON 1mg; SODIUM 846mg; CALC 338mg

Chile Mayo

Prep: 1 minute

⅓ cup low-fat mayonnaise dressing
1 tablespoon chile paste with garlic (such as sambal oelek)

1 teaspoon brown sugar
1 teaspoon lime juice
½ teaspoon fish sauce

1. Combine all ingredients in a small bowl, stirring well. Yield: about ⅓ cup (serving size: 1½ tablespoons).

CALORIES 25; FAT 1.3g (sat 0g, mono 0.3g, poly 1g); PROTEIN 0.1g; CARB 4.6g; FIBER 0g; CHOL 0mg; IRON 0mg; SODIUM 401mg; CALC 1mg

fix it faster

If time is of the essence, take this meal inside. Broil the grouper for the sandwiches about 10 minutes or until desired degree of doneness.

These small sandwiches pack incredible flavor—and it's all about the rub.

Smoked Paprika Salmon Sliders

Prep: 5 minutes • Cook: 10 minutes • Other: 5 minutes

Smoked Paprika Rub
3 (6-ounce) salmon fillets (1 inch thick)
Cooking spray
1 (10-ounce) package hearth-baked French rolls (such as Pepperidge Farm)

2 tablespoons light mayonnaise
½ cup packed arugula or mixed baby salad greens

1. Preheat broiler.
2. Prepare Smoked Paprika Rub; rub over tops of fillets, reserving ½ teaspoon. Place salmon on a broiler pan coated with cooking spray. Broil 10 minutes or until desired degree of doneness. Let cool 5 minutes.
3. While salmon cools, reduce oven temperature to 425°. Heat rolls at 425° according to package directions. Combine mayonnaise and reserved ½ teaspoon rub; spread evenly onto cut sides of rolls.
4. Remove skin from salmon, and cut each fillet in half crosswise. Place salmon on roll bottoms. Top with arugula and roll tops. Yield: 6 servings (serving size: 1 slider).

CALORIES 238; FAT 4.9g (sat 0.6g, mono 2g, poly 2.1g); PROTEIN 21.2g; CARB 26.8g; FIBER 1.5g; CHOL 44mg; IRON 2.3mg; SODIUM 371mg; CALC 115mg

Smoked Paprika Rub

Prep: 2 minutes

1 tablespoon smoked paprika
1 tablespoon brown sugar
1 teaspoon grated orange rind

¼ teaspoon salt
¼ teaspoon freshly ground black pepper

1. Combine all ingredients in a small bowl. Yield: 2½ tablespoons (serving size: 1¼ teaspoons).

CALORIES 13; FAT 0.1g (sat 0g, mono 0g, poly 0.1g); PROTEIN 0.2g; CARB 2.9g; FIBER 0.4g; CHOL 0mg; IRON 0.2mg; SODIUM 99mg; CALC 5mg

quick flip

Part of the beauty of salmon is the way it adapts so well to flavor rubs. Change the Smoked Paprika Rub into Chili Rub by simply combining 1 tablespoon chili powder, 1 tablespoon brown sugar, 1 teaspoon ground cumin, and ¼ teaspoon each of salt and freshly ground black pepper. As the fish cooks, the rub caramelizes.

Crushed Heirloom Tomato and Shrimp Bruschetta

Prep: 9 minutes • Cook: 4 minutes

8 (0.7-ounce) diagonal slices French bread (½ inch thick)
Olive oil-flavored cooking spray
4 large garlic cloves, halved
½ cup (4 ounces) goat cheese, softened

Crushed Heirloom Tomato and Shrimp Topping
¼ teaspoon freshly ground black pepper
1 tablespoon extra-virgin olive oil
24 small fresh basil leaves

1. Preheat grill.
2. Coat bread with cooking spray. Grill 2 minutes on each side or until toasted. Rub cut sides of garlic on 1 side of each piece of toast. Spread goat cheese evenly over garlic on toast. Top each toast with ½ cup Crushed Heirloom Tomato and Shrimp Topping. Sprinkle with pepper, and drizzle with olive oil. Top each serving with basil leaves. Yield: 4 servings (serving size: 2 bruschetta).

CALORIES 355; FAT 13.3g (sat 6g, mono 5.1g, poly 2.1g); PROTEIN 32.3g; CARB 26.1g; FIBER 1.8g; CHOL 185mg; IRON 5.1mg; SODIUM 647mg; CALC 159mg

Crushed Heirloom Tomato and Shrimp Topping

Prep: 4 minutes • Cook: 4 minutes

1 pound peeled and deveined medium shrimp
Olive oil-flavored cooking spray
2 cups heirloom multicolored cherry tomatoes

1 teaspoon grated lemon rind
1 tablespoon fresh lemon juice
¼ teaspoon salt
¼ teaspoon crushed red pepper (optional)

1. Preheat grill.
2. Coat shrimp with cooking spray; place shrimp in a grill basket. Grill 2 to 3 minutes on each side or until shrimp reach desired degree of doneness.
3. While shrimp cook, place tomatoes in a medium bowl. Press tomatoes with the back of a spoon or potato masher until lightly crushed. Add shrimp to tomatoes in bowl; stir in remaining ingredients. Yield: 4 servings (serving size: 1 cup).

CALORIES 139; FAT 2.4g (sat 0.5g, mono 0.7g, poly 1.1g); PROTEIN 23.7g; CARB 4.9g; FIBER 0.9g; CHOL 172mg; IRON 3.1mg; SODIUM 320mg; CALC 64mg

quick flip

Crushed Heirloom Tomato and Shrimp Topping is transformed into Tricolored Pepper Medley and Shrimp Topping with one trade-out. Take out the 2 cups heirloom multicolored cherry tomatoes, and replace with 2 cups diced yellow, orange, and red bell peppers. The bell peppers add a pop of color to the bruschetta along with subtle sweetness and crunch.

These mile-high knife and fork sandwiches highlight heirloom tomatoes, summer's seasonal gems.

Put a new spin on the patty melt using tuna. Top it with a pickle spear, if desired, and serve it while the cheese oozes. The prep time clocks in at under 10 minutes.

Havarti-Dill Tuna Melt
Prep: 7 minutes • Cook: 2 minutes

8 (1-ounce) slices 15-grain bread (such as Pepperidge Farm), toasted
Cucumber Tuna Salad

4 (¾-ounce) slices Havarti cheese with dill
4 (¼-inch-thick) slices tomato

1. Preheat broiler.
2. Place 4 toast slices on a baking sheet; spread evenly with Cucumber Tuna Salad. Top evenly with cheese. Broil 2 minutes or until cheese melts.
3. Top with tomato and remaining toast slices. Yield: 4 servings (serving size: 1 sandwich).

CALORIES 342; FAT 16.7g (sat 6.2g, mono 4.6g, poly 5.8g); PROTEIN 24.1g; CARB 29.1g; FIBER 5.5g; CHOL 47mg; IRON 1.8mg; SODIUM 731mg; CALC 223mg

Cucumber Tuna Salad
Prep: 4 minutes

1 (6.4-ounce) pouch albacore tuna in water (such as StarKist), flaked
⅓ cup finely chopped celery (1 stalk)
⅓ cup light mayonnaise

¼ cup finely chopped seeded cucumber
¼ teaspoon black pepper
⅛ teaspoon salt

1. Combine all ingredients in a medium bowl. Yield: 1½ cups (serving size: ⅓ cup).

CALORIES 124; FAT 7.2g (sat 1g, mono 1.8g, poly 4.4g); PROTEIN 12.2g; CARB 2.3g; FIBER 0.3g; CHOL 28mg; IRON 0.3mg; SODIUM 449mg; CALC 7mg

ingredient spotlight

Albacore tuna has the highest fat and lightest flesh of tuna varieties. It's prized for its white flesh and mild flavor. Dense in texture, it's the priciest of canned tunas.

4-ingredient

10-minute

Bacon adds a little slice of heaven to these quick roll-ups. And let's face it, bacon makes just about any sandwich better.

Veggie Roll-Ups
Prep: 6 minutes • Cook: 1 minute

½ cup refrigerated hummus (such as Athenos Original)
4 (8-inch) 96% fat-free whole-wheat flour tortillas (such as Mission)

4 precooked bacon slices
Carrot-Red Onion Toss
½ cup finely chopped cucumber

1. Spread hummus evenly over tortillas. Microwave bacon slices according to package directions; crumble bacon. Sprinkle bacon evenly over hummus. Top evenly with Carrot–Red Onion Toss and cucumber; roll up. Yield: 4 servings (serving size: 1 roll-up).

CALORIES 220; FAT 6.4g (sat 0.5g, mono 1.9g, poly 3.9g); PROTEIN 7.5g; CARB 34.4g; FIBER 4.8g; CHOL 5mg; IRON 0.6mg; SODIUM 688mg; CALC 11mg

Carrot–Red Onion Toss
Prep: 1 minute

1 cup matchstick-cut carrots
⅓ cup vertically sliced red onion

2 tablespoons light red wine vinaigrette
¼ teaspoon freshly ground black pepper

1. Combine all ingredients in a medium bowl; toss gently. Yield: 1¼ cups (serving size: about ⅓ cup).

CALORIES 18; FAT 0g (sat 0g, mono 0g, poly 0g); PROTEIN 0.4g; CARB 4.1g; FIBER 0.7g; CHOL 0mg; IRON 0.1mg; SODIUM 101mg; CALC 9mg

> **quick flip**
>
> **Give Carrot–Red Onion Toss some Asian flair** by omitting the 2 tablespoons light red wine vinaigrette and adding 2 tablespoons low-fat sesame-ginger dressing (such as Newman's Own). The ingredient swap adds another layer of flavor to roll-ups that are brimming with color and crunch.

4-ingredient

Blue cheese is the surprise ingredient in this burger. It boosts the flavor and keeps it juicy. Top the burger with your favorite condiments, and serve with steak fries to round out your meal.

Blue Cheeseburger

Prep: 6 minutes • Cook: 12 minutes

1 pound 93% lean ground beef	⅛ teaspoon black pepper
¼ cup minced fresh onion	4 (1.8-ounce) white-wheat hamburger buns
¼ cup (1 ounce) crumbled blue cheese	4 (¼-inch-thick) slices tomato (optional)
¼ teaspoon salt	4 green leaf lettuce leaves (optional)

1. Combine first 5 ingredients in a medium bowl; stir well. Divide beef mixture into 4 equal portions, shaping each into a ½-inch-thick patty.
2. Heat a nonstick grill pan over medium-high heat. Place hamburger patties in pan, and cook 6 minutes on each side or until desired degree of doneness.
3. Top bottom half of each bun with 1 patty, tomato, and lettuce, if desired, and remaining half of bun. Yield: 4 servings (serving size: 1 burger).

CALORIES 294; FAT 12.4g (sat 5.1g, mono 5g, poly 2.3g); PROTEIN 26.9g; CARB 22.2g; FIBER 5.2g; CHOL 61mg; IRON 5.5mg; SODIUM 556mg; CALC 297mg

quick flip

Drop the tomato slice on each burger, and add 1 tablespoon fig preserves in its place. The thick, sweet fig preserves bring out the tang of the blue cheese in these mouthwatering burgers.

Overlapping tasks keeps prep and cook time to a minimum for this recipe. Fire up the grill, and season the steak while the oven preheats and the rolls bake. Prepare the slaw while the steak is grilling. Assemble the sandwiches, and you're done.

Flank Steak Sandwiches with Carrot Slaw
Prep: 10 minutes • Cook: 13 minutes • Other: 5 minutes

4 (1.5-ounce) frozen ciabatta rolls	¼ teaspoon freshly ground black pepper
1 (1-pound) flank steak, trimmed	Cooking spray
2 teaspoons olive oil	2 cups bagged baby spinach leaves
1 teaspoon five-spice powder	Carrot Slaw
¼ teaspoon salt	

1. Bake rolls according to package directions. Cut rolls horizontally in half.
2. Preheat grill.
3. Rub steak with oil; sprinkle with five-spice powder, salt, and pepper. Place steak on grill rack coated with cooking spray. Grill 6 minutes on each side or until desired degree of doneness. Remove steak from grill, and let stand 5 minutes. Cut steak diagonally across grain into thin slices.
4. Place ½ cup spinach on roll bottoms. Top evenly with steak and Carrot Slaw. Place roll tops over slaw. Yield: 4 servings (serving size: 1 sandwich).

CALORIES 306; FAT 10g (sat 3.1g, mono 5.5g, poly 1.3g); PROTEIN 28.6g; CARB 23.6g; FIBER 1.8g; CHOL 39mg; IRON 4mg; SODIUM 583mg; CALC 56mg

Carrot Slaw
Prep: 10 minutes

2 teaspoons rice vinegar	2 garlic cloves, minced
1 teaspoon grated peeled fresh ginger	1 cup shredded carrot
1 teaspoon olive oil	¼ cup shredded radishes
¼ teaspoon salt	1 tablespoon chopped fresh cilantro
¼ teaspoon freshly ground black pepper	

1. Combine first 6 ingredients in a medium bowl. Add carrot, radishes, and cilantro; toss to coat. Cover and chill until ready to serve. Yield: 1 cup (serving size: ¼ cup).

CALORIES 26; FAT 1.2g (sat 0.2g, mono 0.8g, poly 0.2g); PROTEIN 0.4g; CARB 3.6g; FIBER 1g; CHOL 0mg; IRON 0.2mg; SODIUM 168mg; CALC 14mg

Soft, pillowy flatbreads hug a spicy lamb filling drizzled with refreshing cucumber-mint sauce in this take on a favorite Greek sandwich. Round out the meal with a healthy side of red grapes.

Lamb Wraps with Tzatziki Sauce
Prep: 16 minutes • Cook: 9 minutes

Cooking spray
¾ pound lean ground lamb
1 cup chopped onion
½ teaspoon black pepper
¼ teaspoon salt

2 cups shredded romaine lettuce
2 (3.8-ounce) Mediterranean-style white flatbreads (such as Toufayan)
Tzatziki Sauce

1. Heat a large nonstick skillet over medium-high heat. Coat pan with cooking spray. Add lamb and onion; cook 8 minutes or until lamb is browned and onion is tender, stirring to crumble lamb. Drain. Stir in pepper and salt.
2. Divide lettuce evenly between flatbreads; spoon lamb mixture evenly over lettuce. Drizzle lamb mixture evenly with Tzatziki Sauce. Roll up flatbreads, and wrap in parchment paper or tie with string. Cut each wrap in half, and serve immediately. Yield: 4 servings (serving size: 1 wrap).

CALORIES 389; FAT 17.6g (sat 6.5g, mono 6.8g, poly 4.2g); PROTEIN 23.6g; CARB 33.1g; FIBER 3.5g; CHOL 58mg; IRON 1.5mg; SODIUM 532mg; CALC 67mg

Tzatziki Sauce
Prep: 5 minutes

½ cup plain 2% reduced-fat Greek yogurt
¼ cup shredded seeded peeled cucumber
1 tablespoon chopped fresh mint

1 tablespoon lemon juice
⅛ teaspoon salt
2 garlic cloves, pressed

1. Combine all ingredients in a small bowl. Yield: about ⅔ cup (serving size: 2½ tablespoons).

CALORIES 26; FAT 0.7g (sat 0.5g, mono 0.2g, poly 0g); PROTEIN 3g; CARB 2.4g; FIBER 0.1g; CHOL 2mg; IRON 0.7mg; SODIUM 84mg; CALC 35mg

Nothing says Southern goodness more than bacon and pimiento cheese, and we've devised a delicious way to combine these regional favorites in sandwich form. Serve with a mixed fruit salad.

BLTs with Pimiento Cheese
Prep: 8 minutes • Cook: 12 minutes

½ cup light pimiento cheese spread (such as Price's)
8 (1-ounce) slices whole-wheat bread
12 reduced-fat bacon slices, cooked

4 green leaf lettuce leaves
12 (¼-inch-thick) slices tomato
¼ teaspoon freshly ground black pepper

1. Spread 1 tablespoon pimiento cheese over each bread slice.
2. Top each of 4 bread slices with 3 bacon slices, 1 lettuce leaf, and 3 tomato slices. Sprinkle with pepper. Cover with remaining 4 bread slices. Cut sandwiches in half; secure with wooden picks. Yield: 4 servings (serving size: 1 sandwich).

CALORIES 272; FAT 9.7g (sat 3.5g, mono 2.9g, poly 3.3g); PROTEIN 15.7g; CARB 29.2g; FIBER 3g; CHOL 25mg; IRON 2.5mg; SODIUM 894mg; CALC 127mg

ingredient spotlight

100% Whole-Wheat Bread Look for bread that has "whole-wheat flour," "whole grain," or "whole oats" in the ingredients label; 100% whole-wheat bread contains more protein and fiber than white bread for the same number of calories.

Turn up the flavor and the fun with this tropical twist on a ham and provolone sandwich with a checkerboard look. Serve with carrot sticks or your other favorite veggies on the side for dunking in the hummus.

Waffled Hawaiian Sandwiches
Prep: 3 minutes • Cook: 4 minutes per batch

8 ounces shaved lower-sodium deli smoked ham
4 (1-ounce) slices reduced-fat provolone cheese
4 (1-ounce) slices fresh pineapple
8 (0.9-ounce) slices white-wheat bread
Butter-flavored cooking spray

1. Preheat waffle iron.
2. Layer ham, cheese, and pineapple slices evenly on 4 bread slices; top with remaining bread slices. Coat sandwiches and waffle iron with cooking spray. Place sandwiches in waffle iron, in batches if necessary, and cook 4 to 6 minutes or until cheese melts and bread is toasted. Yield: 4 servings (serving size: 1 sandwich).

CALORIES 284; FAT 8.2g (sat 4g, mono 2.9g, poly 1.3g); PROTEIN 23.2g; CARB 30.4g; FIBER 2.9g; CHOL 40mg; IRON 0.5mg; SODIUM 901mg; CALC 229mg

serve with
Macadamia Hummus
Prep: 4 minutes • Cook: 10 minutes

2 garlic cloves
½ cup macadamia nuts, toasted
3 tablespoons water
2 tablespoons fresh lemon juice
1 tablespoon extra-virgin olive oil
1 (16-ounce) can chickpeas (garbanzo beans), drained

1. Drop garlic through a food chute with food processor on. Process until minced. Add nuts and remaining ingredients; process 1 minute or until smooth. Cover and store in refrigerator for up to 1 week. Yield: 12 servings (serving size: about 2 tablespoons).

CALORIES 73; FAT 5.9g (sat 0.8g, mono 4.4g, poly 0.5g); PROTEIN 1.4g; CARB 4.7g; FIBER 1.4g; CHOL 0mg; IRON 0.5mg; SODIUM 46mg; CALC 12mg

4-ingredient
10-minute

Italian Sausage Calzones

Prep: 10 minutes • Cook: 21 minutes • Other: 5 minutes

2 (4.5-ounce) hot turkey Italian sausage links
1 (13.8-ounce) can refrigerated pizza crust dough
½ cup fire-roasted tomato-and-garlic pasta sauce
1 cup (4 ounces) shredded reduced-fat Italian cheese blend
Cooking spray

1. Preheat oven to 450°.
2. Remove casings from sausage. Cook sausage in a large nonstick skillet over medium-high heat until browned, stirring to crumble. Drain well.
3. Place dough on a lightly floured surface; divide dough into 6 equal portions. Roll each portion into a 6-inch circle. Spread about 1 tablespoon pasta sauce over each circle, leaving a ¼-inch border. Arrange sausage evenly over half of each circle; top evenly with cheese. Fold other half of dough over filling; press edges together with a fork to seal.
4. Place calzones on a baking sheet coated with cooking spray. Coat calzones with cooking spray.
5. Bake at 450º for 15 minutes or until golden brown. Remove from oven. Let stand 5 minutes before serving. Yield: 6 servings (serving size: 1 calzone).

CALORIES 292; FAT 9.3g (sat 3.9g, mono 3.1g, poly 2.2g); PROTEIN 18g; CARB 33.5g; FIBER 0.3g; CHOL 46mg; IRON 2.6mg; SODIUM 928mg; CALC 142mg

serve with
Chopped Salad with Creamy Dill Dressing

Prep: 5 minutes

1 small garlic clove
¼ cup fat-free cottage cheese
2 tablespoons fat-free milk
1 tablespoon light mayonnaise
2 teaspoons white wine vinegar
¼ teaspoon freshly ground black pepper
⅛ teaspoon salt
1 tablespoon chopped fresh dill
4 cups chopped romaine lettuce
1 cup halved grape tomatoes

1. Drop garlic through food chute with food processor on. Process until minced. Add cottage cheese and next 5 ingredients. Process until smooth. Stir in dill.
2. Combine lettuce and tomatoes in a medium bowl; add dressing, tossing to coat. Yield: 6 servings (serving size: about ¾ cup).

CALORIES 28; FAT 0.9g (sat 0.1g, mono 0.2g, poly 0.5g); PROTEIN 2g; CARB 3.3g; FIBER 1.0g; CHOL 1mg; IRON 0.3mg; SODIUM 108mg; CALC 26mg

Call these quick, family-friendly pies pizza-in-a-pocket. Sprinkle any vegetable topping for pizza—onion, peppers, or mushrooms—on the filling before baking. Add a salad, and dinner's complete.

4-ingredient

10-minute

Rotisserie chicken is a cook's best friend. In this variation of chicken salad, we gave it the "wings" treatment complete with hot sauce, blue cheese, and celery. We used 1 tablespoon hot sauce for a medium kick—adjust up or down depending on your heat preference.

Buffalo Chicken Salad Sandwiches
Prep: 8 minutes

½ cup low-fat mayonnaise dressing
3 tablespoons crumbled blue cheese
1 tablespoon hot sauce (such as Frank's)
¼ teaspoon freshly ground black pepper
2 cups shredded skinless, boneless rotisserie chicken breast

¾ cup chopped celery
5 romaine lettuce leaves
5 (¼-inch-thick) slices tomato
5 (1.8-ounce) white-wheat hamburger buns

1. Combine first 4 ingredients in a medium bowl. Add chicken and celery, tossing to coat. Place 1 lettuce leaf, 1 tomato slice, and ½ cup chicken mixture on bottom half of each bun. Place remaining bun halves on top. Yield: 5 servings (serving size: 1 sandwich).

CALORIES 246; FAT 7.3g (sat 2.1g, mono 1.8g, poly 3.3g); PROTEIN 24g; CARB 26.6g; FIBER 5.8g; CHOL 51mg; IRON 0.8mg; SODIUM 693mg; CALC 354mg

serve with
Two-Potato Peppered Fries
Prep: 3 minutes • Cook: 20 minutes

1¼ cups frozen Yukon Gold fries with sea salt (such as Alexia)
1¼ cups frozen sweet potato fries (such as Alexia)

Olive oil-flavored cooking spray
1 tablespoon grated Parmesan cheese
1 teaspoon freshly ground mixed peppercorns

1. Preheat oven to 450°.
2. Place fries on a large rimmed baking sheet; coat heavily with cooking spray. Combine cheese and pepper. Sprinkle cheese mixture over fries; toss well.
3. Bake at 450° for 15 minutes. Stir, and bake an additional 5 minutes or until fries are lightly browned. Yield: 5 servings (serving size: ½ cup).

CALORIES 110; FAT 4g (sat 0.4g, mono 2.6g, poly 0.8g); PROTEIN 2.1g; CARB 17g; FIBER 1.9g; CHOL 1mg; IRON 0.7mg; SODIUM 143mg; CALC 35mg

Oregano, lemon, and feta cheese brighten the flavor of deli-convenient chicken in this quick Greek-themed sandwich.

Greek Chicken Sandwich with Lemon-Feta Spread
Prep: 10 minutes

Lemon-Feta Spread
4 (1.5-ounce) whole-grain white sandwich thins (such as Arnold)
2 cups bagged baby spinach leaves

8 ounces thinly sliced lemon pepper roasted chicken breast (such as Boar's Head)
¼ cup thinly sliced red onion

1. Prepare Lemon-Feta Spread.
2. Spread 2 tablespoons Lemon-Feta Spread evenly on cut sides of sandwich thins. Layer spinach, chicken, and onion evenly on bottoms of sandwich thins. Top with sandwich thin tops. Yield: 4 servings (serving size: 1 sandwich).

CALORIES 227; FAT 7.4g (sat 1.1g, mono 3.6g, poly 2.6g); PROTEIN 18.9g; CARB 24.9g; FIBER 5.7g; CHOL 37mg; IRON 1.9mg; SODIUM 782mg; CALC 81mg

Lemon-Feta Spread
Prep: 5 minutes

¼ cup canola mayonnaise
3 tablespoons crumbled reduced-fat feta cheese

2 teaspoons grated lemon rind
1 teaspoon minced fresh oregano
½ teaspoon freshly ground black pepper

1. Combine all ingredients in a small bowl. Yield: ½ cup (serving size: 2 tablespoons).

CALORIES 60; FAT 5.4g (sat 0.8g, mono 2.9g, poly 1.6g); PROTEIN 1.4g; CARB 0.6g; FIBER 0.3g; CHOL 2mg; IRON 0mg; SODIUM 178mg; CALC 19mg

fix it faster

Shave 5 minutes off your prep time simply by spreading the sandwich thins with 2 tablespoons of light mayonnaise.

What gives this wrap its charm is the fact that it's a sandwich and a salad rolled up into a convenient, hand-held package. If you want to make a lunch-box version, pack the lettuce, peanuts, and cilantro separate from the filling and assemble at lunchtime.

Lemongrass Chicken Lettuce Wraps
Prep: 9 minutes

3 cups shredded cooked chicken breast
1 cup matchstick-cut carrots
Lemongrass Vinaigrette

12 Boston lettuce leaves
¼ cup chopped dry-roasted peanuts
Fresh cilantro leaves (optional)

1. Combine first 3 ingredients in a medium bowl. Divide mixture evenly among lettuce leaves. Sprinkle with peanuts and, if desired, cilantro leaves. Yield: 4 servings (serving size: 3 wraps).

CALORIES 249; FAT 9.6g (sat 1.9g, mono 4.5g, poly 3g); PROTEIN 34.9g; CARB 5.2g; FIBER 1.2g; CHOL 89mg; IRON 1.6mg; SODIUM 403mg; CALC 34mg

Lemongrass Vinaigrette
Prep: 5 minutes

2 tablespoons fresh lime juice
1 tablespoon lemongrass paste (such as Gourmet Garden)
1 tablespoon chopped fresh cilantro

2 teaspoons canola oil
2 teaspoons fish sauce
1 teaspoon lower-sodium soy sauce
2 garlic cloves, minced

1. Combine all ingredients in a small bowl. Yield: ⅓ cup (serving size: about 1 tablespoon).

CALORIES 29; FAT 2.7g (sat 0.3g, mono 1.3g, poly 1g); PROTEIN 0.3g; CARB 1.8g; FIBER 0.1g; CHOL 0mg; IRON 0.1mg; SODIUM 272mg; CALC 3mg

ingredient spotlight

Lemongrass paste is a ground aromatic herb with a fresh lemony taste. It contains citral, an ingredient found in lemon peel. That essential oil gives lemongrass its prized lemon taste and fragrance. Lemongrass paste is used in Asian dishes to flavor sauces, soups, and curries.

Cut the ciabatta on a sharp diagonal for these big, open-faced chicken sandwiches. A pesto-laced mayonnaise ramps up the flavor of this hearty sandwich.

Mega Crostini Chicken Sandwiches
Prep: 6 minutes • Cook: 1 minute

4 (1-ounce) slices diagonally cut ciabatta, toasted
Olive oil-flavored cooking spray
Pesto Mayo

8 ounces thinly sliced lower-sodium deli chicken (such as Boar's Head EverRoast)
2 (6-ounce) ripe tomatoes, cut into 4 slices each
½ cup alfalfa sprouts

1. Lightly coat ciabatta slices with cooking spray; spread Pesto Mayo evenly on 1 side of each slice. Place chicken evenly over pesto. Top evenly with tomato slices and sprouts. Yield: 4 servings (serving size: 1 sandwich).

CALORIES 208; FAT 8.1g (sat 1.6g, mono 3.3g, poly 3.2g); PROTEIN 16.9g; CARB 21.4g; FIBER 1.6g; CHOL 34mg; IRON 1.7mg; SODIUM 795mg; CALC 14mg

Pesto Mayo
Prep: 2 minutes

3 tablespoons light mayonnaise
1 tablespoon commercial pesto (such as Alessi)

¼ teaspoon ground red pepper

1. Combine all ingredients in a small bowl. Cover and chill. Yield: ¼ cup (serving size: 1 tablespoon).

CALORIES 60; FAT 6g (sat 1.3g, mono 1.9g, poly 2.7g); PROTEIN 0.3g; CARB 1.5g; FIBER 0g; CHOL 4mg; IRON 0.1mg; SODIUM 151mg; CALC 4mg

Shards of crisp apples and sliced cheddar cheese balance sweetness with bite in this flavorful chicken sandwich. Have the deli shave the chicken into paper-thin slices.

Shaved Chicken, Apple, and Cheddar Sandwiches with Basil Mayo
Prep: 5 minutes • Cook: 8 minutes

4 (1.5-ounce) frozen focaccia rolls with Asiago and Parmesan cheese (such as Alexia)
Basil Mayo
6 ounces shaved deli maple-glazed roasted chicken breast (such as Boar's Head)

1 medium Granny Smith apple, thinly sliced
4 (0.7-ounce) slices reduced-fat sharp cheddar cheese

1. Bake focaccia according to package directions. Cut rolls horizontally in half.
2. Prepare Basil Mayo. Spread 1 tablespoon Basil Mayo evenly over cut sides of bread halves.
3. Layer roll bottoms evenly with chicken and apple; top with cheese and roll tops. Yield: 4 servings (serving size: 1 sandwich).

CALORIES 266; FAT 8.1g (sat 3.1g, mono 2.1g, poly 2.9g); PROTEIN 19.2g; CARB 31.1g; FIBER 1.7g; CHOL 40mg; IRON 0.9mg; SODIUM 788mg; CALC 175mg

Basil Mayo
Prep: 3 minutes

¼ cup low-fat mayonnaise dressing
1½ tablespoons chopped fresh basil

1 teaspoon Dijon mustard
½ teaspoon freshly ground pepper

1. Combine all ingredients in a small bowl. Yield: ⅓ cup (serving size: 1 tablespoon).

CALORIES 17; FAT 1g (sat 0g, mono 0.2g, poly 0.8g); PROTEIN 0.1g; CARB 2.5g; FIBER 0.1g; CHOL 0mg; IRON 0.1mg; SODIUM 160mg; CALC 3mg

This California favorite begins with pulled chicken and ends with a smoky paprika aioli. In between are creamy avocado and tomato slices. If the chicken is already smoky, use regular paprika in the aioli.

California Smoked Chicken Sandwiches
Prep: 5 minutes • Cook: 5 minutes

12 (0.7-ounce) slices sourdough bread
Smoked Paprika Aioli
 6 (¼-inch-thick) slices tomato

2 cups pulled skinless smoked chicken
1 medium avocado, cut into 12 slices

1. Toast bread. While bread toasts, prepare Smoked Paprika Aioli.
2. Spread aioli evenly on 6 bread slices. Layer tomato, chicken, and avocado over aioli. Top with remaining bread slices. Yield: 6 servings (serving size: 1 sandwich).

CALORIES 263; FAT 8.5g (sat 1.8g, mono 3.6g, poly 2.9g); PROTEIN 19.9g; CARB 25.8g; FIBER 2.5g; CHOL 42mg; IRON 2.3mg; SODIUM 356mg; CALC 32mg

Smoked Paprika Aioli
Prep: 5 minutes

3 tablespoons light mayonnaise
1 tablespoon finely chopped green onions
1 teaspoon smoked paprika

½ teaspoon grated lemon rind
1 garlic clove, minced

1. Combine all ingredients in a small bowl, stirring with a whisk. Cover and chill until ready to serve. Yield: ¼ cup (serving size: 2 teaspoons).

CALORIES 30; FAT 2.5g (sat 0.4g, mono 0.4g, poly 1.6g); PROTEIN 0.1g; CARB 0.9g; FIBER 0.1g; CHOL 3mg; IRON 0mg; SODIUM 60mg; CALC 2mg

10-minute

This American classic borrows the flavors of Italy. Sun-dried tomatoes, fresh basil, and fontina cheese perk up this cheese sandwich that can be prepared in a panini grill or on a griddle like a traditional grilled cheese.

Italian Grilled Cheese Sandwiches
Prep: 2 minutes • Cook: 7 minutes

2 ounces thinly sliced pancetta
8 (0.8-ounce) slices Chicago Italian bread
¼ teaspoon freshly ground black pepper
4 (¾-ounce) slices fontina cheese

1¾ ounces large sun-dried tomatoes, packed without oil (about 12)
8 large fresh basil leaves
Olive oil-flavored cooking spray

1. Preheat panini grill.
2. Cook pancetta in a large nonstick skillet over medium-high heat 5 minutes, turning often, until crisp. Remove pancetta from pan. Drain on paper towels.
3. Sprinkle 4 bread slices evenly with pepper; top evenly with pancetta, cheese slices, tomatoes, and basil leaves. Top sandwiches with remaining bread slices. Coat outsides of sandwiches with cooking spray.
4. Place sandwiches on panini grill; cook 2 minutes or until golden brown and cheese melts. Cut sandwiches in half, if desired. Yield: 4 servings (serving size: 1 sandwich).

CALORIES 274; FAT 13.1g (sat 6.5g, mono 4.6g, poly 2.1g); PROTEIN 12.4g; CARB 26.5g; FIBER 2g; CHOL 35mg; IRON 2mg; SODIUM 794mg; CALC 161mg

serve with
Watermelon Salad
Prep: 5 minutes

1 tablespoon white balsamic vinegar
2 teaspoons extra-virgin olive oil
1 teaspoon honey
¼ teaspoon freshly ground black pepper
1 shallot, minced

4 cups baby arugula
2 cups cubed watermelon
¼ cup (1 ounce) crumbled reduced-fat feta cheese

1. Combine first 5 ingredients in a large bowl. Add arugula and watermelon; toss gently to coat. Divide watermelon mixture evenly among 4 plates. Sprinkle each serving with 1 tablespoon cheese. Yield: 4 servings (serving size: 1½ cups salad and 1 tablespoon cheese).

CALORIES 79; FAT 3.5g (sat 1g, mono 2g, poly 0.5g); PROTEIN 2.6g; CARB 10.7g; FIBER 0.8g; CHOL 2mg; IRON 0.6mg; SODIUM 105mg; CALC 57mg

Juicy strawberries dress up this cheesy hot turkey sandwich. And the flavor mix doesn't stop there. All that goodness is sandwiched between cinnamon-raisin bread for a perfect pairing with Mint Limeade.

Hot Turkey and Strawberry Sandwiches
Prep: 6 minutes • Cook: 4 minutes

8 (1-ounce) slices whole-wheat cinnamon-raisin bread (such as Pepperidge Farm)
½ cup (4 ounces) tub-style ⅓-less-fat cream cheese
8 ounces thinly sliced 47% lower-sodium skinless turkey (such as Boar's Head)
8 large strawberries

1. Preheat broiler.
2. Place bread slices on a baking sheet; spread each slice with 1 tablespoon cream cheese. Place 2 ounces turkey over cream cheese on each of 4 slices. Broil 4 minutes or until cream cheese melts and turkey is thoroughly heated.
3. Slice and place 2 strawberries over turkey on each sandwich half. Top with remaining bread slices, cheese sides down.
4. Cut sandwiches in half, and serve immediately. Yield: 4 servings (serving size: 1 sandwich).

CALORIES 263; FAT 8.2g (sat 4.2g, mono 3g, poly 1g); PROTEIN 19.9g; CARB 23.2g; FIBER 3.7g; CHOL 41mg; IRON 2.2mg; SODIUM 628mg; CALC 62mg

serve with
Mint Limeade
Prep: 4 minutes

4 cups water, divided
⅓ cup sugar
¼ cup fresh mint leaves
1 lime, cut into quarters
Ice cubes
Mint leaves (optional)

1. Place 2 cups water and next 3 ingredients in a blender; process 1 minute or until mixture is pureed. Pour lime mixture through a sieve into a large pitcher. Stir in remaining 2 cups water. Pour limeade over ice cubes in glasses, and, if desired, garnish with mint leaves. Yield: 4 servings (serving size: about 1 cup).

CALORIES 71; FAT 0g (sat 0g, mono 0g, poly 0g); PROTEIN 0.1g; CARB 18.7g; FIBER 0.6g; CHOL 0mg; IRON 0.1mg; SODIUM 1mg; CALC 4mg

4-ingredient

Toasting the caraway seeds releases their aromatic oils and revs up the flavor of the colorful slaw in these updated hot dogs.

Grilled Chicken Sausages with Caraway Slaw
Prep: 7 minutes • Cook: 6 minutes

1 (12-ounce) package chicken apple sausage (such as Al Fresco)
Cooking spray

4 (1.7-ounce) bakery-style hot dog buns
Caraway Slaw

1. Preheat grill.
2. Place sausages on grill rack coated with cooking spray. Grill 6 minutes or until sausages reach desired degree of doneness, turning once. During last minute of grilling, open buns and place, cut sides down, on grill rack. Toast 1 minute.
3. While sausages cook, prepare slaw.
4. Divide sausages evenly among buns. Top sausages evenly with slaw. Yield: 4 servings (serving size: 1 sandwich).

CALORIES 340; FAT 12.8g (sat 2.4g, mono 5.3g, poly 5g); PROTEIN 19.7g; CARB 36.8g; FIBER 1g; CHOL 88mg; IRON 2.3mg; SODIUM 740mg; CALC 16mg

Caraway Slaw
Prep: 6 minutes • Cook: 1 minute

1 teaspoon caraway seeds
1 tablespoon chopped fresh parsley
2 tablespoons light mayonnaise
2 teaspoons cider vinegar

½ teaspoon sugar
1 cup thinly sliced red cabbage
1 cup packaged angel hair slaw

1. Cook caraway seeds in a small skillet over medium-high heat, stirring constantly, 1 to 2 minutes or until fragrant. Combine seeds, parsley, and next 3 ingredients in a medium bowl. Add cabbage and slaw, tossing to coat. Cover and chill until ready to serve. Yield: 4 servings (serving size: ½ cup).

CALORIES 41; FAT 2.6g (sat 0.4g, mono 0.6g, poly 1.5g); PROTEIN 0.7g; CARB 4g; FIBER 1g; CHOL 3mg; IRON 0.3mg; SODIUM 70mg; CALC 16mg

salads

Candied Balsamic Tomatoes and Mozzarella Salad, 95

Mediterranean Pasta Salad, 96

Antipasto Salad, 98

Chickpea, Feta, and Orzo Salad, 101

Tuna–Pita Chip Panzanella, 103

Crab Salad with Buttermilk Dressing, 104

Grilled Shrimp with Fennel-Orange Salad, 107

Greek Shrimp Salad, 108

Tropical Shrimp Salad, 111

Chipotle Taco Salad, 113

"Black and Blue" Steak Salad, 114

Grilled Pork Tenderloin Salad with Maple-Bacon Vinaigrette, 117

Tarragon-Chicken Quinoa Salad, 118

Curried Chicken and Broccoli Salad, 120

Chicken Caesar, 123

Asian Soba Noodle Salad, 124

Chicken Edamame Salad with Wasabi Vinaigrette, 127

Blueberry Spinach Salad with Grilled Chicken, 129

Turkey–Blue Cheese Salad, 130

Turkey-Cranberry Salad, 133

Succulent grape tomatoes are kissed with sugar, splashed with tangy balsamic vinegar, and finished with mozzarella and fresh basil. Try any combination of colorful tomatoes when they're in season.

Candied Balsamic Tomatoes and Mozzarella Salad
Prep: 4 minutes • Cook: 8 minutes

Cooking spray
4 cups grape tomatoes
1 teaspoon sugar
¼ teaspoon salt
¼ teaspoon pepper

1 tablespoon balsamic vinegar
4 ounces fresh mozzarella cheese, drained and cut into small pieces
¼ cup small fresh basil leaves, torn

1. Heat a large nonstick skillet over medium-high heat. Coat pan with cooking spray. Add tomatoes to pan; cook 5 minutes or until tomatoes release juices. Sprinkle with sugar, salt, and pepper; cook 2 minutes. Drizzle with vinegar; cook 30 seconds or just until vinegar evaporates.
2. Transfer tomato mixture to a serving bowl. Add mozzarella and basil; toss. Yield: 2 servings (serving size: about 1⅓ cups).

CALORIES 233; FAT 12.2g (sat 8.1g, mono 3.5g, poly 0.6g); PROTEIN 12.3g; CARB 17.1g; FIBER 4.3g; CHOL 45mg; IRON 0.6mg; SODIUM 388mg; CALC 384mg

serve with
Garlic-Pepper Toasts
Prep: 1 minute • Cook: 5 minutes

1 large garlic clove, halved
4 (1-ounce) slices ciabatta bread

Olive oil-flavored cooking spray
¼ teaspoon crushed red pepper

1. Preheat oven to 450°.
2. Rub cut sides of garlic over 1 side of each bread slice. Place bread on a baking sheet. Coat bread with cooking spray; sprinkle evenly with pepper. Bake at 450° for 5 minutes or until toasted. Yield: 2 servings (serving size: 2 toasts).

CALORIES 166; FAT 2.9g (sat 0.3g, mono 2.2g, poly 0.4g); PROTEIN 5.1g; CARB 31.5g; FIBER 1.1g; CHOL 0mg; IRON 1.8mg; SODIUM 388mg; CALC 3mg

Who would guess that this hearty Provençal-inspired pasta salad has less than 15 grams of fat per serving? It's studded with sun-dried tomatoes and drizzled with a tapenade-spiked vinaigrette.

Mediterranean Pasta Salad
Prep: 6 minutes • Cook: 10 minutes

8   ounces uncooked multigrain farfalle (bow tie pasta; such as Barilla Plus)
Olive-Parmesan Vinaigrette
1   cup chopped zucchini (about 1 medium)
½   cup julienne-cut sun-dried tomatoes, packed without oil
Fresh basil leaves (optional)

1. Cook pasta according to package directions, omitting salt and fat. While pasta cooks, prepare Olive-Parmesan Vinaigrette. Add zucchini to pasta during the last 1 to 2 minutes of cook time. Drain. Rinse pasta mixture under cold water; drain and place in a large bowl. Add tomatoes; drizzle with Olive-Parmesan Vinaigrette, tossing to coat. Garnish with basil, if desired, and serve immediately. Yield: 6 servings (serving size: 1 cup).

CALORIES 247; FAT 8.1g (sat 1.7g, mono 4.5g, poly 1.7g); PROTEIN 10.4g; CARB 33.1g; FIBER 5.1g; CHOL 3mg; IRON 2.7mg; SODIUM 245mg; CALC 100mg

Olive-Parmesan Vinaigrette
Prep: 4 minutes

¼   cup (1 ounce) grated fresh Parmesan cheese
¼   cup red wine vinegar
¼   cup olive tapenade
1   tablespoon extra-virgin olive oil
1   teaspoon Dijon mustard
¼   teaspoon freshly ground black pepper

1. Place all ingredients in a blender; process until smooth. Cover and refrigerate until ready to serve. Yield: 6 servings (serving size: 2 tablespoons).

CALORIES 73; FAT 6.7g (sat 1.7g, mono 4.1g, poly 0.8g); PROTEIN 2.7g; CARB 0.9g; FIBER 0.7g; CHOL 3mg; IRON 0.5mg; SODIUM 204mg; CALC 81mg

Here's a make-ahead salad that just got even easier. Just toss together all the ingredients and serve. Or toss it, chill it, and relax. The longer it chills, the better it tastes.

Antipasto Salad

Prep: 3 minutes • Cook: 12 minutes

1 (9-ounce) package fresh light 4-cheese ravioli
½ cup fat-free balsamic vinaigrette
¼ cup sliced ripe olives
¼ cup fresh basil leaves

2 tablespoons chopped drained oil-packed sun-dried tomato halves
1 (14-ounce) can quartered artichoke hearts, drained
Freshly ground black pepper (optional)

1. Cook pasta according to package directions, omitting salt and fat; drain.
2. Combine cooked pasta, vinaigrette, and remaining ingredients in a large bowl. Garnish with black pepper, if desired. Serve immediately. Yield: 4 servings (serving size: 1¼ cups).

CALORIES 232; FAT 4.3g (sat 1.6g, mono 1.9g, poly 0.8g); PROTEIN 10.5g; CARB 38.7g; FIBER 2.8g; CHOL 25mg; IRON 2.3mg; SODIUM 871mg; CALC 86mg

fix it faster

Slicing fresh olives can be a little time-consuming.
To make this recipe even faster, consider purchasing canned sliced olives instead.

This Mediterranean-style salad combines the chewy texture of chickpeas with the tangy flavor of feta. Chopped tomato adds a pop of color.

Chickpea, Feta, and Orzo Salad
Prep: 7 minutes • Cook: 10 minutes

1 cup uncooked orzo (rice-shaped pasta)
Cucumber-Thyme Relish
  1 cup refrigerated prechopped tomato
  1 (16-ounce) can chickpeas (garbanzo beans), rinsed and drained

¼ teaspoon salt
⅓ cup (1.3 ounces) crumbled feta cheese with basil and sun-dried tomatoes

1. Cook pasta according to package directions; drain and rinse under cold water. Drain well. While pasta cooks, prepare Cucumber-Thyme Relish.
2. Combine tomato and chickpeas in a large bowl, tossing gently; stir in pasta, salt, and Cucumber-Thyme Relish. Add feta cheese; toss gently. Yield: 4 servings (serving size: 1½ cups).

CALORIES 294; FAT 7.7g (sat 1.6g, mono 4.2g, poly 1.9g); PROTEIN 10.6g; CARB 46.6g; FIBER 5.3g; CHOL 7mg; IRON 1.3mg; SODIUM 488mg; CALC 60mg

Cucumber-Thyme Relish
Prep: 4 minutes

1½ tablespoons fresh lemon juice
  1 tablespoon extra-virgin olive oil
  ½ cup chopped English cucumber
  2 tablespoons finely chopped red onion

1 tablespoon fresh thyme leaves
¼ teaspoon salt
¼ teaspoon freshly ground black pepper

1. Combine lemon juice and olive oil in a medium bowl, stirring with a whisk. Stir in cucumber and remaining ingredients. Yield: ⅔ cup (serving size: about 3 tablespoons).

CALORIES 37; FAT 3.5g (sat 0.5g, mono 2.5g, poly 0.5g); PROTEIN 0.2g; CARB 1.6g; FIBER 0.3g; CHOL 0mg; IRON 0.2mg; SODIUM 146mg; CALC 7mg

ingredient spotlight

Orzo is a tiny rice-shaped pasta. It is perfect in soups and salads and cooks in a flash. It is available in both short, plump "grains" and long, thin "grains."

We borrowed the idea of the traditional Italian bread salad and substituted pita chips for this salad. It's best tossed and eaten right away to enjoy the crunch.

Tuna–Pita Chip Panzanella
Prep: 4 minutes

3 cups plain pita chips, coarsely broken
1½ cups chopped cucumber (about 1 large)
½ cup chopped red onion (about 1 small)
¼ cup pitted kalamata olives, coarsely chopped

1 (12-ounce) can albacore tuna in water, drained and flaked into large chunks
¼ cup light balsamic vinaigrette (such as Kraft)
¼ cup torn fresh mint leaves
¼ teaspoon freshly ground black pepper

1. Combine first 5 ingredients in a bowl; toss gently. Drizzle with vinaigrette; toss. Sprinkle with mint leaves and pepper; toss well. Serve immediately. Yield: 6 servings (serving size: 1½ cups).

CALORIES 165; FAT 5.8g (sat 0.5g, mono 4g, poly 1.2g); PROTEIN 11.9g; CARB 16.8g; FIBER 1.9g; CHOL 16mg; IRON 0.4mg; SODIUM 475mg; CALC 14mg

serve with
Salt and Pepper Tomatoes
Prep: 3 minutes

2 medium-sized red tomatoes, each cut into 5 slices (about ¾ pound)
2 medium-sized yellow tomatoes, each cut into 4 slices (about 9 ounces)

¼ cup (1 ounce) crumbled reduced-fat feta cheese
¼ teaspoon freshly ground black pepper
⅛ teaspoon salt

1. Alternately overlap tomato slices on a platter; sprinkle with cheese, pepper, and salt. Cover and chill until ready to serve. Yield: 6 servings (serving size: 3 tomato slices and 2 teaspoons cheese).

CALORIES 30; FAT 0.9g (sat 0.5g, mono 0.2g, poly 0.1g); PROTEIN 2.1g; CARB 4.3g; FIBER 1.2g; CHOL 1mg; IRON 0.5mg; SODIUM 133mg; CALC 24mg

quick flip

Panzanella is an Italian bread salad that's popular in the summer months. Traditionally, the recipe calls for soaking densely textured, day-old bread in water and then squeezing it out, giving it the name of "leftover salad." Swap out the pita chips for 3 cups of cubed Italian loaf bread for a more authentic dish.

No need to proceed with caution for this creamy seafood salad because low-fat buttermilk provides the creaminess. Lemon zest adds plenty of zing.

Crab Salad with Buttermilk Dressing
Prep: 7 minutes

Buttermilk Dressing
1 pound jumbo lump crabmeat, drained and shell pieces removed

4 large Bibb lettuce leaves
2 cups multicolored cherry tomatoes (about 12 ounces), quartered

1. Prepare Buttermilk Dressing.
2. Combine crabmeat and dressing; toss well. Place a lettuce leaf on each of 4 plates. Spoon about ⅔ cup crab salad on each lettuce leaf; sprinkle ½ cup tomatoes over each salad. Yield: 4 servings (serving size: 1 salad).

CALORIES 129; FAT 3.6g (sat 1.5g, mono 0.9g, poly 1.1g); PROTEIN 18.7g; CARB 7.3g; FIBER 1.1g; CHOL 108mg; IRON 1.4mg; SODIUM 498mg; CALC 90mg

Buttermilk Dressing
Prep: 4 minutes

½ cup low-fat buttermilk
¼ cup light sour cream
2 teaspoons grated lemon rind

1 teaspoon chopped fresh dill
¼ teaspoon freshly ground black pepper
⅛ teaspoon salt

1. Combine all ingredients in a small bowl, stirring with a whisk. Yield: 4 servings (serving size: 3 tablespoons).

CALORIES 31; FAT 1.3g (sat 0.9g, mono 0.2g, poly 0.1g); PROTEIN 1.6g; CARB 3.7g; FIBER 0.1g; CHOL 6mg; IRON 0mg; SODIUM 120mg; CALC 38mg

quick flip

Change out the flavor of the dressing with a quick switch of mint for the dill. One teaspoon of mint brings out the citrusy, zesty flavor of this seafood specialty.

The shrimp and salad are delicious enough
to serve alone, but who wants a one-dimensional salad?
We've combined them and added a final sprinkle of
Parmigiano-Reggiano cheese shards.

Grilled Shrimp with Fennel-Orange Salad

Prep: 13 minutes • Cook: 5 minutes

Fennel-Orange Salad
- 1 tablespoon brown sugar
- 1 tablespoon olive oil
- ¼ teaspoon freshly ground black pepper

- ⅛ teaspoon kosher salt
- 1½ pounds peeled and deveined large shrimp
- Cooking spray
- Parmigiano-Reggiano cheese shards (optional)

1. Preheat grill.

2. Prepare Fennel-Orange Salad. Place reserved 3 tablespoons juice from sectioning oranges in a medium bowl. Stir in brown sugar and next 3 ingredients; add shrimp, tossing well to coat.

3. Remove shrimp from orange juice mixture, and place in a grill topper coated with cooking spray. Place topper on grill rack. Grill 5 minutes or until shrimp reach desired degree of doneness, turning once with a spatula. Serve grilled shrimp over Fennel-Orange Salad. Garnish with cheese shards, if desired. Yield: 4 servings (serving size: 1½ cups salad and 7 to 8 shrimp).

CALORIES 363; FAT 13g (sat 2.1g, mono 8.2g, poly 2.5g); PROTEIN 37g; CARB 25g; FIBER 5.6g; CHOL 259mg; IRON 5.3mg; SODIUM 677mg; CALC 188mg

Fennel-Orange Salad

Prep: 7 minutes

- 2 navel oranges
- 2 tablespoons white wine vinegar
- 1 tablespoon olive oil
- ½ teaspoon freshly ground black pepper
- ¼ teaspoon kosher salt

- 2 medium fennel bulbs, thinly sliced
- ½ cup sliced red onion
- ⅓ cup pitted kalamata olives, halved
- Fennel fronds (optional)

1. Peel and section oranges over a large bowl; squeeze membranes to extract juice. If preparing Grilled Shrimp (above), reserve 3 tablespoons juice. Gently stir vinegar and next 3 ingredients into orange sections and remaining juice in bowl. Add fennel, onion, and olives; toss gently. Garnish with fennel fronds, if desired. Yield: 4 servings (serving size: 1½ cups).

CALORIES 140; FAT 6.7g (sat 0.8g, mono 5g, poly 0.7g); PROTEIN 2.5g; CARB 20g; FIBER 5.6g; CHOL 0mg; IRON 1.1mg; SODIUM 365mg; CALC 96mg

fix it faster

An indoor grill or the broiler is a quick-prep option to grilling outdoors.

The Greek Feta Dressing for this shrimp salad does double duty as both a dressing and a quick-soak marinade.

Greek Shrimp Salad
Prep: 6 minutes • Cook: 6 minutes

Greek Feta Dressing, divided
1 pound peeled and deveined medium shrimp
8 cups coarsely chopped romaine lettuce

1½ cups halved cherry tomatoes
1 cup chopped English cucumber

1. Prepare Greek Feta Dressing. Combine shrimp and ¼ cup Greek Feta Dressing in a bowl. Heat a large nonstick skillet over medium-high heat. Add shrimp mixture; cook, stirring often, 5 minutes or until desired degree of doneness.
2. While shrimp cooks, place 2 cups lettuce on each of 4 plates; top evenly with tomato and cucumber.
3. Spoon shrimp mixture evenly over salads, and drizzle with remaining dressing. Serve immediately. Yield: 4 servings (serving size: 2 cups lettuce, 6 tablespoons tomato, ¼ cup cucumber, ⅔ cup shrimp mixture, and 3 tablespoons dressing).

CALORIES 288; FAT 16.1g (sat 4.2g, mono 8.8g, poly 2.9g); PROTEIN 27.1g; CARB 8.7g; FIBER 3.2g; CHOL 185mg; IRON 4.4mg; SODIUM 634mg; CALC 175mg

Greek Feta Dressing
Prep: 3 minutes

½ cup (2 ounces) finely crumbled feta cheese
½ cup red wine vinegar
2 tablespoons salt-free dried herb-Greek seasoning (such as McCormick)

3 tablespoons extra-virgin olive oil
½ teaspoon salt

1. Combine all ingredients in a small bowl, stirring with a whisk. Yield: 5 servings (serving size: 3 tablespoons).

CALORIES 107; FAT 10.8g (sat 2.9g, mono 6.6g, poly 1.3g); PROTEIN 1.6g; CARB 0.5g; FIBER 0g; CHOL 10mg; IRON 0.2mg; SODIUM 361mg; CALC 58mg

quick flip

Don't have shrimp? Make an easy sub with chicken tenderloins cut into 1-inch pieces. The pluses: price, availability, and ease of preparation.

A stress-free shrimp dinner? Definitely. In under 10 minutes? You bet. Just reach for cooked shrimp, and dress, toss, and enjoy!

Tropical Shrimp Salad
Prep: 7 minutes

Spicy Ginger Dressing
1½ pounds large shrimp, cooked, peeled, and coarsely chopped

1¼ cups coarsely chopped fresh pineapple
⅓ cup sliced radishes (about 5 medium radishes)
Bibb lettuce leaves (optional)

1. Prepare Spicy Ginger Dressing in a large bowl. Add shrimp, pineapple, and radishes; toss well. Drizzle with dressing, and toss well. Serve shrimp salad on Bibb lettuce leaves, if desired. Yield: 4 servings (serving size: 1 cup).

CALORIES 248; FAT 5g (sat 0.8g, mono 1.2g, poly 3g); PROTEIN 34.9g; CARB 14.7g; FIBER 1.2g; CHOL 259mg; IRON 4.7mg; SODIUM 665mg; CALC 102mg

Spicy Ginger Dressing
Prep: 2 minutes

½ cup light sesame-ginger dressing (such as Newman's Own)
¼ cup chopped green onions

1 tablespoon fresh lime juice
1 tablespoon chili garlic sauce (such as Hokan)

1. Combine all ingredients. Cover and chill until ready to serve. Yield: 4 servings (serving size: 3 tablespoons).

CALORIES 44; FAT 2g (sat 0g, mono 0.5g, poly 1.5g); PROTEIN 0g; CARB 6.8g; FIBER 0.4g; CHOL 0mg; IRON 0.5mg; SODIUM 410mg; CALC 6mg

Smoky chipotle salsa replaces sodium-laden taco seasoning mix to flavor the meat in this popular Mexican salad. And it's ready in less than 15 minutes. Let the fiesta begin!

Chipotle Taco Salad
Prep: 3 minutes • Cook: 7 minutes

1 pound ground sirloin
1 cup chipotle salsa (such as Muir Glen), divided
2 tablespoons water
¼ teaspoon salt
6 cups shredded iceberg lettuce
4 cups baked tortilla chips (such as Guiltless Gourmet)

1 cup chopped tomato
½ cup light sour cream
¼ cup sliced green onions (about 2 onions)
1 cup (4 ounces) preshredded reduced-fat 4-cheese Mexican blend cheese

1. Cook beef in a large nonstick skillet over medium heat until browned; stir to crumble. Stir in ½ cup salsa, 2 tablespoons water, and salt; cook 1 minute.
2. Arrange 1½ cups lettuce on each of 4 plates; top each serving with 1 cup tortilla chips, ¼ cup tomato, ⅔ cup meat mixture, 2 tablespoons sour cream, 2 tablespoons salsa, 1 tablespoon green onions, and ¼ cup cheese. Yield: 4 servings (serving size: 1 salad).

CALORIES 400; FAT 14.8g (sat 7.3g, mono 5.4g, poly 2.1g); PROTEIN 34.3g; CARB 32g; FIBER 3.8g; CHOL 80mg; IRON 3.1mg; SODIUM 989mg; CALC 227mg

serve with
Watermelon-Limeade Sparkler
Prep: 4 minutes

2 cups cubed watermelon
2 cups lime-flavored sparkling water
¼ cup frozen limeade concentrate, thawed

Crushed ice
4 lime wedges

1. Place watermelon in a food processor; process until smooth. Pour into a large pitcher. Add 2 cups sparkling water and limeade concentrate, stirring until concentrate dissolves. Serve over crushed ice with lime wedges. Yield: 4 servings (serving size: 1 cup sparkler and 1 lime wedge).

CALORIES 73; FAT 0.1g (sat 0g, mono 0.03g, poly 0.04g); PROTEIN 0.5g; CARB 18.9g; FIBER 0.8g; CHOL 0mg; IRON 0.2mg; SODIUM 6mg; CALC 24mg

"Black and Blue" Steak Salad

Prep: 4 minutes • Cook: 12 minutes • Other: 8 hours and 5 minutes

2 teaspoons olive oil
1½ teaspoons 25%-less-sodium Montreal steak seasoning (such as McCormick)
1 (¾-pound) flank steak, trimmed
Cooking spray

1 (6.5-ounce) package sweet butter lettuce blend salad greens (such as Fresh Express)
⅓ cup extra-virgin olive oil vinaigrette (such as Bolthouse Farms Classic Balsamic)
¾ cup (3 ounces) crumbled blue cheese

1. Rub oil and sprinkle steak seasoning on both sides of steak. Place steak in a large heavy-duty zip-top plastic bag; seal bag. Marinate in refrigerator 8 hours.
2. Preheat grill.
3. Remove steak from bag. Place steak on grill rack coated with cooking spray. Grill 6 to 8 minutes on each side or until desired degree of doneness. Remove steak from grill; cover and let stand 5 minutes. Cut steak diagonally across grain into thin slices.
4. Combine salad greens and vinaigrette in a large bowl, tossing gently to coat. Divide salad evenly among 4 plates. Arrange steak evenly over salads; sprinkle evenly with blue cheese. Yield: 4 servings (serving size: 3 ounces steak, 1¼ cups salad, and 3 tablespoons cheese).

CALORIES 240; FAT 12.7g (sat 6.4g, mono 5.3g, poly 1g); PROTEIN 23.4g; CARB 5.5g; FIBER 0.5g; CHOL 45mg; IRON 2mg; SODIUM 644mg; CALC 146mg

serve with
Balsamic Berries Romanoff

Prep: 3 minutes

1 cup quartered small strawberries
1 cup blueberries
1 cup raspberries

1 tablespoon bottled balsamic glaze
¼ cup light sour cream

1. Combine first 4 ingredients in a medium bowl; let stand 5 minutes. Spoon berry mixture evenly into 4 small bowls. Top evenly with sour cream. Yield: 4 servings (serving size: ¾ cup berry mixture and 1 tablespoon sour cream).

CALORIES 75; FAT 1.5g (sat 0.8g, mono 0.3g, poly 0.3g); PROTEIN 1.4g; CARB 16g; FIBER 3.7g; CHOL 5mg; IRON 0.5mg; SODIUM 19mg; CALC 17mg

Order a "Pittsburgh Rare, black and blue" in an upscale steakhouse, and you'll get a steak charred on the outside and rare on the inside. Our "black and blue" salad is a variation on the theme. Here, flank steak, grilled medium-rare so it's tender and juicy, is teamed with blue cheese, an excellent companion to this flavorful beefy salad.

Enjoy the seasonal splendor of peaches in a new way. They make the crossover from cobbler to the grill and stand next to pork tenderloin atop a flourish of baby greens drizzled with a sweet-smoky vinaigrette.

4-ingredient

Grilled Pork Tenderloin Salad with Maple-Bacon Vinaigrette

Prep: 16 minutes • Cook: 20 minutes • Other: 10 minutes

Maple-Bacon Vinaigrette
1 (1-pound) pork tenderloin, trimmed
¼ teaspoon salt
¼ teaspoon freshly ground black pepper

6 peaches, halved and pitted
Cooking spray
12 cups mixed baby salad greens

1. Prepare Maple-Bacon Vinaigrette.

2. Preheat grill.

3. While grill heats, combine 2 tablespoons Maple-Bacon Vinaigrette and pork in a large heavy-duty zip-top plastic bag; seal. Let stand 10 minutes.

4. Remove pork from vinaigrette, discarding vinaigrette. Sprinkle pork with salt and pepper. Coat peach halves with cooking spray. Place pork and peach halves on grill rack coated with cooking spray.

5. Grill pork 10 minutes on each side or until a thermometer registers 155° (slightly pink). Let pork stand 5 minutes before slicing. Grill peach halves 1 to 2 minutes on each side. While pork stands, cut each peach half into 4 wedges. Cut pork into ½-inch slices.

6. Toss salad greens with 2½ tablespoons Maple-Bacon Vinaigrette. Place 2 cups greens mixture on each of 6 plates; top evenly with pork slices and peach wedges. Drizzle remaining Maple-Bacon Vinaigrette evenly over salads; sprinkle with reserved bacon. Yield: 6 servings (serving size: 2 ounces pork, 2 cups salad, and 1 peach).

CALORIES 286; FAT 10.5g (sat 3.4g, mono 4.3g, poly 2.6g); PROTEIN 30.9g; CARB 16.4g; FIBER 1.1g; CHOL 70mg; IRON 2.1mg; SODIUM 809mg; CALC 241mg

Maple-Bacon Vinaigrette

Prep: 1 minute • Cook: 10 minutes

3 slices applewood-smoked bacon
¼ cup minced Vidalia or other sweet onion
¼ cup white wine vinegar
2½ tablespoons maple syrup

2 teaspoons olive oil
¼ teaspoon dry mustard
¼ teaspoon salt
¼ teaspoon freshly ground black pepper

1. Cook bacon in a large nonstick skillet over medium heat until crisp. Remove bacon from pan, reserving 1½ teaspoons drippings in pan; crumble and set bacon aside. Add onion to drippings in pan; sauté 1½ minutes. Remove from heat; stir in vinegar and remaining ingredients. Yield: 6 servings (serving size: about 1½ tablespoons).

CALORIES 120; FAT 2.5g (sat 0.8g, mono 1g, poly 0.6g); PROTEIN 21.8g; CARB 1.3g; FIBER 0.1g; CHOL 60mg; IRON 0.8mg; SODIUM 252mg; CALC 12mg

Packed with protein, this whole-grain salad combines tender rotisserie chicken and juicy grapes with an apple-yogurt dressing. Granny Smith apple slices make a great accompaniment.

Tarragon-Chicken Quinoa Salad

Prep: 4 minutes • Cook: 18 minutes

1 cup uncooked quinoa
2 cups water
Creamy Apple Dressing

2 cups pulled rotisserie chicken
2 cups halved red seedless grapes
½ teaspoon salt

1. Place quinoa in a fine sieve. Rinse quinoa under cold water until water runs clear; drain well.

2. Combine quinoa and 2 cups water in a medium saucepan; bring to a boil. Cover, reduce heat, and simmer 15 minutes or until grains are translucent and the germ has spiraled out from each grain. While quinoa cooks, prepare Creamy Apple Dressing. Rinse quinoa under cold water until cool; drain well.

3. Place quinoa, chicken, and grapes in a large bowl. Combine Creamy Apple Dressing and salt, stirring with a whisk; add to quinoa mixture, tossing until coated. Serve immediately, or cover and refrigerate until thoroughly chilled. Yield: 6 servings (serving size: 1 cup).

CALORIES 273; FAT 6.1g (sat 1.4g, mono 3g, poly 1.6g); PROTEIN 20.6g; CARB 35.4g; FIBER 2.6g; CHOL 41mg; IRON 3.4mg; SODIUM 444mg; CALC 52mg

Creamy Apple Dressing

Prep: 5 minutes

½ cup plain low-fat Greek yogurt
1 Granny Smith apple, cored and quartered
1 tablespoon olive oil

1 teaspoon fresh tarragon
¼ teaspoon salt
¼ teaspoon white pepper

1. Place all ingredients a blender; process 1 minute or until apple is pureed. Cover and chill until ready to serve. Yield: 6 servings (serving size: about 3 tablespoons).

CALORIES 54; FAT 2.7g (sat 0.6g, mono 1.7g, poly 0.3g); PROTEIN 2g; CARB 6.2g; FIBER 0.4g; CHOL 1mg; IRON 0.1mg; SODIUM 105mg; CALC 23mg

4-ingredient

It's all about the crunch from the crisp apples and crunchy broccoli coleslaw. Fresh ginger and curry deliver the flavor to this chicken salad. Serve over red leaf lettuce, if desired, with whole-wheat crackers to complete the meal.

Curried Chicken and Broccoli Salad
Prep: 8 minutes

Curry-Yogurt Dressing
- 3 cups pulled rotisserie chicken
- 2 cups chopped Fuji apple (2 apples)
- ½ cup raisins
- 1 (12-ounce) package broccoli coleslaw

1. Prepare Curry-Yogurt Dressing in a large bowl. Add chicken and remaining ingredients; toss well. Cover and chill until ready to serve. Yield: 6 servings (serving size: 1½ cups).

CALORIES 333; FAT 3.9g (sat 1.3g, mono 1.6g, poly 0.9g); PROTEIN 39.7g; CARB 34.5g; FIBER 6g; CHOL 89mg; IRON 2.6mg; SODIUM 505mg; CALC 90mg

Curry-Yogurt Dressing
Prep: 4 minutes

- ¾ cup vanilla fat-free Greek yogurt
- 1 tablespoon chopped fresh cilantro
- 1 tablespoon grated peeled fresh ginger
- 1¼ teaspoons curry powder
- ¼ teaspoon salt

1. Combine all ingredients. Cover and refrigerate until ready to use. Yield: 6 servings (serving size: 2 tablespoons).

CALORIES 17; FAT 0.1g (sat 0g, mono 0.1g, poly 0g); PROTEIN 2.5g; CARB 1.6g; FIBER 0.2g; CHOL 0mg; IRON 0.1mg; SODIUM 108mg; CALC 21mg

Rotisserie chicken stars in this chopped salad with a light Caesar dressing. One rotisserie chicken yields about 3 cups chopped chicken. Save the remaining 1 cup as a topping for pizza.

10-minute

Chicken Caesar
Prep: 7 minutes

Dijon Chicken
3 (1-ounce) slices ciabatta bread, toasted
1 large garlic clove, halved
1 romaine heart, chopped (5 cups)

½ cup (2 ounces) grated fresh Parmesan cheese
¼ cup reduced-calorie Caesar dressing (such as Ken's Steak House Lite Caesar)

1. Prepare Dijon Chicken.
2. Rub cut sides of toast with garlic halves. Cut toast vertically into ¾-inch-wide strips; cut strips in half to make croutons.
3. Combine lettuce, Dijon Chicken, and cheese in a large bowl; toss. Drizzle with dressing; toss. Add croutons. Yield: 4 servings (serving size: ½ cup chicken, about 1¾ cups salad, and 1 tablespoon dressing).

CALORIES 286; FAT 10.5g (sat 3.4g, mono 4.3g, poly 2.6g); PROTEIN 30.9g; CARB 16.4g; FIBER 1.1g; CHOL 70mg; IRON 2.1mg; SODIUM 809mg; CALC 241mg

Dijon Chicken
Prep: 2 minutes

½ teaspoon grated lemon rind
2 tablespoons fresh lemon juice
1 tablespoon water
1½ teaspoons Dijon mustard

½ teaspoon freshly ground black pepper
2 cups skinless, boneless rotisserie chicken breast, pulled

1. Combine first 5 ingredients in a bowl; add chicken and toss. Yield: 2 cups (serving size: ½ cup).

CALORIES 121; FAT 2.5g (sat 0.2g, mono 1g, poly 0.6g); PROTEIN 21.8g; CARB 1.3g; FIBER 0.1g; CHOL 60mg; IRON 0.8mg; SODIUM 252mg; CALC 12mg

fix it faster

Romaine is an elongated head of lettuce with leaves that are juicy and sweet. It's the traditional lettuce for Caesar salad because it's sturdy and can hold up well to strong-flavored dressings and garnishes. If you're in a crunch for time, substitute 1 (10-ounce) package chopped romaine.

Soba noodles are made from buckwheat and wheat flour; if unavailable, use whole-wheat spaghetti.

Asian Soba Noodle Salad
Prep: 10 minutes • Cook: 10 minutes

1 (8-ounce) package soba noodles
1½ cups frozen shelled edamame (green soybeans)
1½ cups matchstick-cut carrots
Orange Vinaigrette

Cooking spray
1 pound chicken breast tenders, cut into thin strips
¼ teaspoon salt
¼ teaspoon freshly ground black pepper

1. Cook noodles in boiling water 7 minutes or until almost al dente. Add edamame and carrots to pan; cook 1 minute or until tender. Drain; rinse under cold water. While noodle mixture cooks, prepare Orange Vinaigrette in a large bowl. Add noodle mixture to bowl; set aside.
2. While noodles cook, heat a large nonstick skillet over medium-high heat. Coat pan with cooking spray. Sprinkle chicken evenly with salt and pepper. Add chicken to pan. Cook 3 minutes on each side or until browned. Add chicken to noodle mixture; toss gently to coat. Cover and chill until ready to serve. Yield: 6 servings (serving size: about 1 cup).

CALORIES 322; FAT 7.6g (sat 1.2g, mono 2.9g, poly 3.4g); PROTEIN 25.6g; CARB 36.3g; FIBER 4g; CHOL 42mg; IRON 1.2mg; SODIUM 446mg; CALC 16mg

Orange Vinaigrette
Prep: 6 minutes

3 tablespoons fresh orange juice
1 tablespoon finely chopped green onions
1 tablespoon mirin (sweet rice wine)
1 tablespoon lower-sodium soy sauce

1 tablespoon dark sesame oil
2 teaspoons grated peeled fresh ginger
2 large garlic cloves, minced

1. Combine all ingredients in a bowl, stirring with a whisk. Yield: 6 servings (serving size: 1 tablespoon).

CALORIES 33; FAT 2.4g (sat 0.3g, mono 0.9g, poly 1.1g); PROTEIN 0.3g; CARB 2.4g; FIBER 0.1g; CHOL 0mg; IRON 0.1mg; SODIUM 101mg; CALC 4mg

Edamame are green soybeans. These folate-rich gems are packed with protein and fiber. They can be simmered, steamed, microwaved, boiled, and sautéed. You can even puree edamame to make hummus.

Chicken Edamame Salad with Wasabi Vinaigrette
Prep: 13 minutes

1½ cups frozen shelled edamame (green soybeans)
6 cups shredded napa (Chinese) cabbage
3 cups shredded cooked chicken breast
4 green onions, sliced
¾ cup Wasabi Vinaigrette

1. Place edamame in a wire mesh strainer; rinse with cold water until thawed. Drain well. Combine edamame and next 3 ingredients in a large bowl. Prepare Wasabi Vinaigrette. Add Wasabi Vinaigrette to edamame mixture; toss well. Yield: 4 servings (serving size: 2 cups).

CALORIES 404; FAT 13.8g (sat 2.1g, mono 6.4g, poly 5.2g); PROTEIN 42.9g; CARB 25.8g; FIBER 6.3g; CHOL 89mg; IRON 1.4mg; SODIUM 261mg; CALC 120mg

Wasabi Vinaigrette
Prep: 3 minutes

⅔ cup rice vinegar
2 tablespoons canola oil
3 tablespoons honey
2 teaspoons wasabi paste
¼ teaspoon salt
2 garlic cloves, pressed

1. Combine all ingredients, stirring well with a whisk. Yield: 1 cup (serving size: 3 tablespoons).

CALORIES 104; FAT 5.8g (sat 0.4g, mono 3.4g, poly 2g); PROTEIN 0.1g; CARB 12.1g; FIBER 0.1g; CHOL 0mg; IRON 0.1mg; SODIUM 159mg; CALC 3mg

quick flip

Substitute 2 (6-ounce) bags fresh baby spinach for the 6 cups napa cabbage. Drizzle the leftover vinaigrette over the spinach, and add mandarin oranges, sliced almonds, and thinly sliced red onions.

4-ingredient

This salad is the prescription for a healthful meal—blueberries for antioxidants; spinach for iron, folate, and vitamins A and C; and chicken for protein—just what the doctor ordered.

Blueberry Spinach Salad with Grilled Chicken

Prep: 9 minutes • Cook: 11 minutes • Other: 3 minutes

Blueberry-Thyme Dressing, divided
3 (6-ounce) skinless, boneless chicken
   breast halves
Cooking spray

1 (6-ounce) package fresh baby spinach
1 cup (4 ounces) crumbled goat cheese
1 cup blueberries (optional)

1. Prepare Blueberry-Thyme Dressing.
2. Place chicken breasts in a medium bowl. Add ⅓ cup dressing; toss to coat.
3. Heat a nonstick grill pan over medium-high heat. Coat pan with cooking spray. Add chicken mixture to pan; cook 5 minutes on each side or until desired degree of doneness. Let chicken stand 3 minutes before cutting crosswise into ½-inch slices. Cover and keep warm.
4. While chicken cooks, place 1½ cups spinach on each of 4 plates.
5. Top salads evenly with chicken slices; sprinkle evenly with goat cheese and, if desired, blueberries. Drizzle evenly with remaining dressing. Yield: 4 servings (serving size: 1½ cups spinach, 3 ounces chicken, 2 tablespoons cheese, and about 3 tablespoons dressing).

CALORIES 546; FAT 27.8g (sat 16.2g, mono 9.1g, poly 2.5g); PROTEIN 41.3g; CARB 16.4g; FIBER 2g; CHOL 141mg; IRON 2mg; SODIUM 793mg; CALC 143mg

Blueberry-Thyme Dressing

Prep: 3 minutes

1 cup blueberries
2 tablespoons lemon juice
2 tablespoons extra-virgin olive oil

2 tablespoons honey
2 teaspoons chopped fresh thyme
½ teaspoon salt

1. Place all ingredients in a blender; process 30 seconds or until smooth. Yield: 5 servings (serving size: about 3 tablespoons).

CALORIES 93; FAT 5.7g (sat 0.8g, mono 4g, poly 0.8g); PROTEIN 0.3g; CARB 11.9g; FIBER 0.8g; CHOL 0mg; IRON 0.2mg; SODIUM 233mg; CALC 4mg

Here's the perfect lunch-break salad; it's simple, quick, and delicious. Substitute sliced deli chicken breast for the turkey, and feta cheese for blue cheese, if you like.

Turkey–Blue Cheese Salad

Prep: 4 minutes

4 ounces thinly sliced deli smoked turkey breast
4 cups mixed salad greens
2 cups grape tomatoes
2 tablespoons crumbled blue cheese
¼ cup light balsamic vinaigrette

1. Stack turkey slices; roll up. Cut into 1-inch pieces.
2. Arrange greens on 4 plates. Top each with turkey, tomatoes, blue cheese, and vinaigrette. Yield: 4 servings (serving size: 1 cup greens, 1 ounce turkey, ½ cup tomatoes, ½ tablespoon blue cheese, and 1 tablespoon vinaigrette).

CALORIES 81; FAT 2.4g (sat 0.7g, mono 1.1g, poly 0.6g); PROTEIN 8.7g; CARB 7.2g; FIBER 2.2g; CHOL 18mg; IRON 0.9mg; SODIUM 509mg; CALC 26mg

ingredient spotlight

Blue Cheese The distinctively robust and sharp flavor of blue cheese drives people to love it or hate it. Its most distinguishable feature is its white interior, which is streaked with bluish veins. The texture can vary from crumbly to creamy. Blue cheese pairs well with fruits, such as apples, pears, and strawberries, which balance and accentuate its flavor.

No need to roast a turkey for this after-the-holiday favorite. Just visit your local deli and pick up the fixings.

Turkey-Cranberry Salad
Prep: 6 minutes

1 (8-ounce) bag romaine, green leaf, and butter lettuce hearts mix (such as Fresh Express Triple Hearts)
1 (8-ounce) slice deli turkey breast, cubed
1 (8¼-ounce) can mandarin oranges in light syrup, drained

1 cup seasoned croutons
½ cup dried cranberries
¼ teaspoon black pepper
5 tablespoons chopped pecans (optional)
¼ cup fat-free raspberry vinaigrette (such as Maple Grove Farms of Vermont)

1. Divide lettuce evenly among 5 plates. Top evenly with turkey and next 4 ingredients. Sprinkle with pecans, if desired. Drizzle salads evenly with vinaigrette. Yield: 5 servings (serving size: about 2¼ cups).

CALORIES 159; FAT 2.2g (sat 0.5g, mono 1g, poly 0.5g); PROTEIN 12.4g; CARB 23.5g; FIBER 2.5g; CHOL 21mg; IRON 1.3mg; SODIUM 388mg; CALC 39mg

ingredient spotlight

Pecans add a toasty crunch to salads and are a source of heart-healthy monounsaturated fat. You can buy them in many forms—halves, pieces, and chopped—but whole pecans in the shell are best for freshness and flavor. A good rule of thumb is that 1 pound of unshelled pecans yields about half a pound, or about 2 cups, of nutmeat. Any leftover unshelled pecans can be stored in a cool, dry place for up to six months.

meatless main dishes

Roasted Beet Risotto with Walnuts and Goat Cheese, 136
Grilled Eggplant with Feta and Greek Couscous, 138
Chili-Cheese Sweet Potato Fries, 141
Succotash-Stuffed Tomatoes, 143
Spicy Vegetable Burritos, 144
Tropical Black Beans, 147
Tostadas, 149
Apple and Olive Quesadillas, 150
Garlic–Mashed Potato Pizza, 153
Goat Cheese–Mushroom Naan Pizza, 154
Fig and Arugula Pizzas with Goat Cheese, 156
Stromboli, 159
Spanakopita, 160
Asparagus and Basil Omelet, 163
Lemon-Artichoke Frittata, 165
Southwest Rice Frittata, 166
Mushroom Macaroni and Cheese, 169
Pappardelle with Roasted Zucchini, Mascarpone, and Pine Nuts, 170
Penne with Roasted Ratatouille, 172
Baked Ravioli with Butternut Squash Cream Sauce, 175

Roasted Beet Risotto with Walnuts and Goat Cheese

Prep: 6 minutes • Cook: 26 minutes

Roasted Beets
2 teaspoons olive oil
1¼ cups Arborio rice
1 (32-ounce) carton organic vegetable broth
1¼ cups water
¼ teaspoon salt
½ cup (2 ounces) crumbled goat cheese, divided
¼ teaspoon freshly ground black pepper
½ cup chopped walnuts, toasted
Parsley leaves (optional)

1. Prepare Roasted Beets.
2. While beets bake, heat oil in a Dutch oven over medium-high heat. Add rice; sauté 2 minutes or until lightly toasted.
3. Combine broth, 1¼ cups water, and salt. Add broth mixture to pan. Cook, stirring frequently, until almost all liquid is absorbed, about 20 minutes.
4. Stir ¼ cup goat cheese and pepper into rice mixture. Divide mixture evenly among 6 plates. Top evenly with Roasted Beets, remaining ¼ cup goat cheese, and walnuts. Garnish with parsley leaves, if desired. Yield: 6 servings (serving size: ¾ cup risotto, ½ cup beets, about 1 tablespoon cheese, and about 1 tablespoon walnuts).

CALORIES 387; FAT 16.4g (sat 5.9g, mono 4.4g, poly 5.7g); PROTEIN 11.5g; CARB 46.1g; FIBER 4.6g; CHOL 24mg; IRON 1.5mg; SODIUM 795mg; CALC 60mg

Roasted Beets

Prep: 5 minutes • Cook: 26 minutes

1½ pounds beets (about 7 small), peeled and cut into wedges
2 teaspoons olive oil
¼ teaspoon salt
¼ teaspoon freshly ground black pepper
Cooking spray
¼ cup fresh parsley leaves

1. Preheat oven to 450°.
2. Combine first 4 ingredients on a large rimmed baking sheet coated with cooking spray. Bake at 450° for 26 minutes or until tender, stirring once. Toss with parsley just before serving. Yield: 6 servings (serving size: ½ cup).

CALORIES 62; FAT 1.7g (sat 0.3g, mono 1.2g, poly 0.2g); PROTEIN 1.9g; CARB 11.1g; FIBER 2.3g; CHOL 0mg; IRON 1mg; SODIUM 182mg; CALC 21mg

ingredient spotlight

Arborio rice is a short-grained white rice used in making risotto, the creamy long-stirred specialty of northern Italy. The liquid used to make risotto is key to its taste, so buy the best chicken or vegetable broth or stock.

Beets, a hearty root vegetable like carrots, parsnips, and turnips, make a good substitute for meat when roasted. The beauty of beets is in the variety of their available colors—from yellow to candy-striped and deep purple. When preparing beets, cut them into similar sizes so they will cook evenly.

Grilled Eggplant with Feta and Greek Couscous

Prep: 2 minutes • Cook: 14 minutes

2 small eggplants (about 1 pound each), each cut into 4 lengthwise slices
1 tablespoon extra-virgin olive oil
1 tablespoon chopped fresh oregano
¼ teaspoon salt

¼ teaspoon freshly ground black pepper
1½ cups (6 ounces) crumbled reduced-fat feta cheese
Greek Couscous
Oregano sprigs (optional)

1. Preheat grill.
2. Drizzle eggplant slices with olive oil. Sprinkle evenly with oregano, salt, and pepper. Grill 6 minutes on each side or until tender. Sprinkle eggplant with cheese; grill 2 minutes or until cheese melts.
3. While eggplant grills, prepare Greek Couscous.
4. Place 2 eggplant slices on each of 4 plates. Top each serving with 1 cup couscous. Garnish with oregano sprigs, if desired. Yield: 4 servings (serving size: 2 eggplant slices and 1 cup couscous).

CALORIES 416; FAT 18.5g (sat 5.4g, mono 9.4g, poly 3.6g); PROTEIN 18.2g; CARB 49.1g; FIBER 12.8g; CHOL 13mg; IRON 2.2mg; SODIUM 913mg; CALC 187mg

Greek Couscous

Prep: 3 minutes • Other: 10 minutes

2 cups hot cooked whole-wheat couscous
¼ cup pitted kalamata olives, halved
2 tablespoons balsamic vinegar
1 tablespoon olive oil

20 grape tomatoes, quartered
1 (15-ounce) can no-salt-added cannellini beans, rinsed and drained

1. Combine all ingredients in a medium bowl. Cover and refrigerate 10 minutes. Yield: 4 servings (serving size: 1 cup).

CALORIES 269; FAT 9.1g (sat 1.1g, mono 5.2g, poly 2.8g); PROTEIN 8.3g; CARB 41.1g; FIBER 8.3g; CHOL 0mg; IRON 1.9mg; SODIUM 170mg; CALC 72mg

fix it faster

Streamline prep time by using an indoor grill to cook this eggplant. Eggplant is a versatile vegetable that can be grilled, mashed, pureed, or sautéed. It's best eaten in peak season—summer to early fall—when the flesh is mild, not bitter.

Eggplant takes a Mediterranean turn when warm off the grill and topped with melted feta and Greek Couscous. Eggplant's mild flavor makes it the perfect foil for assertive flavors like briny feta cheese and tangy kalamata olives.

Just scatter sweet potato fries on a plate, and top with chili with beans. No one will miss the meat. Promise!

Chili-Cheese Sweet Potato Fries
Prep: 1 minute • Cook: 18 minutes

1 (20-ounce) package frozen julienne-cut sweet potato fries (such as Alexia)
Butter-flavored cooking spray
1 (15-ounce) can vegetarian chili with beans (such as Hormel)
1 cup (4 ounces) reduced-fat shredded sharp cheddar cheese
¼ cup sliced green onions

1. Preheat oven to 450°.
2. Arrange fries on a large rimmed baking sheet. Coat fries with cooking spray. Bake at 450° for 18 to 22 minutes or until crisp.
3. While fries bake, cook chili in a small saucepan over medium heat 3 minutes or until thoroughly heated.
4. Transfer fries to a serving platter. Spoon chili over fries; sprinkle with cheese and green onions. Serve hot. Yield: 6 servings (serving size: ⅙ chili-cheese fries).

CALORIES 282; FAT 11.5g (sat 3.5g, mono 3.5g, poly 4.4g); PROTEIN 10.5g; CARB 37.8g; FIBER 6.4g; CHOL 15mg; IRON 0.9mg; SODIUM 381mg; CALC 193mg

serve with
Mini Strawberry Milk Shakes
Prep: 5 minutes

2½ cups vanilla low-fat ice cream (such as Edy's)
2 cups sliced strawberries
½ cup 1% low-fat milk
½ teaspoon vanilla extract

1. Place all ingredients in a blender; process just until smooth. Yield: 6 servings (serving size: about ⅔ cup).

CALORIES 111; FAT 3.3g (sat 1.8g, mono 1.1g, poly 0.3g); PROTEIN 3.5g; CARB 17.8g; FIBER 1.1g; CHOL 18mg; IRON 0.2mg; SODIUM 48mg; CALC 84mg

4-ingredient

Keep your eyes on the prized summer staples
of just-picked corn, plump beans, and juicy ripe tomatoes.
If they're not in season, substitute frozen corn, frozen limas,
and canned tomatoes.

Succotash-Stuffed Tomatoes

Prep: 10 minutes • Cook: 21 minutes

Summer Succotash
4 (8-ounce) tomatoes
¼ teaspoon salt
¼ teaspoon freshly ground black pepper

2 (1-ounce) slices sourdough bread, torn
¼ cup (1 ounce) grated fresh Parmigiano-Reggiano cheese
1 teaspoon olive oil

1. Preheat oven to 450°.
2. Prepare Summer Succotash.
3. Cut tomatoes in half crosswise; scoop out and discard pulp.
4. Place tomato halves, cut sides up, in a 13 x 9–inch baking dish. Sprinkle with salt and pepper. Spoon Summer Succotash evenly into each tomato half.
5. Place bread in a food processor; process until coarse crumbs form. Add cheese and olive oil; process 30 seconds. Sprinkle breadcrumb mixture over succotash.
6. Bake at 450° for 10 to 12 minutes or until tomatoes are thoroughly heated and crumb topping is brown. Yield: 4 servings (serving size: 2 tomato halves).

CALORIES 288; FAT 5.7g (sat 2.4g, mono 2g, poly 1.1g); PROTEIN 11.2g; CARB 49.2g; FIBER 8.9g; CHOL 9mg; IRON 2.5mg; SODIUM 720mg; CALC 96mg

Summer Succotash

Prep: 2 minutes • Cook: 11 minutes

1 tablespoon butter
1 cup refrigerated prechopped onion
3 garlic cloves, minced
1½ cups frozen baby lima beans
1½ cups frozen baby gold and white whole-kernel corn (such as Birds Eye)

¾ cup organic vegetable broth
¼ teaspoon salt
¼ teaspoon freshly ground black pepper
¼ cup chopped fresh basil

1. Melt butter in a large nonstick skillet over medium heat. Add onion and garlic; cook 3 minutes or until tender, stirring often. Stir in lima beans and next 4 ingredients. Cover, bring to a boil, and cook 3 minutes. Uncover and cook 3 minutes or until vegetables are tender and liquid almost evaporates, stirring often. Stir in basil. Yield: 4 servings (serving size: ¾ cup).

CALORIES 187; FAT 3.5g (sat 1.9g, mono 1g, poly 0.5g); PROTEIN 6.9g; CARB 31.4g; FIBER 5.7g; CHOL 8mg; IRON 1.3mg; SODIUM 455mg; CALC 49mg

Warning: Smoky-sweet chipotle peppers pack plenty of heat. If you prefer a tamer taste, just use the sauce from the chipotle peppers.

Spicy Vegetable Burritos
Prep: 4 minutes • Cook: 8 minutes

½ (8.8-ounce) package precooked brown rice (such as Minute Ready to Serve)
2 teaspoons canola oil
2 cups frozen corn, black bean, and bell pepper mix (such as Pictsweet)
2 garlic cloves, minced
¼ cup organic vegetable broth
1 tablespoon chopped chipotle peppers canned in adobo sauce

1 teaspoon ground cumin
4 (8-inch) 96% fat-free whole-wheat tortillas (such as Mission), warmed
½ cup reduced-fat sour cream
Reduced-fat shredded sharp cheddar cheese, fresh salsa, chopped fresh cilantro (optional)

1. Microwave rice according to package directions.
2. While rice cooks, heat oil in a large nonstick skillet over medium-high heat. Add corn mix and garlic. Cook 5 minutes or until tender, stirring occasionally. Stir in broth, chipotle peppers, and cumin. Cook 30 seconds or until liquid almost evaporates.
3. Spread tortillas evenly with sour cream. Spoon one-fourth of rice down center of each tortilla. Top evenly with corn mixture; roll up, and secure with wooden picks. Top with reduced-fat shredded sharp cheddar cheese, fresh salsa, and chopped fresh cilantro, if desired. Yield: 4 servings (serving size: 1 burrito).

CALORIES 384; FAT 9.6g (sat 3g, mono 3.8g, poly 2.8g); PROTEIN 9.6g; CARB 66.8g; FIBER 7.3g; CHOL 12mg; IRON 1.4mg; SODIUM 567mg; CALC 39mg

serve with
Pineapple Agua Fresca
Prep: 5 minutes

3 cups cubed fresh pineapple
2 cups cold water
1 tablespoon sugar

1 tablespoon fresh lime juice
1 tablespoon chopped fresh mint
Fresh pineapple wedges (optional)

1. Combine first 4 ingredients in a blender; process 1 minute or until smooth. Strain mixture through a sieve into a pitcher; discard solids. Stir in mint. Cover and chill until ready to serve. Serve over ice, and, if desired, garnish with pineapple wedges. Yield: 4 servings (serving size: 1 cup).

CALORIES 69; FAT 0.2g (sat 0g, mono 0g, poly 0.1g); PROTEIN 0.7g; CARB 18.2g; FIBER 1.7g; CHOL 0mg; IRON 0.4mg; SODIUM 1mg; CALC 17mg

Light coconut milk, not to be confused with coconut cream, adds a creamy finish and exotic flavor boost to this nutty-flavored brown rice side dish that partners with the hearty black bean main dish.

Tropical Black Beans

Prep: 7 minutes • Cook: 8 minutes

2 teaspoons olive oil
1½ cups refrigerated prechopped tricolor
    bell pepper mix
¾ cup chopped red onion
2 garlic cloves, minced
1 cup (½-inch) chunks mango (1 mango)

⅓ cup fresh orange juice
½ teaspoon ground allspice
½ teaspoon black pepper
2 (15-ounce) cans reduced-sodium black beans
    (such as Bush's), rinsed and drained
½ cup (4 ounces) crumbled queso fresco

1. Heat oil in a large nonstick skillet over medium-high heat. Add bell pepper mix, onion, and garlic; sauté 4 minutes or until tender. Stir in mango and next 4 ingredients. Cook 3 to 4 minutes or until thoroughly heated. Sprinkle with cheese. Yield: 4 servings (serving size: 1¼ cups bean mixture and 2 tablespoons cheese).

CALORIES 237; FAT 5.4g (sat 1.8g, mono 2.6g, poly 0.8g); PROTEIN 12.2g; CARB 40.8g; FIBER 8.4g; CHOL 9mg; IRON 3.4mg; SODIUM 198mg; CALC 177mg

serve with
Coconut Rice

Prep: 2 minutes • Cook: 13 minutes • Other: 5 minutes

1 cup light coconut milk
¼ teaspoon salt
1 cup instant brown rice
¼ cup chopped green onions

1½ teaspoons Pickapeppa sauce
2 tablespoons flaked sweetened coconut,
    toasted

1. Combine coconut milk and salt in a 2-quart saucepan. Bring to a boil; gradually stir in rice. Cover, reduce heat, and simmer 10 minutes or until liquid is absorbed. Remove from heat; let stand, covered, 5 minutes. Fluff with a fork. Stir in remaining ingredients. Yield: 4 servings (serving size: ½ cup).

CALORIES 122; FAT 4.4g (sat 3.5g, mono 0.4g, poly 0.4g); PROTEIN 2.3g; CARB 21g; FIBER 1.5g; CHOL 0mg; IRON 0.6mg; SODIUM 175mg; CALC 5mg

quick flip

Consider subbing coconut curry broth (such as College Inn) for the light coconut milk. Lighter than light coconut milk, this broth nicely mingles flavors of coconut and curry. The hint of curry adds an ever-so-mild touch of heat.

What makes this fun to eat is the mix of crunchy textures and creamy flavors. Add a sliver of avocado, just for good measure, if desired.

Tostadas
Prep: 4 minutes • Cook: 7 minutes

Black Bean Topping
- ½ cup reduced-fat sour cream
- ¼ cup chopped fresh cilantro
- 2 tablespoons water
- ¼ teaspoon freshly ground black pepper
- 4 (8-inch) carb balance flour tortillas (such as Mission)

Cooking spray
- 1⅓ cups shredded iceberg lettuce
- Sliced avocado (optional)
- Cilantro leaves (optional)

1. Preheat broiler.
2. Prepare Black Bean Topping. Combine sour cream and next 3 ingredients; set aside.
3. Coat both sides of tortillas with cooking spray. Arrange tortillas in a single layer on a large baking sheet. Broil 2 minutes on each side or until crisp and beginning to char around edges.
4. Spread about 7 tablespoons Black Bean Topping over each tortilla; top each with ⅓ cup lettuce. Drizzle with 3½ tablespoons sour cream mixture. Garnish with avocado and cilantro, if desired. Yield: 4 servings (serving size: 1 tostada).

CALORIES 268; FAT 8.5g (sat 4.1g, mono 2.4g, poly 1.8g); PROTEIN 14.7g; CARB 31.1g; FIBER 7.6g; CHOL 12mg; IRON 2.6mg; SODIUM 617mg; CALC 60mg

Black Bean Topping
Prep: 1 minute • Cook: 3 minutes

Cooking spray
- 2 cups frozen vegetarian meatless crumbles (such as Morningstar Farms Meal Starters)
- ½ cup fat-free spicy black bean dip (such as Guiltless Gourmet)

- 3 tablespoons fresh salsa
- 2 tablespoons chopped fresh cilantro

1. Heat a large nonstick skillet over medium-high heat. Coat pan with cooking spray. Add crumbles to pan; cook 2 minutes. Stir in bean dip, salsa, and cilantro. Cook 1 minute or until thoroughly heated. Yield: 4 servings (serving size: about 7 tablespoons).

CALORIES 95; FAT 1.9g (sat 0.4g, mono 0.4g, poly 1.1g); PROTEIN 9.6g; CARB 9.2g; FIBER 4.3g; CHOL 0mg; IRON 2.5mg; SODIUM 313mg; CALC 24mg

This version of a Mexican favorite balances sweet, crisp apples with briny olives, tempered by creamy, oozing cheese. Think of this as an upscale grilled cheese quesadilla.

Apple and Olive Quesadillas
Prep: 4 minutes • Cook: 12 minutes

2   cups shredded Braeburn apple (2 apples)
1¼ cups (5 ounces) reduced-fat sharp cheddar cheese (such as Cracker Barrel)
½   cup pimiento-stuffed olives, finely chopped
4   (8-inch) fat-free flour tortillas
Butter-flavored cooking spray

1. Press apple between paper towels until barely moist. Combine apple, cheese, and olives. Spoon 1 cup apple mixture onto half of each tortilla. Fold each tortilla in half. Coat tops with cooking spray.
2. Heat a large nonstick skillet over medium-high heat. Coat pan with cooking spray. Place 2 quesadillas in pan, coated sides up. Cook 3 minutes on each side or until golden and cheese melts. Repeat procedure with remaining 2 quesadillas. Cut each quesadilla into 3 wedges. Yield: 4 servings (serving size: 1 quesadilla).

CALORIES 283; FAT 9.4g (sat 4.4g, mono 4g, poly 1g); PROTEIN 11.9g; CARB 35.4g; FIBER 3.3g; CHOL 25mg; IRON 1.3mg; SODIUM 911mg; CALC 315mg

serve with
Cranberry-Apple Spritzer
Prep: 1 minute

2   cups cranberry-apple juice drink
1   cup apple juice
1   cup lime sparkling water
Ice cubes (optional)
Frozen cranberries (optional)
Frozen thin lime wedges (optional)

1. Combine juice drink and apple juice in a pitcher. Gently stir in 1 cup sparkling water. Serve over ice, and garnish with cranberries and lime wedges, if desired. Yield: 4 cups (serving size: 1 cup).

CALORIES 110; FAT 0g (sat 0g, mono 0g, poly 0g); PROTEIN 0.1g; CARB 27.9g; FIBER 0.1g; CHOL 0mg; IRON 0.1mg; SODIUM 10mg; CALC 9mg

4-ingredient

Pizza with potatoes? This one delivers. Mashed potatoes replace tomato sauce as the topping. As an option to the potatoes with skins, try refrigerated mashed potatoes for an amazingly different version if you can afford a little more sodium.

Garlic–Mashed Potato Pizza
Prep: 4 minutes • Cook: 26 minutes

Tomato Topping
1½ cups country-style refrigerated mashed
    potatoes (such as Simply Potatoes)
1 tablespoon bottled roasted minced garlic

¼ teaspoon freshly ground black pepper
1 (10-ounce) thin pizza crust (such as Boboli)
Olive oil-flavored cooking spray

1. Preheat oven to 450°.
2. Prepare Tomato Topping.
3. Place potatoes in a microwave-safe bowl. Cover with plastic wrap; vent. Microwave at HIGH 3 minutes or until thoroughly heated, stirring after 1½ minutes. Stir in garlic and pepper.
4. While potatoes cook, coat crust with cooking spray. Spread potato mixture onto crust to within 1 inch of edge. Sprinkle Tomato Topping over pizza.
5. Bake pizza at 450°, directly on oven rack, for 8 minutes or until crust is browned. Yield: 4 servings (serving size: 2 slices).

CALORIES 337; FAT 9.9g (sat 2.8g, mono 3.5g, poly 3.5g); PROTEIN 9.6g; CARB 51.2g; FIBER 3.9g; CHOL 8mg; IRON 2.9mg; SODIUM 704mg; CALC 137mg

Tomato Topping
Prep: 1 minute • Cook: 15 minutes

2 cups grape tomatoes
2 teaspoons olive oil
¼ teaspoon salt

¼ teaspoon freshly ground black pepper
¼ teaspoon crushed red pepper
1 tablespoon chopped fresh rosemary

1. Preheat oven to 450°.
2. Spread tomatoes on a rimmed baking sheet; drizzle with oil. Sprinkle with salt and peppers; toss gently.
3. Bake at 450° for 15 minutes (do not stir). Sprinkle with rosemary. Yield: 4 servings (serving size: about ½ cup).

CALORIES 36; FAT 2.3g (sat 0.3g, mono 1.6g, poly 0.3g); PROTEIN 0.6g; CARB 3.4g; FIBER 1.1g; CHOL 0mg; IRON 0.2mg; SODIUM 149mg; CALC 18mg

Goat Cheese–Mushroom Naan Pizza

Prep: 9 minutes • Cook: 18 minutes

2 teaspoons olive oil
2 (4-ounce) packages presliced exotic mushroom blend (such as shiitake, cremini, and oyster)
2 (3-ounce) whole-wheat naan

Cooking spray
¼ cup sun-dried tomato pesto (such as Classico)
¾ cup (3 ounces) crumbled goat cheese with herbs

1. Preheat oven to 450°.
2. Heat oil in a large nonstick skillet over medium-high heat. Add mushrooms; cook 7 minutes or until lightly browned, stirring once.
3. While mushrooms cook, place naan on a large baking sheet coated with cooking spray. Spread 2 tablespoons pesto over each naan, spreading to within ½ inch of edges. Sprinkle mushrooms evenly over each; top with goat cheese.
4. Bake at 450° for 10 minutes or until cheese softens. Cut each pizza in half. Yield: 4 servings (serving size: ½ pizza).

CALORIES 235; FAT 9.7g (sat 3.6g, mono 3.6g, poly 2.4g); PROTEIN 10.3g; CARB 27.8g; FIBER 5g; CHOL 8mg; IRON 2.3mg; SODIUM 420mg; CALC 34mg

serve with
Butter Lettuce–Orange Salad with Sweet and Sour Dressing

Prep: 5 minutes

1 large navel orange
3 tablespoons white wine vinegar
1 tablespoon olive oil
1 tablespoon honey
¼ teaspoon salt

⅛ teaspoon black pepper
1 (6.5-ounce) package sweet butter lettuce blend salad greens (such as Fresh Express)
¼ cup fresh mint leaves, torn

1. Peel and section orange over a large bowl, squeezing membranes to extract juice and placing sections in a separate bowl. Add vinegar and next 4 ingredients to orange juice, stirring with a whisk. Add orange sections, lettuce, and mint; toss gently. Serve immediately. Yield: 4 servings (serving size: 1¼ cups).

CALORIES 70; FAT 3.4g (sat 0.5g, mono 2.5g, poly 0.4g); PROTEIN 0.9g; CARB 10.1g; FIBER 1.5g; CHOL 0mg; IRON 0.8mg; SODIUM 147mg; CALC 33mg

quick flip

A prebaked pizza crust (such as mini prebaked Italian pizza crusts by Boboli) easily stands in for naan. Baking the crust before topping with the mushrooms and goat cheese helps keep it crispy.

Rustic naan, an East Indian yeast flatbread traditionally baked in a tandoor oven, makes a flavorful, sturdy base for this meatless pizza. Look for it with pita breads, wraps, and other flatbreads in your grocery store.

4-ingredient

We subbed naan, a ready-made flatbread, for crust in this cheesy, fruity pizza variation. Flatbreads, such as naan, make quick and easy pizza crusts.

Fig and Arugula Pizzas with Goat Cheese

Prep: 15 minutes • Cook: 15 minutes

Fig-Arugula Pesto
2 (4.4-ounce) naan (such as Fabulous Flats)
Cooking spray
4 ounces goat cheese, sliced

1 cup thinly sliced red Bartlett pear (1 pear)
2 tablespoons walnuts, toasted and coarsely chopped

1. Preheat oven to 450°.
2. Prepare Fig-Arugula Pesto. Place naan on a baking sheet coated with cooking spray. Spread half of Fig-Arugula Pesto on each naan, spreading to within 1 inch of edges. Arrange goat cheese slices evenly over pizzas.
3. Bake at 450° for 15 minutes or until naan is crisp and goat cheese is golden and bubbly. Top evenly with pear and walnuts. Cut each pizza into 4 slices. Yield: 4 servings (serving size: 2 slices).

CALORIES 412; FAT 19.1g (sat 5.8g, mono 5.7g, poly 7.4g); PROTEIN 12.1g; CARB 50.4g; FIBER 4.6g; CHOL 13mg; IRON 2.3mg; SODIUM 595mg; CALC 118mg

Fig-Arugula Pesto

Prep: 10 minutes

½ cup fig preserves
¼ cup chopped toasted walnuts
1 tablespoon extra-virgin olive oil

½ teaspoon salt
¼ teaspoon freshly ground black pepper
1 (5-ounce) package arugula

1. Place first 5 ingredients in a food processor; pulse 5 times or until blended. Add arugula; pulse 10 times or until arugula is finely chopped. Yield: 1⅓ cups (serving size: about 10 tablespoons).

CALORIES 177; FAT 8.5g (sat 1g, mono 3.2g, poly 4.1g); PROTEIN 2g; CARB 24.4g; FIBER 1.1g; CHOL 0mg; IRON 0.7mg; SODIUM 300mg; CALC 65mg

Introduce your family to a new stromboli. Meet the meatless version. We swapped traditional ground beef for a protein-based vegetarian staple. For a little crunch, bake the stromboli on a greased baking sheet dusted with a tablespoon of yellow cornmeal.

4-ingredient

Stromboli

Prep: 15 minutes • Cook: 18 minutes

"Meaty" Filling
Olive oil-flavored cooking spray
1 (11-ounce) can refrigerated thin pizza
crust dough

1½ tablespoons prepared mustard
5 (⅔-ounce) reduced-fat provolone
cheese slices

1. Preheat oven to 425°.
2. Prepare "Meaty" Filling.
3. Coat a baking sheet with cooking spray. Unroll dough onto a large baking sheet; press into a 12 x 8–inch rectangle. Thinly spread mustard over dough to within ½ inch of edges. Spread "Meaty" Filling lengthwise down center third of dough, leaving a 1-inch border at both ends. Top filling with cheese.
4. Cut slits from edge of filling to edge of dough at 1-inch intervals on long sides of rectangle. Alternating sides, fold strips at an angle across filling. Coat top of dough with cooking spray.
5. Bake at 425° for 12 minutes or until browned. Cut crosswise into 6 equal portions. Yield: 6 servings (serving size: 1 sandwich).

CALORIES 239; FAT 8.7g (sat 2.6g, mono 4g, poly 1.9g); PROTEIN 11.2g; CARB 29.3g; FIBER 2.2g; CHOL 8mg; IRON 2.1mg; SODIUM 628mg; CALC 51mg

"Meaty" Filling

Prep: 2 minutes • Cook: 4 minutes

Olive oil-flavored cooking spray
1 cup frozen vegetarian meatless crumbles
(such as Morningstar Farms Meal Starters)
½ cup chopped red onion

½ cup tomato-and-basil pasta sauce
(such as Classico)
¼ cup sliced ripe olives
¼ cup thinly sliced fresh basil

1. Heat a large nonstick skillet over medium-high heat. Coat pan with cooking spray. Add meatless crumbles and onion to pan; sauté 3 minutes or until onion is tender. Stir in pasta sauce and remaining ingredients. Yield: 6 servings.

CALORIES 42; FAT 1.6g (sat 0.1g, mono 0.6g, poly 0.7g); PROTEIN 3.1g; CARB 4.4g; FIBER 1.3g; CHOL 0mg; IRON 0.8mg; SODIUM 175mg; CALC 29mg

fix it faster

If braiding dough across the top is too fussy, just roll up the dough starting at one long side. Tuck the ends under, and pinch to seal. Then cut three or four slits (steam vents) across the top of the dough.

Spanakopita
Prep: 11 minutes • Cook: 37 minutes

Spinach Filling
12 (12 x 9-inch) sheets frozen phyllo dough
    (such as Athens), thawed

Olive oil-flavored cooking spray
2 tablespoons grated fresh Parmesan cheese

1. Preheat oven to 375°.
2. Prepare Spinach Filling.
3. Place 1 phyllo sheet on a large cutting board or work surface (cover remaining dough to prevent drying); coat with cooking spray. Top with 1 dough sheet; coat with cooking spray. Repeat procedure with 4 additional dough sheets and cooking spray.
4. Fit dough stack in an 11 x 7–inch baking dish coated with cooking spray, allowing phyllo to extend up sides of pan. Spread Spinach Filling over phyllo. Fold edges over filling even with edges of dish. Sprinkle with Parmesan cheese.
5. Place 1 phyllo sheet on work surface (cover remaining phyllo to prevent drying); coat with cooking spray. Top with 1 dough sheet; coat with cooking spray. Repeat procedure with 4 remaining sheets and cooking spray.
6. Place dough stack over spinach mixture. Fold edges over dough even with edges of dish. Coat dough with cooking spray.
7. Bake at 375° for 30 minutes or until golden. Cut into rectangles. Yield: 8 servings (serving size: 1 rectangle).

CALORIES 191; FAT 7g (sat 2.6g, mono 3.4g, poly 0.8g); PROTEIN 10.1g; CARB 21g; FIBER 2.3g; CHOL 56mg; IRON 2.6mg; SODIUM 481mg; CALC 155mg

Spinach Filling
Prep: 1 minute • Cook: 7 minutes

2 teaspoons olive oil
1 (8-ounce) container refrigerated
   prechopped onion
2 (6-ounce) packages fresh baby spinach
¾ cup part-skim ricotta cheese

1 (3.5-ounce) package crumbled reduced-fat
   feta cheese with basil and sun-dried
   tomatoes
¼ teaspoon salt
2 large eggs, lightly beaten

1. Heat oil in a large nonstick skillet over medium heat. Add onion; sauté 5 minutes or until tender. Gradually add 1 package spinach. Cook, stirring constantly, 1 minute or just until spinach wilts slightly. Gradually add remaining package spinach; cook, stirring constantly, just until spinach wilts. Remove from heat. Drain spinach mixture through a fine sieve, pressing with the back of a spoon; place in a bowl. Stir in cheeses, salt, and eggs. Yield: 3½ cups.

CALORIES 98; FAT 4.7g (sat 1.9g, mono 2.2g, poly 0.5g); PROTEIN 7.3g; CARB 6g; FIBER 1.8g; CHOL 54mg; IRON 1.7mg; SODIUM 312mg; CALC 127mg

This Greek spinach pie with a fancy name requires some special tips. When working with phyllo, always keep the remaining portion covered with a damp cloth towel to prevent it from drying out. And be sure to drain the spinach well before combining with cheeses to keep the crust from becoming soggy.

4-ingredient

Simple to prepare, this garden-fresh omelet is a quick-fix brunch, lunch, or dinner. Serve it with whole-wheat toast and orange juice.

Asparagus and Basil Omelet
Prep: 4 minutes • Cook: 7 minutes

Cooking spray
12 asparagus spears, diagonally cut into 1-inch pieces (about 1 cup)
2 large eggs
½ cup egg substitute
¼ cup water
¼ teaspoon salt
¼ teaspoon coarsely ground black pepper
½ cup (2 ounces) reduced-fat shredded Swiss cheese
2 tablespoons fresh basil leaves

1. Heat an 8-inch nonstick skillet over medium-high heat; coat pan with cooking spray. Add asparagus, and sauté 3 minutes; set aside.
2. Combine eggs and next 4 ingredients in a medium bowl; stir with a whisk until blended.
3. Wipe pan with paper towels. Heat pan over medium heat; recoat pan with cooking spray. Add egg mixture, and cook 3 minutes or until set (do not stir). Sprinkle with asparagus, cheese, and basil. Loosen omelet with a spatula; fold in half. Cook 1 to 2 minutes or until cheese melts. Slide omelet onto a plate. Cut in half. Yield: 2 servings (serving size: ½ omelet).

CALORIES 203; FAT 7.7g (sat 2.7g, mono 3g, poly 1.9g); PROTEIN 24.1g; CARB 7g; FIBER 2.1g; CHOL 191mg; IRON 4.5mg; SODIUM 548mg; CALC 360mg

ingredient spotlight

Asparagus has a mild flavor and a delicate texture, although it becomes tougher as it ages. During its peak season (February through June), pencil-thin spears are plentiful. To maintain freshness, wrap a moist paper towel around the stem ends, or stand upright in about 2 inches of cold water.

This lemony frittata with a sunny flavor is similar to an omelet but easier. Packed with artichoke hearts, it makes a great light main course for the time-starved cook.

Lemon-Artichoke Frittata

Prep: 1 minute • Cook: 17 minutes

1 tablespoon olive oil
1 lemon
6 large eggs
4 large egg whites

⅓ cup light garlic-and-herbs spreadable cheese (such as Alouette light)
1 (14-ounce) can quartered artichoke hearts, drained

1. Preheat oven to 450°.
2. Heat oil in a 10-inch ovenproof skillet over medium heat.
3. While oil heats, grate rind and squeeze juice from lemon to measure 2 teaspoons rind and 2 teaspoons juice. Combine lemon rind, lemon juice, eggs, egg whites, and cheese, stirring with a whisk. Stir in artichoke hearts.
4. Add egg mixture to pan; reduce heat to medium-low, and cook until edges begin to set, about 2 minutes. Gently lift edge of egg mixture, tilting pan to allow uncooked egg mixture to come in contact with pan. Cook 2 minutes or until egg mixture is almost set.
5. Bake at 450° for 11 minutes or until center is set. Transfer frittata to a serving platter immediately; cut into 8 wedges. Yield: 4 servings (serving size: 2 wedges).

CALORIES 182; FAT 11.9g (sat 4.2g, mono 5.8g, poly 1.8g); PROTEIN 15.8g; CARB 7g; FIBER 0.1g; CHOL 282mg; IRON 2.3mg; SODIUM 325mg; CALC 44mg

serve with
Blueberry Citrus Salad

Prep: 5 minutes • Other: 30 minutes

3 navel oranges
2 tablespoons chopped fresh mint

2 tablespoons honey
2 cups blueberries

1. Peel and section oranges over a bowl; squeeze membranes to extract juice. Stir in mint and honey. Add blueberries, and toss gently. Cover and chill 30 minutes. Yield: 4 servings (serving size: about ⅔ cup).

CALORIES 126; FAT 0.4g (sat 0g, mono 0.1g, poly 0.2g); PROTEIN 1.6g; CARB 32.7g; FIBER 4.2g; CHOL 0mg; IRON 0.4mg; SODIUM 3mg; CALC 52mg

Spicy rice and sweet bell peppers make this open-faced frittata a standout. Bake it until it's golden brown and crispy on top.

Southwest Rice Frittata

Prep: 5 minutes • Cook: 35 minutes • Other: 10 minutes

1 (8.5-ounce) package Santa Fe–flavored microwavable precooked whole-grain rice medley (such as Uncle Ben's Ready Rice)
Cooking spray

1 (16-ounce) package frozen bell pepper stir-fry
3 large eggs
3 large egg whites
½ cup all-natural salsa (such as Newman's Own)

1. Preheat oven to 400°.
2. Microwave rice according to package directions. Heat a large skillet over medium-high heat. Coat pan with cooking spray. Add bell pepper stir-fry to pan; cook 3 minutes or until thawed and thoroughly heated, stirring frequently. Drain.
3. While bell pepper stir-fry cooks, combine eggs and egg whites in a large bowl, stirring with a whisk. Stir rice, bell pepper stir-fry, and salsa into egg mixture.
4. Spoon rice mixture into an 8-inch springform pan coated with cooking spray, pressing down firmly with the back of a spoon.
5. Bake at 400° for 35 minutes or until set and golden. Let cool 10 minutes on a wire rack. Cut frittata into 4 wedges. Yield: 4 servings (serving size: 1 wedge).

CALORIES 198; FAT 4.2g (sat 0.9g, mono 2g, poly 1.2g); PROTEIN 11.5g; CARB 26.3g; FIBER 4.1g; CHOL 135mg; IRON 1.3mg; SODIUM 446mg; CALC 40mg

serve with
Jalapeño Black Beans and Corn

Prep: 2 minutes • Cook: 8 minutes

1 (15-ounce) can no-salt-added black beans, drained
1 (11-ounce) can whole-kernel corn, drained

¼ cup sliced drained pickled jalapeños
2 tablespoons fresh lime juice
2 tablespoons chopped fresh cilantro

1. Combine first 4 ingredients in a medium saucepan. Cook over medium-high heat 8 minutes or until bubbly and thoroughly heated, stirring occasionally. Stir in cilantro. Yield: 4 servings (serving size: ¾ cup).

CALORIES 151; FAT 1.5g (sat 0g, mono 0.4g, poly 1g); PROTEIN 7.1g; CARB 25.6g; FIBER 7.1g; CHOL 0mg; IRON 1.8mg; SODIUM 266mg; CALC 61mg

4-ingredient

Fontina dresses up this hearty macaroni and cheese. Its creamy texture and nutty flavor are a delicious counterpoint to the earthiness of roasted mushrooms.

Mushroom Macaroni and Cheese
Prep: 1 minute • Cook: 33 minutes

Sherry-Roasted Wild Mushrooms
8 ounces uncooked multigrain elbow macaroni (such as Barilla Plus)
1.1 ounces all-purpose flour (about ¼ cup)
2½ cups evaporated fat-free milk
1 cup (4 ounces) shredded fontina cheese
¼ teaspoon salt
¼ teaspoon freshly ground black pepper
Cooking spray
Fresh oregano leaves (optional)

1. Prepare Sherry-Roasted Wild Mushrooms. While mushrooms roast, cook pasta according to package directions, omitting salt and fat. Drain well.
2. While mushrooms roast and pasta cooks, weigh or lightly spoon flour into a dry measuring cup; level with a knife. Place flour in a large saucepan; gradually add milk, stirring with a whisk until blended. Cook over medium heat 6 minutes or until thick and bubbly; stir constantly with a whisk. Add cheese, salt, and pepper, stirring until cheese melts. Remove from heat. Stir in Sherry-Roasted Wild Mushrooms and pasta. Spoon into a 2-quart baking dish coated with cooking spray.
3. Lower oven temperature to 400°. Bake pasta mixture at 400° for 25 minutes or until bubbly. Sprinkle with oregano leaves, if desired, and serve immediately. Yield: 6 servings (serving size: about 1 cup).

CALORIES 349; FAT 9.1g (sat 4g, mono 3.7g, poly 1.3g); PROTEIN 20.7g; CARB 45.7g; FIBER 3.5g; CHOL 22mg; IRON 1.9mg; SODIUM 499mg; CALC 392mg

Sherry-Roasted Wild Mushrooms
Prep: 3 minutes • Cook: 15 minutes

3 (4-ounce) packages fresh gourmet-blend mushrooms
1 tablespoon olive oil
¼ teaspoon salt
¼ teaspoon freshly ground black pepper
2 garlic cloves, thinly sliced
Cooking spray
2 tablespoons dry sherry
2 teaspoons chopped fresh oregano

1. Preheat oven to 450°.
2. Combine first 5 ingredients on a large rimmed baking sheet coated with cooking spray. Bake at 450° for 15 to 20 minutes or until browned. Stir in sherry and oregano. Yield: 6 servings (serving size: about ½ cup).

CALORIES 38; FAT 2.5g (sat 0.3g, mono 1.7g, poly 0.4g); PROTEIN 1.9g; CARB 2.4g; FIBER 0.6g; CHOL 0mg; IRON 0.3mg; SODIUM 100mg; CALC 6mg

The creamy, rich-tasting mascarpone sauce swirled into pappardelle ribbons and then topped with crunchy pine nuts makes a delicious play on textures. It's a company-worthy dish.

Pappardelle with Roasted Zucchini, Mascarpone, and Pine Nuts

Prep: 19 minutes • Cook: 15 minutes

8 small zucchini, halved lengthwise and sliced (2 pounds)
1 tablespoon olive oil
½ teaspoon salt
½ teaspoon freshly ground black pepper, divided

8 ounces uncooked pappardelle (wide ribbon pasta)
2 tablespoons chopped fresh basil (optional)
½ cup (4 ounces) mascarpone cheese
3 tablespoons pine nuts

1. Preheat broiler.
2. Spread zucchini on a large rimmed baking sheet. Drizzle zucchini with olive oil, and sprinkle with salt and ¼ teaspoon pepper, tossing to coat. Broil, on center oven shelf, 15 minutes or until zucchini is tender and edges are browned.
3. While zucchini broils, cook pasta according to package directions, omitting salt and fat. Drain pasta, reserving ½ cup cooking liquid.
4. Stir roasted zucchini and its accumulated juices, hot cooking liquid, remaining ¼ teaspoon pepper, and, if desired, basil into hot pasta. Gradually add mascarpone, stirring gently until it melts. Sprinkle with pine nuts. Yield: 6 servings (serving size: 1 cup pasta and 1½ teaspoons pine nuts).

CALORIES 303; FAT 15.6g (sat 6.1g, mono 5.3g, poly 4.1g); PROTEIN 9.2g; CARB 31.4g; FIBER 3.2g; CHOL 98mg; IRON 2mg; SODIUM 236mg; CALC 67mg

serve with
Marinated Hearts of Palm Salad

Prep: 5 minutes

1 cup halved grape tomatoes
¼ cup vertically sliced red onion
¼ cup light balsamic and basil vinaigrette (such as Wish-Bone)

1 (15-ounce) can hearts of palm, drained and sliced into ½-inch rounds
1 (14-ounce) can quartered artichoke hearts, drained

1. Combine all ingredients in a medium bowl; toss well. Yield: 6 servings (serving size: about ¾ cup).

CALORIES 61; FAT 2g (sat 0.2g, mono 0.6g, poly 1.1g); PROTEIN 2.8g; CARB 9g; FIBER 3g; CHOL 0mg; IRON 1.4mg; SODIUM 359mg; CALC 32mg

Mild-flavored eggplant, the key ingredient in ratatouille, harmonizes well with bold ingredients such as onion, garlic, and bell peppers. A popular dish from the Provence region of France, it can be served hot, cold, or at room temperature.

Penne with Roasted Ratatouille
Prep: 5 minutes • Cook: 20 minutes

2 cups (1-inch) cubed unpeeled eggplant (1 small)
2 cups refrigerated presliced green, yellow, and red bell pepper strips
1½ cups (1-inch) pieces red onion (about 1 medium)
1 tablespoon olive oil
½ teaspoon salt
½ teaspoon freshly ground black pepper
4 large garlic cloves, chopped
Fresh Tomato Sauce with Penne
Shredded fresh Parmesan cheese (optional)

1. Preheat oven to 450°.
2. Combine first 7 ingredients in a large roasting pan. Bake at 450° for 15 minutes; stir gently. Bake an additional 5 minutes or until vegetables are tender.
3. While vegetables bake, prepare Fresh Tomato Sauce with Penne.
4. Combine roasted vegetables and Fresh Tomato Sauce with Penne in a large bowl. Sprinkle with Parmesan cheese, if desired. Yield: 4 servings (serving size: 1½ cups).

CALORIES 273; FAT 7.4g (sat 0.8g, mono 4.7g, poly 1.7g); PROTEIN 9.9g; CARB 42.3g; FIBER 7.4g; CHOL 0mg; IRON 11.6mg; SODIUM 471mg; CALC 38mg

Fresh Tomato Sauce with Penne
Prep: 3 minutes • Cook: 11 minutes

6 ounces uncooked multigrain penne pasta (such as Barilla Plus)
2 teaspoons olive oil
2 (8-ounce) tomatoes, cored and chopped
⅓ cup chopped fresh basil
2 tablespoons balsamic vinegar
¼ teaspoon salt

1. Cook pasta according to package directions, omitting salt and fat. Drain.
2. Heat oil in a large nonstick skillet over medium-high heat. Add tomato; cook 4 to 5 minutes or until tomato is tender and forms a chunky sauce. Add basil, vinegar, and salt; cook 1 minute. Stir in pasta. Yield: 4 servings (serving size: about 1 cup).

CALORIES 197; FAT 3.9g (sat 0.3g, mono 2.2g, poly 1.2g); PROTEIN 8.2g; CARB 32.9g; FIBER 4.3g; CHOL 0mg; IRON 11.1mg; SODIUM 171mg; CALC 21mg

A creamy butternut squash, brown butter, and sage sauce livens up frozen cheese-filled ravioli. A quick visit under the broiler just before serving, and the end result is crispy perfection.

Baked Ravioli with Butternut Squash Cream Sauce

Prep: 10 minutes • Cook: 14 minutes

1 (22-ounce) package frozen light cheese ravioli (such as Celentano)
Butternut Squash Cream Sauce
Cooking spray

2 tablespoons butter
12 fresh sage leaves
¾ cup (3 ounces) shredded reduced-fat 4-cheese Italian blend cheese

1. Preheat broiler.
2. Cook ravioli according to package directions, omitting salt and fat. Drain.
3. While ravioli cooks, prepare Butternut Squash Cream Sauce.
4. Divide ravioli evenly among 6 shallow baking dishes coated with cooking spray. Spoon cream sauce evenly over ravioli in dishes.
5. Melt butter in a large nonstick skillet over medium-high heat. Add sage; sauté 3 minutes or until bubbles subside and butter begins to brown. Drizzle butter mixture evenly over sauce. Sprinkle evenly with cheese.
6. Place dishes on a large rimmed baking sheet. Broil 3 minutes or until cheese melts and begins to brown. Yield: 6 servings.

CALORIES 381; FAT 19.2g (sat 7.7g, mono 4.7g, poly 6.5g); PROTEIN 16.2g; CARB 36.7g; FIBER 2.9g; CHOL 45mg; IRON 1.8mg; SODIUM 706mg; CALC 299mg

Butternut Squash Cream Sauce

Prep: 3 minutes • Cook: 4 minutes

½ cup chopped walnuts, toasted
½ cup organic vegetable broth
6 tablespoons (3 ounces) ⅓-less-fat cream cheese
1 tablespoon chopped fresh chives

¼ teaspoon salt
¼ teaspoon freshly ground black pepper
1 (12-ounce) package butternut squash puree (such as Mckenzie's), thawed

1. Place all ingredients in a food processor; process until smooth. Yield: 6 servings (serving size: 6 tablespoons).

CALORIES 135; FAT 10.9g (sat 2.9g, mono 2.2g, poly 5.6g); PROTEIN 3.5g; CARB 7.1g; FIBER 1.2g; CHOL 10mg; IRON 0.7mg; SODIUM 340mg; CALC 30mg

fix it faster

To save even more time, consider substituting 6 tablespoons of light tub-style cream cheese with chives and onion for the ⅓-less-fat cream cheese and 1 tablespoon of chopped fresh chives.

fish and shellfish

Pan-Seared Flounder with Fried Rosemary and Garlic, 178
Halibut with Bacon and Balsamic Tomatoes, 181
Mahimahi with Grilled Pineapple Relish, 183
Sweet and Smoky Glazed Salmon, 184
Horseradish-Dill Salmon, 187
Baked Lemon Sole, 188
Parmesan-Broiled Tilapia, 191
Baja Fish Tostadas, 192
Trout with Onion Jam and Bacon, 194
Cornmeal-Crusted Trout with Bourbon-Pecan Butter Sauce, 197
Risotto Milanese with Mussels, 199
Crispy Curry Scallops, 200
Green Curry Scallops with Shiitakes, 202
Sesame-Crusted Scallops with Teriyaki Glaze, 205
Shrimp Quesadilla with Tropical Salsa, 206
Smoky BBQ Shrimp, 209
Shrimp Fried Rice, 211
Shrimp and Artichokes with Wild Rice, 212
Shrimp Jambalaya, 215
Shrimp Scampi, 216

Pan-Seared Flounder with Fried Rosemary and Garlic

Prep: 2 minutes • Cook: 9 minutes

1½ tablespoons olive oil
3 large garlic cloves, thinly sliced
4 rosemary sprigs
4 (6-ounce) flounder fillets

¼ teaspoon salt
¼ teaspoon freshly ground black pepper
¼ teaspoon paprika
Lemon wedges (optional)

1. Heat oil in a large nonstick skillet over medium heat. Add garlic and rosemary. Cook 3 minutes or until garlic is browned and rosemary is crisp. Using a slotted spoon, transfer garlic and rosemary to paper towels, reserving oil in pan.
2. Return oil to medium-high heat. Sprinkle fish evenly with salt, pepper, and paprika. Cook fish in hot oil 3 minutes on each side or until desired degree of doneness. Divide fish evenly among 4 plates. Top with reserved garlic and rosemary. Serve with lemon wedges, if desired. Yield: 4 servings (serving size: 1 fillet).

CALORIES 204; FAT 7.1g (sat 1.4g, mono 4.3g, poly 1.3g); PROTEIN 32.2g; CARB 1g; FIBER 0.2g; CHOL 82mg; IRON 0.7mg; SODIUM 284mg; CALC 37mg

serve with
Lemony Mashed Potatoes

Prep: 5 minutes • Cook: 8 minutes

1½ pounds Yukon Gold potatoes, peeled and cut into 1-inch chunks
1 tablespoon water
⅓ cup 1% low-fat milk
¼ cup reduced-fat sour cream

1½ teaspoons grated lemon rind
½ teaspoon garlic powder
¼ teaspoon salt
¼ teaspoon freshly ground black pepper

1. Place potato in a single layer in a microwave-safe bowl; add 1 tablespoon water. Cover bowl with plastic wrap (do not allow plastic wrap to touch food); vent. Microwave at HIGH 8 minutes or until tender.
2. Add remaining ingredients to potato in bowl; mash with a potato masher to desired consistency. Yield: 4 servings (serving size: about ⅔ cup).

CALORIES 171; FAT 2g (sat 1.3g, mono 0.6g, poly 0.1g); PROTEIN 5.2g; CARB 32.1g; FIBER 2.2g; CHOL 7mg; IRON 1.5mg; SODIUM 172mg; CALC 43mg

fix it faster

Put down the potato peeler, open up a package of refrigerated mashed potatoes, and turn up the flavor with a dash of garlic powder, a pinch of pepper, and a sprinkle of lemon zest. In just a few minutes, your side dish is ready to serve.

Cooking garlic and rosemary in the oil infuses it with flavor. This double dose of tastiness is imparted to the fish as it cooks.

4-ingredient

Sweet tomatoes and smoky bacon enhance the mild flavor of halibut. A flat fish with a medium-firm white flesh, halibut hails from the cold waters of the northern Pacific and Atlantic Oceans.

4-ingredient

Halibut with Bacon and Balsamic Tomatoes

Prep: 1 minute • Cook: 18 minutes

4   slices center-cut bacon
4   (6-ounce) skinless halibut fillets (about ½ to ¾ inch thick)
¼   teaspoon salt
¼   teaspoon freshly ground black pepper
2   cups grape tomatoes
2   tablespoons balsamic vinegar
Chopped fresh parsley (optional)

1. Cook bacon in a large nonstick skillet over medium-high heat 4 minutes or until crisp. Remove bacon from pan, reserving drippings in pan; crumble.
2. While bacon cooks, sprinkle fish evenly with salt and pepper. Add fillets to hot drippings in pan; cook 4 to 5 minutes on each side or until desired degree of doneness. Remove from pan, and keep warm.
3. Add tomatoes to pan. Sauté 4 minutes or until tomatoes begin to burst. Add vinegar; cook 1 minute or until sauce thickens, pressing tomatoes with the back of a spoon to release juice.
4. Spoon tomato mixture evenly over each fillet. Sprinkle with crumbled bacon and, if desired, parsley. Yield: 4 servings (serving size: 1 fillet, 6 tablespoons tomato mixture, and 1 tablespoon bacon).

CALORIES 228; FAT 5.2g (sat 1.3g, mono 2g, poly 1.8g); PROTEIN 38g; CARB 4.5g; FIBER 1g; CHOL 59mg; IRON 1.5mg; SODIUM 329mg; CALC 95mg

serve with
Grilled Asparagus with Shallot-Dijon Vinaigrette

Prep: 4 minutes • Cook: 5 minutes

1   pound fresh asparagus, trimmed
Cooking spray
1   shallot, minced
1   tablespoon chopped fresh parsley
1   tablespoon sherry vinegar
1   tablespoon extra-virgin olive oil
1   teaspoon Dijon mustard
¼   teaspoon salt
¼   teaspoon freshly ground black pepper

1. Preheat grill.
2. Place asparagus on grill rack coated with cooking spray. Cook 4 to 5 minutes or until tender, turning occasionally.
3. While asparagus cooks, combine shallot and next 6 ingredients in a large bowl, stirring well with a whisk.
4. Place asparagus on a serving plate; drizzle with vinaigrette. Serve immediately. Yield: 4 servings (serving size: ¼ of asparagus).

CALORIES 67; FAT 3.7g (sat 0.6g, mono 2.5g, poly 0.6g); PROTEIN 2.7g; CARB 6g; FIBER 2.5g; CHOL 0mg; IRON 2.6mg; SODIUM 179mg; CALC 32mg

Like meat, fish is marinated to bring out the flavor. But unlike meat, it doesn't need to linger long because fish doesn't need tenderizing. We recommend a 15-minute soak for fish or seafood. Longer and the lime juice will make it mushy. Serve with rice to round out your meal.

Mahimahi with Grilled Pineapple Relish

Prep: 4 minutes • Cook: 10 minutes • Other: 15 minutes

3 tablespoons light coconut milk
3 tablespoons fresh lime juice
1 tablespoon lower-sodium soy sauce
4 (6-ounce) mahimahi or other firm white fish fillets

Grilled Pineapple Relish
¼ teaspoon salt
¼ teaspoon freshly ground black pepper
Cooking spray

1. Preheat grill.
2. Combine first 3 ingredients in a shallow dish; add fish, turning to coat. Cover and marinate at room temperature 15 minutes. While fish marinates, prepare Grilled Pineapple Relish.
3. Remove fish from dish, and discard marinade. Sprinkle fish with salt and pepper.
4. Place fish on grill rack coated with cooking spray. Grill 5 minutes on each side or until desired degree of doneness. Spoon Grilled Pineapple Relish evenly over fish. Yield: 4 servings (serving size: 1 fillet and about ⅔ cup relish).

CALORIES 276; FAT 2g (sat 1g, mono 0.4g, poly 0.5g); PROTEIN 33.1g; CARB 32.8g; FIBER 2.9g; CHOL 124mg; IRON 3mg; SODIUM 604mg; CALC 68mg

Grilled Pineapple Relish

Prep: 7 minutes • Cook: 10 minutes

4 green onions
1 (1¼-pound) cored fresh pineapple, cut into ½-inch-thick slices
1 small red bell pepper, halved vertically and seeded

Cooking spray
3 tablespoons brown sugar
1 tablespoon seasoned rice vinegar
⅛ teaspoon salt

1. Preheat grill.
2. Coat first 3 ingredients heavily with cooking spray. Place on grill rack coated with cooking spray. Grill onions 6 minutes or until lightly browned, turning once. Grill pineapple and bell pepper 10 minutes or until lightly browned and tender.
3. Combine brown sugar, vinegar, and salt in a medium bowl, stirring until sugar dissolves. Coarsely chop pineapple and bell pepper. Cut onion into 1-inch pieces, and add to bowl. Toss well. Yield: 4 servings (serving size: about ⅔ cup).

CALORIES 120; FAT 0.2g (sat 0g, mono 0g, poly 0.1g); PROTEIN 1.2g; CARB 30.9g; FIBER 2.8g; CHOL 0mg; IRON 0.9mg; SODIUM 156mg; CALC 39mg

Crisp and glazed on the outside, this salmon cooks up tender and moist inside. The citrusy-sweet glaze with the smoky note adds a flavorful finish.

Sweet and Smoky Glazed Salmon
Prep: 3 minutes • Cook: 10 minutes • Other: 10 minutes

2 tablespoons frozen lemonade
   concentrate, thawed
1 tablespoon water
1 tablespoon honey
1 teaspoon smoked paprika

4 (6-ounce) salmon fillets
2 teaspoons canola oil
¼ teaspoon salt
¼ teaspoon freshly ground black pepper

1. Preheat broiler.
2. Combine first 4 ingredients in a large heavy-duty zip-top plastic bag. Add fish to bag; seal. Refrigerate 10 minutes, turning bag once.
3. Remove fish from bag, reserving marinade. Place marinade in a microwave-safe bowl; microwave at HIGH 40 seconds or until bubbly.
4. Heat oil in a cast-iron skillet over medium-high heat; sprinkle fish with salt and pepper. Add fish to pan; cook 3 minutes. Turn fish over; brush marinade evenly over fish. Broil 5 minutes or until desired degree of doneness. Yield: 4 servings (serving size: 1 fillet).

CALORIES 253; FAT 8.3g (sat 1.4g, mono 3.4g, poly 3.4g); PROTEIN 34.1g; CARB 9g; FIBER 0.2g; CHOL 89mg; IRON 1.5mg; SODIUM 260mg; CALC 25mg

serve with
Petite Green Peas with Mint Butter
Prep: 2 minutes • Cook: 5 minutes

¼ cup finely chopped onion
2 tablespoons water
2½ cups frozen petite green peas
1 tablespoon ⁵⁰/₅₀ non-hydrogenated buttery
   blend stick spread (such as Smart Balance)

2 tablespoons chopped fresh mint
¼ teaspoon salt
¼ teaspoon freshly ground black pepper

1. Combine onion and 2 tablespoons water in a medium microwave-safe bowl; cover and microwave at HIGH 2 minutes. Add peas; cover and microwave 3 minutes or until peas and onion are tender.
2. Add buttery blend spread and remaining ingredients to peas; toss well. Yield: 4 servings (serving size: about ⅔ cup).

CALORIES 72; FAT 2.3g (sat 0.6g, mono 0.9g, poly 0.6g); PROTEIN 3.9g; CARB 11.6g; FIBER 4.1g; CHOL 0mg; IRON 1.1mg; SODIUM 301mg; CALC 24mg

10-minute

The essence of horseradish in this creamy sauce wakes up the flavor of the fish, which has a medium-firm flesh. Prepared horseradish is grated fresh horseradish root preserved in vinegar. It can be kept refrigerated for several months or until it begins to darken or hits a sour note.

Horseradish-Dill Salmon
Prep: 1 minute • Cook: 7 minutes

4 (6-ounce) skinless salmon fillets (1 inch thick)
¼ teaspoon salt
¼ teaspoon freshly ground black pepper
Olive oil-flavored cooking spray
2 tablespoons fat-free sour cream
2 tablespoons light mayonnaise

1 tablespoon prepared horseradish
1 tablespoon chopped fresh dill
1 tablespoon chopped drained capers
1 teaspoon grated lemon rind
2 teaspoons fresh lemon juice

1. Sprinkle fillets evenly with salt and pepper.
2. Heat a large nonstick skillet over medium-high heat; coat pan with cooking spray. Add fillets to pan; cook 3 to 4 minutes on each side or until desired degree of doneness.
3. While fillets cook, combine sour cream and next 6 ingredients in a small bowl. Spoon 2 tablespoons sauce over each fillet. Yield: 4 servings (serving size: 1 fillet and 2 tablespoons sauce).

CALORIES 235; FAT 8.6g (sat 1.6g, mono 2.8g, poly 4.1g); PROTEIN 34.6g; CARB 2.8g; FIBER 0.3g; CHOL 92mg; IRON 1.4mg; SODIUM 376mg; CALC 42mg

serve with
Roasted Broccoli with Garlic and Pine Nuts
Prep: 3 minutes • Cook: 17 minutes

1 (12-ounce) package fresh broccoli florets
4 garlic cloves, crushed
2 teaspoons olive oil
¼ teaspoon salt

¼ teaspoon crushed red pepper (optional)
Cooking spray
2 tablespoons pine nuts
2 teaspoons fresh lemon juice

1. Preheat oven to 450°.
2. Combine first 4 ingredients and, if desired, red pepper on a rimmed baking sheet coated with cooking spray.
3. Bake at 450° for 15 minutes or until browned and almost tender. Add pine nuts. Bake an additional 2 minutes or until nuts are toasted. Drizzle broccoli with lemon juice just before serving. Yield: 4 servings (serving size: ¾ cup).

CALORIES 77; FAT 5.5g (sat 0.7g, mono 2.8g, poly 1.9g); PROTEIN 3.3g; CARB 6.2g; FIBER 2.7g; CHOL 0mg; IRON 1.1mg; SODIUM 169mg; CALC 47mg

A little fat translates into a lot of flavor for this mild, delicate white fish.

Baked Lemon Sole
Prep: 7 minutes • Cook: 9 minutes

1 tablespoon olive oil
1 cup panko (Japanese breadcrumbs)
¼ cup (1 ounce) grated fresh Romano cheese
1 teaspoon grated lemon rind
8 (3-ounce) sole fillets
2 tablespoons fresh lemon juice

¼ teaspoon salt
¼ teaspoon freshly ground black pepper
Cooking spray
Lemon wedges (optional)
Chopped fresh parsley (optional)

1. Preheat oven to 450°.
2. Coat a rimmed baking sheet with oil. Place in oven while oven preheats to 450°.
3. Combine panko, cheese, and lemon rind in a small bowl. Brush fish with lemon juice; sprinkle evenly with salt and pepper. Dredge fish in panko mixture.
4. Place fish on preheated baking sheet. Coat tops with cooking spray. Bake at 450° for 9 to 11 minutes or until desired degree of doneness. Serve with lemon wedges, and sprinkle with parsley, if desired. Yield: 4 servings (serving size: 2 fillets).

CALORIES 269; FAT 7.8g (sat 2.4g, mono 3.8g, poly 1.6g); PROTEIN 36.3g; CARB 11.1g; FIBER 0.8g; CHOL 87mg; IRON 0.7mg; SODIUM 451mg; CALC 100mg

serve with
Zucchini and Tomato Couscous
Prep: 3 minutes • Cook: 6 minutes • Other: 5 minutes

¾ cup fat-free, lower-sodium chicken broth
½ cup uncooked couscous
1 teaspoon grated lemon rind
¼ teaspoon salt
¼ teaspoon freshly ground black pepper
2 teaspoons olive oil

1 cup halved grape tomatoes
2 garlic cloves, minced
1 medium zucchini, halved lengthwise and thinly sliced
¼ cup pitted kalamata olives, halved
1 tablespoon chopped fresh parsley

1. Bring broth to a boil in a small saucepan. Stir in couscous and next 3 ingredients. Cover, remove from heat, and let stand 5 minutes.
2. While couscous cooks, heat oil in a large nonstick skillet over medium-high heat. Add tomatoes, garlic, and zucchini; sauté 3 to 4 minutes or until tender. Add vegetables, olives, and parsley to couscous; fluff with a fork. Yield: 4 servings (serving size: about 1 cup).

CALORIES 147; FAT 4.9g (sat 0.6g, mono 3.5g, poly 0.6g); PROTEIN 4.1g; CARB 21.6g; FIBER 2.3g; CHOL 0mg; IRON 0.6mg; SODIUM 403mg; CALC 27mg

Sustainable tilapia and a rich-tasting cheesy coating combine the best of good eats. Grouper and orange roughy fillets work equally well in this simple-to-fix entrée.

Parmesan-Broiled Tilapia
Prep: 4 minutes • Cook: 11 minutes

6 (6-ounce) tilapia fillets
Cooking spray
¼ cup (1 ounce) grated fresh Parmesan cheese
3 tablespoons chopped green onions
3 tablespoons light mayonnaise

1 tablespoon yogurt-based spread (such as Brummel & Brown)
¼ teaspoon salt
¼ teaspoon black pepper
1 garlic clove, pressed

1. Preheat broiler.
2. Pat fish dry with a paper towel. Arrange fish on the rack of a broiler pan coated with cooking spray.
3. Combine cheese and next 6 ingredients in a small bowl. Spread mixture evenly over fish.
4. Broil 11 minutes or until desired degree of doneness. Yield: 6 servings (serving size: 1 fillet).

CALORIES 217; FAT 7.5g (sat 2.2g, mono 2.3g, poly 2.8g); PROTEIN 36.3g; CARB 1g; FIBER 0.2g; CHOL 88mg; IRON 1mg; SODIUM 339mg; CALC 88mg

serve with
Lavender Potatoes
Prep: 3 minutes • Cook: 20 minutes

1½ pounds baby Yukon gold potatoes (about 24 potatoes)
1 tablespoon olive oil

1½ teaspoons dried lavender
¼ teaspoon salt
¼ teaspoon freshly ground black pepper

1. Preheat oven to 450°.
2. Cut potatoes in half crosswise. Place potato, oil, and remaining ingredients in a bowl, tossing to coat. Spread potato mixture in a single layer on a large rimmed baking sheet. Bake at 450° for 20 minutes. Yield: 6 servings (serving size: ½ cup).

CALORIES 114; FAT 2.3g (sat 0.3g, mono 1.6g, poly 0.2g); PROTEIN 2.7g; CARB 20.2g; FIBER 1.4g; CHOL 0mg; IRON 1mg; SODIUM 104mg; CALC 0mg

quick flip
Lavender, a signature seasoning from Provence, France, imparts a flowery scent to potatoes. If you prefer a bolder flavor, substitute rosemary, an herb favored in Mediterranean cuisine.

Try these fun "knife and fork" tacos. Typically, premade tostada shells are deep-fried, but baking your own shells makes them waistline-worthy and dollar-wise. Pico de Gallo Slaw and guacamole double the nutritional dividends.

Baja Fish Tostadas
Prep: 5 minutes • Cook: 18 minutes

4 (6-inch) corn tortillas
Cooking spray
Pico de Gallo Slaw
4 (6-ounce) tilapia fillets

¼ teaspoon salt
¼ teaspoon freshly ground black pepper
½ cup refrigerated guacamole (such as Wholly)
2 tablespoons chopped fresh cilantro

1. Preheat oven to 400°.
2. Coat both sides of corn tortillas with cooking spray. Place tortillas directly on oven rack placed in center of oven. Bake at 400° for 5 minutes; turn tortillas with tongs, and bake an additional 5 minutes or until crispy. Remove from oven with tongs, and place on paper towels.
3. While tortillas bake, prepare Pico de Gallo Slaw.
4. Preheat grill.
5. Coat both sides of fish with cooking spray. Sprinkle fish with salt and pepper. Place fish on grill rack coated with cooking spray; grill 4 minutes on each side or until desired degree of doneness. Using 2 forks, break fish into large chunks.
6. Place 1 tortilla on each of 4 plates. Spread 2 tablespoons guacamole on each tortilla; spoon Pico de Gallo Slaw evenly over guacamole. Divide fish evenly among tortillas, and sprinkle with cilantro. Yield: 4 servings (serving size: 1 tostada).

CALORIES 313; FAT 11.9g (sat 4.2g, mono 4.2g, poly 3.5g); PROTEIN 36.6g; CARB 20.6g; FIBER 1.8g; CHOL 85mg; IRON 1.1mg; SODIUM 729mg; CALC 32mg

Pico de Gallo Slaw
Prep: 3 minutes

1½ cups packaged shredded iceberg lettuce
1½ cups packaged 3-color deli coleslaw (such as Fresh Express)

1 cup fresh pico de gallo
⅓ cup light lime vinaigrette (such as Newman's Own)

1. Combine all ingredients in a medium bowl; toss well. Yield: 4 servings (serving size: about ¾ cup).

CALORIES 59; FAT 4g (sat 0.7g, mono 1.4g, poly 1.9g); PROTEIN 0.4g; CARB 8.5g; FIBER 0.7g; CHOL 0mg; IRON 0.1mg; SODIUM 250mg; CALC 4mg

We turned up the flavor of trout fillets and cilantro slaw using sweet-savory garlic and onion jam with both. If you can't get trout fillets in your area, substitute farm-raised tilapia or other thin white fish fillets. If you have time to chill the companion slaw, all the better to boost the flavor.

Trout with Onion Jam and Bacon
Prep: 4 minutes • Cook: 8 minutes

4 (6-ounce) trout fillets
¼ teaspoon salt
¼ teaspoon freshly ground black pepper
¼ cup roasted garlic onion jam (such as Stonewall Kitchen)

Cooking spray
4 precooked bacon slices

1. Preheat broiler.
2. Sprinkle trout with salt and pepper. Stir jam well; brush tops of fillets evenly with jam. Place fillets on the rack of a broiler pan coated with cooking spray. Broil 8 to 10 minutes or until desired degree of doneness.
3. Heat bacon according to package directions. Coarsely crumble 1 bacon slice over each fillet before serving. Yield: 4 servings (serving size: 1 fillet and 1 bacon slice).

CALORIES 247; FAT 7.5g (sat 2.4g, mono 3.1g, poly 1.9g); PROTEIN 30.5g; CARB 13.1g; FIBER 0g; CHOL 146mg; IRON 0.5mg; SODIUM 331mg; CALC 30mg

serve with
Cilantro Slaw
Prep: 1 minute • Cook: 1 minute

¼ cup roasted garlic onion jam (such as Stonewall Kitchen)
1 tablespoon brown sugar
1 tablespoon white vinegar

2 cups packaged 3-color coleslaw (such as Fresh Express)
¼ cup chopped fresh cilantro

1. Combine first 3 ingredients in a microwave-safe bowl. Microwave at HIGH 45 seconds or until jam melts. Cool slightly. Stir in coleslaw and cilantro. Yield: 2 cups (serving size: ½ cup).

CALORIES 72; FAT 0g (sat 0g, mono 0g, poly 0g); PROTEIN 0.4g; CARB 18.1g; FIBER 0.7g; CHOL 0mg; IRON 0.1mg; SODIUM 9mg; CALC 4mg

4-ingredient

Trout fillets can vary in size. Generally, one 6-ounce uncooked fillet is the standard serving size. If trout isn't available, try grouper, the "other flaky white fish." Serve with sautéed spinach.

Cornmeal-Crusted Trout with Bourbon-Pecan Butter Sauce
Prep: 4 minutes • Cook: 13 minutes

¼ cup stone-ground yellow cornmeal
3 tablespoons panko (Japanese breadcrumbs)
4 (6-ounce) rainbow trout fillets
¼ teaspoon salt
¼ teaspoon freshly ground black pepper
2 teaspoons olive oil
Bourbon-Pecan Butter Sauce

1. Combine cornmeal and panko in a shallow dish; sprinkle fish with salt and pepper. Heat oil in a large nonstick skillet over medium-high heat. Dredge tops of fish in cornmeal mixture.
2. Place fish, breading sides down, in pan; cook 4 minutes or until browned. Turn fish over; cook 3 to 4 minutes or until desired degree of doneness. Remove fish from pan; cover and keep warm.
3. Prepare Bourbon-Pecan Butter Sauce; spoon sauce evenly over fish. Yield: 4 servings (serving size: 1 fillet and about 1 tablespoon Bourbon-Pecan Butter Sauce).

CALORIES 376; FAT 15.9g (sat 3.5g, mono 7.7g, poly 4.7g); PROTEIN 36.6g; CARB 12.2g; FIBER 2.1g; CHOL 104mg; IRON 1.8mg; SODIUM 242mg; CALC 127mg

Bourbon-Pecan Butter Sauce
Prep: 1 minute • Cook: 5 minutes

Butter-flavored cooking spray
¼ cup pecan pieces
¼ cup bourbon
1 tablespoon light brown sugar
2 tablespoons fat-free, lower-sodium chicken broth
1 tablespoon light butter
Dash of ground red pepper

1. Heat a medium nonstick skillet over medium-high heat. Coat pan with cooking spray. Add pecans; sauté 2 minutes or until toasted. Remove from pan. Add bourbon, brown sugar, and broth to pan; bring to a boil. Boil 1 minute or until reduced by half. Remove from heat; add butter and pepper, stirring until butter melts. Yield: 4 servings (serving size: about 1 tablespoon).

CALORIES 115; FAT 7.4g (sat 1.7g, mono 3.7g, poly 1.8g); PROTEIN 0.8g; CARB 4.4g; FIBER 0.7g; CHOL 4mg; IRON 0.3mg; SODIUM 33mg; CALC 10mg

Using a risotto mix shaves off time and keeps the dish easy and hands-off. Serve with crusty bread to soak up the flavors.

Risotto Milanese with Mussels
Prep: 1 minute • Cook: 15 minutes • Other: 3 minutes

1¼ cups water
½ (8-ounce) package risotto alla Milanese (such as Alessi; ½ cup)
Steamed Mussels with Tomato and Fennel

2 tablespoons grated fresh Parmigiano-Reggiano cheese
¼ teaspoon freshly ground black pepper
¼ cup chopped fresh parsley

1. Bring 1¼ cups water to a boil in a medium saucepan. Stir in risotto; cover, reduce heat, and simmer 15 minutes. Prepare Steamed Mussels with Tomato and Fennel while risotto is cooking. Uncover risotto, and let stand 3 minutes. Stir in cheese and pepper. Divide mixture evenly among 4 shallow bowls. Spoon Steamed Mussels with Tomato and Fennel evenly over risotto. Sprinkle with parsley. Yield: 6 servings (serving size: ¼ cup risotto, about 11 mussels, ⅔ cup broth, and 2 teaspoons parsley).

CALORIES 329; FAT 7.4g (sat 2.1g, mono 3g, poly 2.3g); PROTEIN 30.7g; CARB 33.3g; FIBER 3.3g; CHOL 65mg; IRON 10.1mg; SODIUM 994mg; CALC 127mg

Steamed Mussels with Tomato and Fennel
Prep: 7 minutes • Cook: 9 minutes

2 teaspoons olive oil
3 cups coarsely chopped tomato
2 cups vertically sliced onion
2 cups sliced fennel bulb

3 garlic cloves, minced
½ cup dry white wine
70 mussels (3 pounds), scrubbed and debearded

1. Heat oil in a large Dutch oven over medium-high heat. Add tomato, onion, fennel, and garlic. Cook, stirring constantly, 4 minutes or until fennel is tender. Add wine and mussels; cover, reduce heat, and simmer 4 minutes or until shells open. Remove from heat; discard any unopened shells. Yield: 6 servings (serving size: about 11 mussels and ⅔ cup broth).

CALORIES 270; FAT 6.9g (sat 1.7g, mono 2.8g, poly 2.3g); PROTEIN 28.8g; CARB 21.8g; FIBER 2.9g; CHOL 64mg; IRON 9.8mg; SODIUM 791mg; CALC 99mg

Panko—or Japanese breadcrumbs—is swoon material! It gives these succulent scallops a light, crispy crust and a delightful crunch. Look for panko on the baking aisle along with other varieties of breadcrumbs or on the ethnic foods aisle of your supermarket.

Crispy Curry Scallops
Prep: 5 minutes • Cook: 5 minutes

1½ pounds large sea scallops (about 12)
½ cup panko (Japanese breadcrumbs)
2 teaspoons lower-sodium soy sauce
1 teaspoon curry powder
2 teaspoons canola oil
Lime wedges

1. Pat scallops dry with paper towels. Place panko in a shallow dish.
2. Toss scallops with soy sauce in a medium bowl; sprinkle evenly with curry powder. Dredge in panko.
3. Heat oil in a large nonstick skillet over medium-high heat. Add scallops to pan; cook 2 to 3 minutes on each side or until browned. Serve with lime wedges. Yield: 4 servings (serving size: 3 scallops).

CALORIES 207; FAT 3.9g (sat 0.3g, mono 1.6g, poly 1.1g); PROTEIN 29.4g; CARB 11.1g; FIBER 1.3g; CHOL 56mg; IRON 0.6mg; SODIUM 388mg; CALC 43mg

serve with
Chile-Ginger Sugar Snaps
Prep: 2 minutes • Cook: 4 minutes

3 tablespoons water
½ teaspoon grated peeled fresh ginger
½ teaspoon chile paste with garlic (such as sambal oelek)
⅛ teaspoon salt
Cooking spray
1 (8-ounce) package fresh sugar snap peas

1. Combine 3 tablespoons water and next 3 ingredients in a small bowl; stir with a whisk.
2. Heat a large nonstick skillet over medium-high heat. Coat pan with cooking spray. Add sugar snap peas, and sauté 1 minute. Add water mixture to pan, tossing to coat peas. Cook 2 minutes or until sugar snap peas are crisp-tender. Yield: 4 servings (serving size: ½ cup).

CALORIES 31; FAT 0.2g (sat 0g, mono 0.2g, poly 0g); PROTEIN 1.4g; CARB 6.5g; FIBER 1.4g; CHOL 0mg; IRON 0.5mg; SODIUM 87mg; CALC 29mg

Green curry paste is a fiery blend of spices and chiles used in Indian and Pakistani cuisines.

Green Curry Scallops with Shiitakes

Prep: 2 minutes • Cook: 11 minutes

1½ pounds sea scallops (about 16 scallops)
¼ teaspoon salt
¼ teaspoon freshly ground black pepper
Olive oil-flavored cooking spray
1 pound shiitake mushrooms, stems removed

1 cup light coconut milk
2 tablespoons green curry paste
2 cups cooked basmati rice (optional)
2 tablespoons chopped fresh basil (optional)

1. Rinse scallops. Drain well, and pat dry with paper towels. Sprinkle scallops with salt and pepper. Heat a large nonstick skillet over medium-high heat. Coat pan with cooking spray. Add scallops to pan; cook 3 minutes on each side or until done. Remove scallops from pan; keep warm.

2. Recoat pan with cooking spray; add mushrooms to pan. Sauté 3 minutes or until tender. Add coconut milk and curry paste. Bring to a simmer, stirring often. Pour sauce over scallops. Serve over basmati rice, and sprinkle with basil, if desired. Yield: 4 servings (serving size: 4 scallops and about ⅔ cup sauce).

CALORIES 253; FAT 4.8g (sat 3.2g, mono 0.8g, poly 0.7g); PROTEIN 31.1g; CARB 23.6g; FIBER 2.4g; CHOL 56mg; IRON 1.3mg; SODIUM 574mg; CALC 45mg

serve with
Mango Lassi

Prep: 4 minutes

2 cups vanilla fat-free yogurt
½ cup fat-free milk

1/16 teaspoon salt
2 peeled ripe mangoes, sliced

1. Place all ingredients in a blender; process until smooth. Cover and refrigerate until ready to serve. Yield: 6 servings (serving size: ¾ cup).

CALORIES 140; FAT 0.3g (sat 0.1g, mono 0.1g, poly 0.1g); PROTEIN 5.2g; CARB 29.8g; FIBER 1.6g; CHOL 2mg; IRON 0.1mg; SODIUM 97mg; CALC 180mg

ingredient spotlight

Green curry paste is typically made with fresh ingredients and all things Asian such as lemongrass, galangal (a cousin of ginger), garlic, onions, green or red chiles, and cilantro. The paste also comes in red and yellow, depending on the ingredients used. The heat index for green curry paste can soar!

4-ingredient

To get the desirable finish on scallops, be sure to pat them dry with a paper towel before cooking. Any moisture on scallops, and they'll steam instead of sear. Try them with the easy 2-ingredient sauce. Use the sauce for dipping spring rolls, lettuce wraps, or other Asian-inspired dishes.

4-ingredient

Sesame-Crusted Scallops with Teriyaki Glaze

Prep: 3 minutes • Cook: 14 minutes

1½ pounds large sea scallops (about 12)
¼ teaspoon salt
¼ teaspoon freshly ground black pepper
3½ tablespoons sesame seeds
1 tablespoon olive oil, divided

5 tablespoons salt-free spicy teriyaki marinade (such as Mrs. Dash)
1½ tablespoons mirin (sweet rice wine)
1½ tablespoons water
Sliced green onions (optional)

1. Pat scallops dry with paper towels. Sprinkle scallops with salt and pepper; dredge in sesame seeds.
2. Heat 1½ teaspoons oil in a large nonstick skillet over medium-high heat. Add half of scallops; cook 3 minutes on each side. Remove scallops from pan; keep warm. Repeat procedure with remaining oil and scallops.
3. Combine teriyaki marinade, mirin, and 1½ tablespoons water, stirring with a whisk. Add to pan; cook 1 minute. Spoon sauce over scallops. Garnish with onions, if desired. Yield: 4 servings (serving size: 3 scallops and 2 tablespoons sauce).

CALORIES 269; FAT 9.2g (sat 1.4g, mono 4.6g, poly 3g); PROTEIN 30g; CARB 12.7g; FIBER 1g; CHOL 56mg; IRON 1.7mg; SODIUM 420mg; CALC 119mg

serve with
Green Onion Soba Noodles

Prep: 3 minutes • Cook: 7 minutes

3 ounces uncooked soba noodles
1 teaspoon dark sesame oil
½ cup sliced green onions

2 garlic cloves, minced
1 tablespoon lower-sodium soy sauce

1. Prepare noodles according to package directions, omitting salt and fat. Drain.
2. While noodles cook, heat oil in a nonstick skillet over medium-high heat. Add onions; sauté 2 minutes. Add garlic; cook 30 seconds. Add drained noodles and soy sauce to pan; toss well. Yield: 4 servings (serving size: ½ cup).

CALORIES 96; FAT 1.5g (sat 0.2g, mono 0.6g, poly 0.6g); PROTEIN 2.6g; CARB 17.1g; FIBER 1g; CHOL 0mg; IRON 0.6mg; SODIUM 273mg; CALC 14mg

quick flip

A Japanese noodle, soba is made from buckwheat flour. If you can't find soba noodles, whole-wheat spaghetti is a close second.

Woo your family and friends with this lighter, modern take on the Mexican specialty. Trade the traditional meat filling and frying method for quesadillas with healthful sautéed shrimp and a knockout fruity salsa.

Shrimp Quesadilla with Tropical Salsa
Prep: 3 minutes • Cook: 12 minutes

2 tablespoons salt-free Fiesta Lime seasoning (such as Mrs. Dash)
1 pound peeled and deveined medium shrimp
1½ teaspoons canola oil
4 (8-inch) 98% fat-free whole-wheat tortillas (such as Mission)

1 cup (4 ounces) preshredded reduced-fat Mexican blend cheese
Cooking spray
Tropical Salsa
Fresh cilantro (optional)

1. Sprinkle seasoning over shrimp; toss well.
2. Heat oil in a large nonstick skillet over medium-high heat; add shrimp. Sauté 3 minutes or until shrimp reach desired degree of doneness; remove from pan. Wipe drippings from pan with a paper towel.
3. Arrange shrimp over half of each tortilla; sprinkle each with ¼ cup cheese. Fold tortillas in half.
4. Return pan to heat. Coat pan and both sides of quesadillas evenly with cooking spray. Place 2 quesadillas in pan; cook 2 minutes on each side or until browned. Repeat procedure with remaining quesadillas. Cut each quesadilla into 2 wedges; serve with Tropical Salsa and, if desired, sprinkle with fresh cilantro. Yield: 4 servings (serving size: 1 quesadilla and ½ cup Tropical Salsa).

CALORIES 452; FAT 12.4g (sat 4.3g, mono 5.2g, poly 2.8g); PROTEIN 36.1g; CARB 49.4g; FIBER 4.7g; CHOL 183mg; IRON 3mg; SODIUM 714mg; CALC 285mg

Tropical Salsa
Prep: 10 minutes

2 tablespoons lime juice
2 teaspoons honey
2 ripe kiwifruit, peeled and chopped

1½ teaspoons canola oil
1½ cups diced peeled mango (1 large mango)
2 tablespoons minced red onion

1. Combine first 3 ingredients in a medium bowl, stirring with a whisk. Add mango, onion, and kiwifruit; toss well. Yield: 4 servings (serving size: ½ cup).

CALORIES 106; FAT 2.2g (sat 0.2g, mono 1.1g, poly 0.7g); PROTEIN 0.9g; CARB 23.3g; FIBER 2.7g; CHOL 0mg; IRON 0.3mg; SODIUM 3mg; CALC 23mg

Like your 'cue cooked low and slow? The enticing aroma of this speedy grilled shrimp just might change your mind. We liked the smoky flavor that bacon and barbecue sauce add to the shrimp.

Smoky BBQ Shrimp
Prep: 8 minutes • Cook: 6 minutes

32 peeled and deveined large shrimp (about 1½ pounds)
⅓ cup spicy barbecue sauce (such as Stubbs)
2 slices applewood-smoked bacon, cooked and finely crumbled

1½ tablespoons low-sugar orange marmalade
Cooking spray

1. Preheat grill.
2. Thread shrimp onto 4 (12-inch) metal skewers.
3. Combine barbecue sauce, bacon, and marmalade; brush evenly over shrimp, using all sauce. Place skewers on grill rack coated with cooking spray; grill 3 to 4 minutes on each side or until shrimp reach desired degree of doneness. Yield: 4 servings (serving size: about 8 shrimp).

CALORIES 227; FAT 5.2g (sat 1.6g, mono 1.6g, poly 1.9g); PROTEIN 37g; CARB 7.4g; FIBER 0g; CHOL 264mg; IRON 4.1mg; SODIUM 502mg; CALC 89mg

serve with
Grilled Avocado with Lime-Cilantro Cream
Prep: 8 minutes • Cook: 2 minutes

2 avocados, peeled, seeded, and halved
Olive oil-flavored cooking spray
2 teaspoons turbinado sugar
¼ teaspoon salt

¼ teaspoon freshly ground black pepper
¼ cup light sour cream
1 tablespoon chopped fresh cilantro
1½ tablespoons fresh lime juice

1. Preheat grill.
2. Coat both sides of avocado with cooking spray; sprinkle evenly with sugar, salt, and pepper. Place avocado, pit sides down, on grill rack coated with cooking spray. Grill 1 to 2 minutes on each side or until lightly charred.
3. Combine sour cream, cilantro, and lime juice. Cut each avocado half in half; drizzle with sour cream mixture. Yield: 4 servings (serving size: 2 avocado wedges and 1 tablespoon cream).

CALORIES 166; FAT 13.2g (sat 3.2g, mono 8.2g, poly 1.6g); PROTEIN 3g; CARB 11.8g; FIBER 4.9g; CHOL 5mg; IRON 0.5mg; SODIUM 515mg; CALC 27mg

Fried rice is the ideal Asian recipe for using quick-start, quick-finish precooked rice. Simply open the pouch, and add it to the stir-fry for the last 3 minutes of cooking. Red pepper, garlic, ginger, and soy sauce put the accent on Asian in this lively shrimp dish.

Shrimp Fried Rice
Prep: 9 minutes • Cook: 9 minutes

Seasoned Shrimp
Cooking spray
1 large egg, lightly beaten
½ cup frozen petite green peas
⅓ cup diagonally sliced green onions
1 (8.8-ounce) pouch microwavable cooked brown rice, chilled (such as Uncle Ben's Whole Grain Brown Ready Rice)

1. Prepare Seasoned Shrimp; keep warm.
2. Wipe pan with paper towels; recoat with cooking spray. Return to medium-high heat. Add egg; cook 1½ minutes or until set. Remove egg from pan; cool and thinly slice.
3. While egg cools, add peas and onions to pan; stir-fry 1 minute. Add rice; stir-fry 2 minutes or until heated. Add egg and Seasoned Shrimp; stir-fry 1 minute. Yield: 4 servings (serving size: 1 cup).

CALORIES 270; FAT 5.2g (sat 1g, mono 1.9g, poly 2.2g); PROTEIN 28.1g; CARB 24.3g; FIBER 2.1g; CHOL 217mg; IRON 3.8mg; SODIUM 528mg; CALC 74mg

Seasoned Shrimp
Prep: 2 minutes • Cook: 3 minutes

Cooking spray
1 pound peeled and deveined large shrimp
¼ teaspoon crushed red pepper
1 tablespoon minced garlic
2 teaspoons minced peeled fresh ginger
2 tablespoons lower-sodium soy sauce

1. Heat a wok or large nonstick skillet over medium-high heat. Coat pan with cooking spray. Add shrimp and crushed red pepper to pan; stir-fry 1 minute. Add garlic and ginger to pan; stir-fry 1 minute. Add soy sauce; stir-fry 1 minute or until shrimp reach desired degree of doneness. Yield: 4 servings (serving size: about 6 shrimp).

CALORIES 137; FAT 2.4g (sat 0.5g, mono 0.6g, poly 1.2g); PROTEIN 23.5g; CARB 2.8g; FIBER 0.1g; CHOL 172mg; IRON 2.9mg; SODIUM 468mg; CALC 61mg

Takeout? Not a chance. This creamy-rich shrimp casserole gives new meaning to the term convenience food. Ready-to-cook shrimp, precooked rice, and refrigerated Alfredo sauce streamline this family favorite that's on the table in 10 minutes flat.

Shrimp and Artichokes with Wild Rice
Prep: 3 minutes • Cook: 6 minutes

1 (8.8-ounce) package precooked long-grain and wild rice (such as Uncle Ben's Ready Rice)
Cream Sauce
1 (9-ounce) package frozen artichoke hearts (such as Birds Eye)

Cooking spray
12 ounces peeled and deveined large shrimp, coarsely chopped
¼ teaspoon freshly ground black pepper
3 tablespoons shredded fresh Parmesan cheese

1. Microwave rice according to package directions. Prepare Cream Sauce. Microwave artichoke hearts according to package directions; drain and chop.
2. While artichokes cook, heat a large nonstick skillet over medium-high heat. Coat pan with cooking spray. Coat shrimp with cooking spray; add shrimp and pepper to pan. Sauté 3 minutes or until desired degree of doneness. Stir in artichoke hearts, rice, and Cream Sauce; cook 1 minute or just until thoroughly heated. Sprinkle with cheese. Serve hot. Yield: 4 servings (serving size: about 1¼ cups).

CALORIES 431; FAT 8.9g (sat 4.4g, mono 2.3g, poly 2.1g); PROTEIN 30.4g; CARB 57g; FIBER 5g; CHOL 149mg; IRON 4.3mg; SODIUM 1345mg; CALC 258mg

Cream Sauce
Prep: 1 minute • Cook: 1 minute

¾ cup refrigerated light Alfredo sauce (such as Buitoni)
2 tablespoons fat-free milk

2 teaspoons bottled minced garlic
¼ teaspoon ground red pepper

1. Combine all ingredients in a microwave-safe bowl or 2-cup glass measuring cup. Microwave at HIGH 1 minute or until thoroughly heated. Yield: 1 cup (serving size: ¼ cup).

CALORIES 71; FAT 4g (sat 2.6g, mono 0.8g, poly 0.6g); PROTEIN 3.3g; CARB 4.7g; FIBER 0g; CHOL 15mg; IRON 0mg; SODIUM 282mg; CALC 83mg

10-minute

Authentic-tasting jambalaya in only 8 minutes? This Creole dish comes together quickly using precooked spicy rice, seasoned canned tomatoes, ready-to-cook shrimp, and ham.

Shrimp Jambalaya

Prep: 1 minute • Cook: 7 minutes

1 teaspoon extra-virgin olive oil
½ cup refrigerated prechopped celery
¾ pound peeled and deveined medium shrimp
1 (14.5-ounce) can diced tomatoes with green pepper, celery, and onion, undrained
¼ cup chopped ham

¼ teaspoon ground red pepper
1 (8.8-ounce) package microwavable precooked Spanish-style rice with tomatoes and peppers (such as Uncle Ben's Ready Rice)
2 tablespoons coarsely chopped fresh parsley

1. Heat oil in a large nonstick skillet over medium-high heat. Add celery; sauté 2 minutes. Add shrimp; sauté 2 minutes or until shrimp reach desired degree of doneness. Stir in tomatoes, ham, and red pepper. Cook, stirring constantly, 1 to 2 minutes or until thoroughly heated.
2. While shrimp mixture cooks, microwave rice according to package directions; stir into shrimp mixture. Sprinkle with parsley. Yield: 4 servings (serving size: about 1 cup).

CALORIES 242; FAT 4.9g (sat 1.1g, mono 2g, poly 1.6g); PROTEIN 22.4g; CARB 26.8g; FIBER 3g; CHOL 135mg; IRON 2.8mg; SODIUM 1051mg; CALC 79mg

serve with
Watercress Salad with Balsamic Orange Vinaigrette

Prep: 5 minutes

2 tablespoons balsamic vinegar
1 tablespoon fresh orange juice
2 teaspoons extra-virgin olive oil

¼ teaspoon salt
¼ teaspoon freshly ground black pepper
4 cups trimmed watercress

1. Whisk together first 5 ingredients in a large bowl; add watercress, and toss gently to coat. Yield: 4 servings (serving size: 1 cup).

CALORIES 33; FAT 2.4g (sat 0.3g, mono 1.7g, poly 0.4g); PROTEIN 0.9g; CARB 2.3g; FIBER 0.2g; CHOL 0mg; IRON 0.1mg; SODIUM 161mg; CALC 44mg

This intensely flavored, garlic-infused scampi served over angel hair pasta won us over for its flavor and quick prep time. You're in and out of the kitchen superfast.

Shrimp Scampi

Prep: 3 minutes • Cook: 7 minutes

1½ tablespoons olive oil
1½ tablespoons bottled minced garlic
1½ pounds peeled and deveined jumbo shrimp
¼ cup finely chopped fresh flat-leaf parsley

1½ tablespoons fresh lemon juice
½ teaspoon salt
⅛ teaspoon ground red pepper

1. Heat oil in a large nonstick skillet over medium-low heat; add garlic, and cook 1 minute. Add shrimp, and cook 5 minutes or until shrimp reach desired degree of doneness, stirring occasionally; remove pan from heat. Stir in parsley and remaining ingredients. Yield: 4 servings (serving size: about 5 shrimp).

CALORIES 233; FAT 8.1g (sat 1.3g, mono 4.1g, poly 1.7g); PROTEIN 34.9g; CARB 3.4g; FIBER 0.2g; CHOL 259mg; IRON 4.4mg; SODIUM 549mg; CALC 100mg

ingredient spotlight

Bottled minced garlic is a handy time-saving product. Instead of taking the time to mince garlic cloves, this makes a great substitution. One teaspoon bottled minced garlic is the equivalent of 2 minced cloves.

10-minute

meats

Dolmathes, 221
Shepherd's Pie, 222
Beef and Pepperoni Pizza, 224
Beef and Bok Choy Stir-Fry, 227
Chili-Lime Flank Steak, 228
Steak Soft Tacos with Grilled Onion, 231
Jamaican-Spiced Hanger Steak with Banana-Mango Chutney, 233
Apricot-Glazed Beef Tenderloin, 234
Beef Tenderloin with Mushroom Gravy, 237
Grecian Steaks, 238
Grilled Lamb Chops with Honey Figs, 241
Veal Piccata, 243
Pork Schnitzel, 244
Grilled Peach Barbecue Pork Chops, 246
Sweet and Spicy Chili Pork Chops, 249
Fiery Grilled Pork Tenderloin, 250
Sage Pork Medallions with Maple Glaze, 253
Ham and Roasted Asparagus Crepes with Gruyère Cheese Sauce, 254
Baked Eggs in Crispy Ham Cups with Petite Peas, 256
Pasta Puttanesca, 259

Dolmathes is a traditional Greek dish of meat and rice stuffed in grape leaves and topped with a delicate lemon avgolemono sauce.

Dolmathes
Prep: 18 minutes • Cook: 31 minutes

18 bottled large grape leaves
1 pound ground round
1 cup butter-and-garlic-flavored
   microwavable cooked rice (such
   as Uncle Ben's Ready Rice)
½ teaspoon freshly ground black pepper

¼ teaspoon salt
Cooking spray
1 cup fat-free, lower-sodium chicken broth
2 teaspoons olive oil
Avgolemono Sauce
Chopped fresh mint or parsley (optional)

1. Rinse grape leaves under cold water; drain and pat dry with paper towels. Remove stems, and discard.
2. Combine beef and next 3 ingredients in a medium bowl. Spoon 2 tablespoons beef mixture onto center of each grape leaf. Bring 2 opposite points of leaf to center, and fold over filling. Beginning at 1 short side, roll up leaf tightly, jelly-roll fashion. Repeat procedure with remaining grape leaves.
3. Place stuffed grape leaves close together, seam sides down, in a Dutch oven coated with cooking spray. Add broth and oil; bring to a boil. Cover, reduce heat, and simmer 30 minutes. Using a slotted spoon, transfer to a serving platter, and keep warm until ready to serve.
4. Prepare Avgolemono Sauce. Serve dolmathes with Avgolemono Sauce, and garnish with chopped mint or parsley, if desired. Yield: 6 servings (serving size: 3 dolmathes and about 1½ tablespoons sauce).

CALORIES 209; FAT 10.7g (sat 3.9g, mono 5.4g, poly 1.2g); PROTEIN 17.6g; CARB 9.3g; FIBER 1.4g; CHOL 79mg; IRON 2.5mg; SODIUM 407mg; CALC 61mg

Avgolemono Sauce
Prep: 2 minutes • Cook: 4 minutes

1 large egg
1 tablespoon fresh lemon juice
⅓ cup fat-free, lower-sodium chicken broth

1 tablespoon chopped fresh parsley
1 tablespoon chopped fresh mint

1. Place egg and lemon juice in a blender; process until egg is well beaten.
2. Place chicken broth in a 1-cup glass measure; microwave at HIGH 30 seconds or until hot. Remove center piece of blender lid; with blender on, gradually add hot broth to egg mixture. Process until blended.
3. Pour mixture into a small saucepan. Cook over medium-high heat, stirring constantly with a whisk, 2 minutes or until slightly thick (do not boil). Stir in parsley and mint. Yield: 6 servings (serving size: about 1½ tablespoons).

CALORIES 14; FAT 0.7g (sat 0.2g, mono 0.3g, poly 0.1g); PROTEIN 1.1g; CARB 0.6g; FIBER 0.1g; CHOL 30mg; IRON 0.2mg; SODIUM 43mg; CALC 6mg

An English meat pie originally devised as a way to use leftover lamb, shepherd's pie just might be the first-ever casserole. This all-in-one meal features beef joined by a medley of veggies and topped with a pillow-soft mountain of mashed potatoes.

Shepherd's Pie

Prep: 2 minutes • Cook: 13 minutes

¾ pound 93% lean ground beef
1½ cups frozen baby vegetable mix (such as Birds Eye)
1 (14.5-ounce) can diced tomatoes with basil, garlic, and oregano, undrained
1 (8-ounce) can no-salt-added tomato sauce
2 cups country-style refrigerated mashed potatoes (such as Simply Potatoes)
Cooking spray
⅛ teaspoon freshly ground black pepper

1. Preheat broiler.
2. Cook beef in a large nonstick skillet over medium-high heat until browned, stirring to crumble. Add vegetable mix, tomatoes, and tomato sauce. Cook 5 minutes or until mixture is slightly thick and thoroughly heated, stirring occasionally.
3. While beef mixture cooks, place potatoes in a microwave-safe bowl. Cover with plastic wrap; vent. Microwave at HIGH 2 minutes or until thoroughly heated.
4. Spoon beef mixture evenly into each of 4 (8-ounce) broiler-safe ramekins coated with cooking spray. Top evenly with potatoes; sprinkle with pepper. Place ramekins on a baking sheet. Broil 2 to 3 minutes or until potatoes are golden. Yield: 4 servings (serving size: 1 pie).

CALORIES 305; FAT 10.7g (sat 5.6g, mono 3.8g, poly 0.4g); PROTEIN 20.6g; CARB 32.4g; FIBER 4.8g; CHOL 56mg; IRON 3.7mg; SODIUM 490mg; CALC 59mg

We reduced the fat, calories, and sodium in this pizzeria-style meat pizza by opting for lighter turkey pepperoni. This trims the fat by 50 percent and still delivers the zesty, spicy flavor of regular pepperoni.

Beef and Pepperoni Pizza

Prep: 2 minutes • Cook: 13 minutes

1 (10-ounce) Italian whole-wheat thin pizza crust (such as Boboli)
Olive oil-flavored cooking spray
½ pound ground beef, extra lean
1 (8-ounce) package presliced mushrooms
¾ cup marinara sauce (such as Newman's Own)
¼ cup turkey pepperoni (about 15 slices)
⅔ cup (2.67 ounces) shredded part-skim mozzarella cheese
¼ teaspoon crushed red pepper

1. Preheat oven to 450°.
2. Place pizza crust on rack in oven while oven preheats; heat 5 minutes.
3. While crust heats, heat a large nonstick skillet over medium-high heat. Coat pan with cooking spray. Add beef and mushrooms; sauté 5 minutes or until beef is browned. Drain.
4. Remove crust from oven; place on an ungreased baking sheet. Coat crust with cooking spray; spread marinara sauce over crust, leaving a 1-inch border. Top with beef mixture, pepperoni, and cheese. Sprinkle evenly with red pepper.
5. Bake at 450° for 7 to 10 minutes or until crust is golden and cheese melts. Cut into 8 wedges. Serve immediately. Yield: 4 servings (serving size: 2 wedges).

CALORIES 366; FAT 11.6g (sat 5.3g, mono 3.9g, poly 1.1g); PROTEIN 29.1g; CARB 7.4g; FIBER 6.8g; CHOL 49mg; IRON 2.8mg; SODIUM 810mg; CALC 216mg

serve with
Classic Vinaigrette Salad

Prep: 7 minutes

¼ cup red wine vinegar
1 tablespoon Dijon mustard
1 teaspoon sugar
2 teaspoons olive oil
¼ teaspoon salt
¼ teaspoon pepper
1 garlic clove, minced
2 cups thinly sliced cucumber
4 radishes, sliced
1 (6.5-ounce) package sweet butter lettuce blend salad greens (such as Fresh Express)

1. Combine first 7 ingredients in a small bowl, stirring with a whisk. Combine cucumber, radishes, and lettuce in a large bowl. Pour dressing over lettuce mixture; toss well. Yield: 4 servings (serving size: 2 cups).

CALORIES 47; FAT 2.3g (sat 0.3g, mono 1.6g, poly 0.3g); PROTEIN 1g; CARB 5.6g; FIBER 1g; CHOL 0mg; IRON 0.9mg; SODIUM 246mg; CALC 27mg

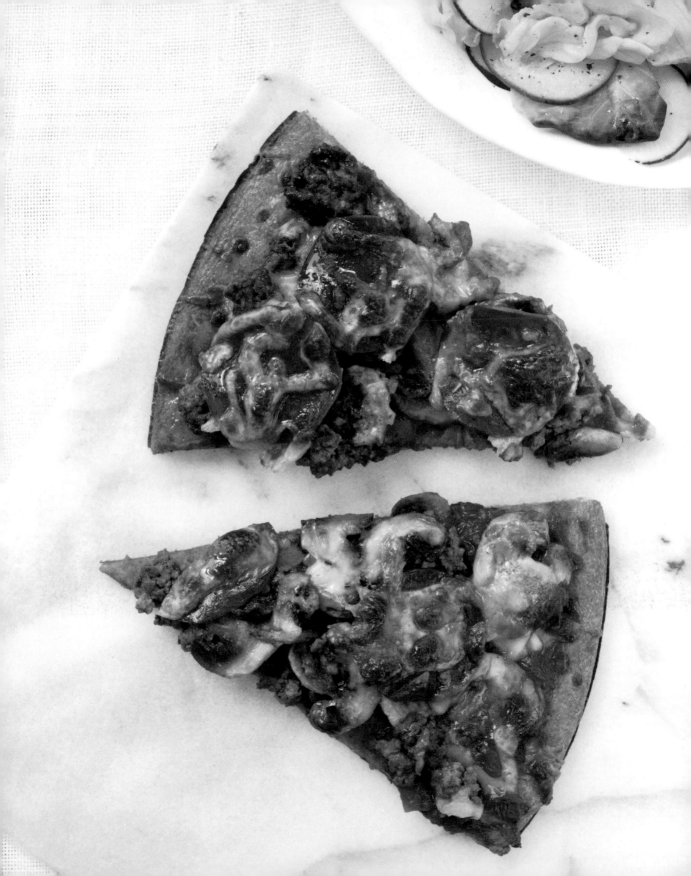

We like to use baby bok choy because the young leaves are so tender. If you can't find it, just use 3½ cups of very coarsely chopped bok choy leaves.

Beef and Bok Choy Stir-Fry

Prep: 10 minutes • Cook: 13 minutes

Orange Stir-Fry Sauce
2 teaspoons canola oil, divided
1 pound sirloin steak, trimmed and cut into thin strips
¼ teaspoon salt
¼ teaspoon freshly ground black pepper
3 baby bok choy, cut into 1-inch pieces

1 medium-sized red bell pepper, cut into ¼-inch strips
1 (8.5-ounce) package microwavable precooked jasmine rice (such as Uncle Ben's Ready Rice)
Sesame seeds (optional)

1. Prepare Orange Stir-Fry Sauce; set aside.
2. Heat 1 teaspoon oil in a large nonstick skillet over medium-high heat. Sprinkle steak strips with salt and pepper. Stir-fry steak in hot oil 5 to 6 minutes or until browned. Remove steak from pan; keep warm.
3. Heat remaining 1 teaspoon oil in pan; add bok choy and bell pepper. Stir-fry 2 minutes or until crisp-tender. Return steak to pan. Stir in sauce; remove from heat.
4. Microwave rice according to package directions. Serve beef mixture over rice. Garnish with sesame seeds, if desired. Yield: 4 servings (serving size: about 1 cup beef mixture and 6 tablespoons rice).

CALORIES 354; FAT 8.9g (sat 1.6g, mono 4.4g, poly 2.8g); PROTEIN 29g; CARB 39.3g; FIBER 2g; CHOL 81mg; IRON 5mg; SODIUM 834mg; CALC 32mg

Orange Stir-Fry Sauce

Prep: 3 minutes • Cook: 4 minutes

1 tablespoon cornstarch
1 tablespoon brown sugar
¼ cup orange juice
¼ cup lower-sodium soy sauce
1 tablespoon rice vinegar

2 teaspoons dark sesame oil
Cooking spray
1 tablespoon minced peeled fresh ginger
2 garlic cloves, minced

1. Combine cornstarch and brown sugar in a small bowl; gradually add orange juice, soy sauce, and vinegar, stirring with a whisk until smooth.
2. Heat oil in a small saucepan coated with cooking spray. Add ginger and garlic; sauté 1 minute or until tender. Stir in orange juice mixture. Cook, stirring constantly, over medium heat 2 minutes or until thick. Yield: 4 servings (serving size: 3 tablespoons).

CALORIES 61; FAT 2.4g (sat 0.3g, mono 1g, poly 1g); PROTEIN 1.2g; CARB 9.1g; FIBER 0.3g; CHOL 0mg; IRON 0.5mg; SODIUM 602mg; CALC 11mg

Chicken tenders substitute deliciously for sirloin steak strips in this stir-fry dish. The accompanying orange-kissed sauce and aromatic jasmine rice make it a winning weeknight dish.

Chili-Lime Flank Steak

Prep: 5 minutes • Cook: 14 minutes • Other: 5 minutes

1 tablespoon chili powder
2 teaspoons grated lime rind
½ teaspoon salt
½ teaspoon freshly ground black pepper
1 (1½-pound) flank steak, trimmed

2 tablespoons fresh lime juice
Cooking spray
3 tablespoons chopped fresh cilantro or cilantro leaves

1. Preheat grill.
2. Combine first 4 ingredients in a small bowl. Sprinkle steak with lime juice. Rub steak with spice mixture.
3. Place steak on grill rack coated with cooking spray. Grill 7 to 8 minutes on each side or until desired degree of doneness. Let stand 5 minutes. Cut steak diagonally across grain into thin slices. Sprinkle each serving with cilantro. Yield: 6 servings (serving size: 3 ounces).

CALORIES 158; FAT 5.7g (sat 2.6g, mono 2.5g, poly 0.5g); PROTEIN 24.4g; CARB 0.7g; FIBER 0.2g; CHOL 39mg; IRON 1.8mg; SODIUM 294mg; CALC 27mg

serve with
Roasted Bell Peppers, Potatoes, and Onion

Prep: 5 minutes • Cook: 25 minutes • Other: 5 minutes

3 medium bell peppers (1 each, green, red, and yellow)
9 small red potatoes (about 1 pound), cut into wedges
1 medium-sized sweet onion, cut into wedges
1 tablespoon olive oil

1 teaspoon garlic powder
½ teaspoon paprika
¼ teaspoon salt
¼ teaspoon freshly ground black pepper
Cooking spray

1. Preheat oven to 450°.
2. Cut bell peppers in half, discarding seeds and membranes. Combine bell pepper, potato, and next 6 ingredients on a large rimmed baking sheet coated with cooking spray. Bake at 450° for 25 minutes or until vegetables are browned and tender. Place peppers in a zip-top plastic bag; seal. Let stand 5 minutes.
3. While peppers stand, place potato mixture in a bowl. Peel and cut bell pepper into bite-sized pieces; add to potato mixture, and toss well. Yield: 6 servings (serving size: about 1 cup).

CALORIES 117; FAT 2.5g (sat 0.4g, mono 1.7g, poly 0.3g); PROTEIN 2.9g; CARB 21.3g; FIBER 2.7g; CHOL 0mg; IRON 1.1mg; SODIUM 109mg; CALC 17mg

This boneless steak from a well-exercised part of the cow requires some TLC—and that's where the smoky-citrusy rub comes in. It brings out the flavor, while the zesty lime juice tenderizes it. A trio of colorful roasted bell peppers brightens this Southwestern-style favorite.

Prepared Southwest chipotle seasoning is a merry mix of red pepper, lime juice, onion, garlic, and salt, blended with smoky chipotle chiles.

Steak Soft Tacos with Grilled Onion
Prep: 15 minutes • Cook: 14 minutes • Other: 5 minutes

1 (¾-pound) flank steak
1 tablespoon olive oil, divided
1 tablespoon salt-free Southwest chipotle seasoning (such as Mrs. Dash), divided
½ teaspoon salt, divided
½ teaspoon freshly ground black pepper, divided

1 large sweet onion, cut into ½-inch-thick slices
Cooking spray
Cilantro Cream
4 (8-inch) flour tortillas with chipotle chili and peppers (such as Gourmet Tortillas)

1. Preheat grill.
2. Rub flank steak with 1 teaspoon oil; sprinkle with 1 teaspoon chipotle seasoning, ¼ teaspoon salt, and ¼ teaspoon black pepper.
3. Coat both sides of onion slices with cooking spray. Combine remaining 2 teaspoons oil, 2 teaspoons chipotle seasoning, ¼ teaspoon salt, and ¼ teaspoon pepper in a small bowl; brush on both sides of onion slices.
4. Place steak and onion slices on grill rack coated with cooking spray. Grill 7 minutes on each side or until steak reaches desired degree of doneness and onion is slightly charred and almost tender. Remove steak and onion from grill; cover steak, and let stand 5 minutes. Cut steak diagonally across grain into thin slices.
5. While steak stands, prepare Cilantro Cream. Stack onion slices, and cut crosswise into quarters. Microwave tortillas according to package directions until warm. Place 1 tortilla on each of 4 plates. Spread tortillas evenly with Cilantro Cream; top evenly with steak and onion. Fold sides of tortillas over, and serve immediately. Yield: 4 servings (serving size: 1 taco).

CALORIES 317; FAT 12g (sat 4.1g, mono 6.2g, poly 1.5g); PROTEIN 23.5g; CARB 30.6g; FIBER 1.9g; CHOL 35mg; IRON 3.4mg; SODIUM 459mg; CALC 175mg

Cilantro Cream
Prep: 4 minutes

¼ cup reduced-fat sour cream
2 tablespoons chopped fresh cilantro

⅛ teaspoon ground cumin
2 large garlic cloves, minced

1. Combine all ingredients in a small bowl, stirring with a whisk. Yield: 4 servings (serving size: 1 tablespoon).

CALORIES 23; FAT 1.8g (sat 1.1g, mono 0.5g, poly 0.1g); PROTEIN 0.6g; CARB 1.1g; FIBER 0.1g; CHOL 6mg; IRON 0.1mg; SODIUM 7mg; CALC 19mg

4-ingredient

Hanger steak shares texture and flavor with flank steak. Here, the spicy Jamaican wet rub makes it tender, juicy, and flavorful.

Jamaican-Spiced Hanger Steak with Banana-Mango Chutney

Prep: 7 minutes • Cook: 23 minutes • Other: 1 hour and 5 minutes

Jamaican Rub
 1 (1-pound) hanger steak
Cooking spray

½ cup chopped banana
½ cup mango chutney

1. Prepare Jamaican Rub.
2. Reserve 2 tablespoons Jamaican Rub. Pat remaining rub onto steak. Place steak in a large heavy-duty zip-top plastic bag; seal bag, and marinate in refrigerator at least 1 hour.
3. Preheat oven to 450°.
4. Heat a large cast-iron or ovenproof skillet over medium-high heat. Coat pan with cooking spray. Add steak; cook 3 minutes on each side or until browned. Bake at 450° for 15 minutes or to desired degree of doneness. Transfer steak to a serving platter; cover and let steak rest 5 minutes.
5. Place reserved rub in a small saucepan. Add banana and chutney; cook, stirring constantly, over medium-high heat 1 minute or until thoroughly heated.
6. Thinly cut steak across grain into thin slices. Spoon chutney over steak. Yield: 4 servings (serving size: 3 ounces steak and ½ cup chutney).

CALORIES 305; FAT 8.2g (sat 3.6g, mono 3.6g, poly 0.9g); PROTEIN 24.4g; CARB 30.8g; FIBER 1.3g; CHOL 39mg; IRON 0.4mg; SODIUM 615mg; CALC 23mg

Jamaican Rub

Prep: 4 minutes

 2 tablespoons dark brown sugar
 1 tablespoon fresh thyme leaves
 2 tablespoons white vinegar
 2 tablespoons grated peeled fresh ginger

 2 teaspoons ground allspice
 1 teaspoon crushed red pepper
 ½ teaspoon salt
 4 garlic cloves, minced

1. Place all ingredients in a small bowl; mash to a paste with a fork. Yield: 4 servings (serving size: 2 tablespoons).

CALORIES 39; FAT 0.2g (sat 0g, mono 0g, poly 0.1g); PROTEIN 0.4g; CARB 9.4g; FIBER 0.9g; CHOL 0mg; IRON 0.4mg; SODIUM 295mg; CALC 23mg

Apricot-Glazed Beef Tenderloin
Prep: 1 minute • Cook: 8 minutes

1 tablespoon butter
4 (4-ounce) beef tenderloin steaks, trimmed (about 1 inch thick)
½ teaspoon ground cumin
½ teaspoon freshly ground black pepper
¼ teaspoon salt
½ cup apricot preserves
2 tablespoons water

1. Melt butter in a large nonstick skillet over medium-high heat.
2. While butter melts, sprinkle steaks evenly with cumin, pepper, and salt. Cook steaks in melted butter 3 minutes on each side or until desired degree of doneness. Transfer steaks to a serving platter; keep warm. Reduce heat to medium.
3. Stir preserves and 2 tablespoons water into drippings, scraping pan to loosen browned bits. Cook, stirring constantly, over medium heat 1 minute or until bubbly.
4. Place 1 steak on each of 4 plates. Spoon sauce evenly over steaks. Yield: 4 servings (serving size: 1 steak and 2 tablespoons sauce).

CALORIES 300; FAT 10.3g (sat 5.1g, mono 4.2g, poly 0.9g); PROTEIN 25.2g; CARB 26.3g; FIBER 0.2g; CHOL 84mg; IRON 1.9mg; SODIUM 230mg; CALC 31mg

serve with
Jalapeño Grits
Prep: 2 minutes • Cook: 7 minutes

1½ cups water
¼ teaspoon salt
½ cup uncooked quick-cooking grits
1½ tablespoons minced seeded jalapeño pepper (1 pepper)
½ cup fat-free milk
2 (0.5-ounce) slices reduced-fat Monterey Jack cheese with jalapeño peppers, chopped
Freshly ground black pepper (optional)

1. Bring 1½ cups water and salt to a boil in a medium saucepan. Gradually stir in grits. Add jalapeño pepper; cover, reduce heat, and simmer 5 minutes or until thick. Stir in milk. Remove from heat; add cheese, stirring until cheese melts. Garnish with freshly ground black pepper, if desired. Yield: 4 servings (serving size: ½ cup).

CALORIES 105; FAT 1.8g (sat 0.9g, mono 0.6g, poly 0.2g); PROTEIN 4.7g; CARB 17.6g; FIBER 0.4g; CHOL 5mg; IRON 0.8mg; SODIUM 223mg; CALC 83mg

fix it faster

These grits are a cinch to make using Monterey Jack cheese studded with jalapeño pepper. The all-in-one cheese eliminates seeding and mincing the chile pepper and gives the grits the desired creamy texture with a hit of hot.

Spicy and creamy meet savory and sweet in this comforting meal with a little kick. The tangy-sweet apricot glaze on the beef balances the lively jalapeño grits sidekick.

4-ingredient

10-minute

4-ingredient

Tenderloin, prized for its rich flavor and tenderness, can be a bit pricey, but the melt-in-your-mouth results are worth the splurge. It's the most tender cut of beef you can buy. Beef tenderloin steaks are often labeled "filet mignon." Round out your meal with Garlicky Smashed Potatoes and a side of steamed haricots verts.

Beef Tenderloin with Mushroom Gravy
Prep: 3 minutes • Cook: 12 minutes

4 (4-ounce) beef tenderloin steaks, trimmed
½ teaspoon freshly ground black pepper
¼ teaspoon salt
Cooking spray
½ cup minced shallots

1 (8-ounce) package presliced baby portobello mushrooms
1 (1.25-ounce) package mushroom-and-herb gravy mix (such as McCormick)
1 cup water

1. Sprinkle steaks with pepper and salt. Heat a large nonstick skillet over medium-high heat. Add steaks to pan, and cook 3 to 4 minutes on each side or until desired degree of doneness. Remove steaks from pan; keep warm.
2. Coat pan with cooking spray. Add shallots and mushrooms; cook 5 minutes. Empty gravy mix into a small bowl. Gradually add 1 cup water, stirring with a whisk until blended. Add gravy to pan, scraping pan to loosen browned bits. Cook 1 minute. Spoon gravy over steaks. Yield: 4 servings (serving size: 1 steak and ¼ cup gravy).

CALORIES 242; FAT 8.7g (sat 2.8g, mono 3.3g, poly 0.4g); PROTEIN 28g; CARB 10.8g; FIBER 1.1g; CHOL 81mg; IRON 2.3mg; SODIUM 716mg; CALC 48mg

serve with
Garlicky Smashed Potatoes
Prep: 2 minutes • Cook: 4 minutes

1 (24-ounce) package country-style mashed potatoes (such as Simply Potatoes)
¼ cup light garlic-and-herbs spreadable cheese (such as Alouette Light)

¼ teaspoon freshly ground black pepper

1. Heat potatoes according to package directions. Stir in cheese and pepper. Yield: 6 servings (serving size: ½ cup).

CALORIES 108; FAT 4.5g (sat 3.3g, mono 0.9g, poly 0.1g); PROTEIN 2.5g; CARB 15g; FIBER 1.9g; CHOL 16mg; IRON 0.7mg; SODIUM 214mg; CALC 29mg

Grecian Steaks

Prep: 2 minutes • Cook: 5 minutes

4 (4-ounce) beef tenderloin steaks, trimmed (about 1 inch thick)
½ teaspoon freshly ground black pepper
Olive oil-flavored cooking spray
2 tablespoons fresh lemon juice
¼ cup (1 ounce) crumbled feta cheese
2 tablespoons coarsely chopped pitted kalamata olives
Fresh oregano leaves (optional)

1. Press steaks with palm of hand to flatten, if desired. Sprinkle steaks with pepper; coat with cooking spray. Heat a large cast-iron skillet over medium-high heat. Coat pan with cooking spray. Add steaks to pan; cook 2 to 3 minutes on each side or until desired degree of doneness. Remove pan from heat. Drizzle steaks with lemon juice, and sprinkle with cheese and olives. Garnish with oregano, if desired. Yield: 4 servings (serving size: 1 steak, about 1½ teaspoons pan juices, and 1 tablespoon cheese).

CALORIES 185; FAT 11g (sat 4.9g, mono 5.2g, poly 0.9g); PROTEIN 19.1g; CARB 1.5g; FIBER 0.1g; CHOL 60mg; IRON 2.5mg; SODIUM 199mg; CALC 3mg

serve with
Lemon-Pepper Fries

Prep: 1 minute • Cook: 17 minutes

3 cups frozen extra-crispy crinkle-cut fries (such as Ore-Ida Golden Crinkles)
Cooking spray
2 teaspoons salt-free lemon pepper seasoning (such as Mrs. Dash)
2 teaspoons grated lemon rind

1. Preheat oven to 450°.
2. Place fries on a large baking sheet coated with cooking spray. Coat fries with cooking spray, and sprinkle with seasoning; toss well. Arrange fries in a single layer.
3. Bake at 450° for 17 minutes or until browned, stirring once. Stir in lemon rind. Yield: 4 servings (serving size: about ¾ cup).

CALORIES 151; FAT 4.1g (sat 2.3g, mono 1.3g, poly 0.5g); PROTEIN 2.3g; CARB 24.5g; FIBER 2.4g; CHOL 0mg; IRON 0mg; SODIUM 360mg; CALC 1mg

quick flip

Substitute ¼ cup (1 ounce) crumbled blue cheese for the feta and kalamata olives. Assertive blue cheese is a small but bold modification for these succulent steaks. Just a sprinkling adds more wow!

Tangy feta cheese and briny kalamata olives add Mediterranean flair to these steaks. Flatten the fillets with your palm to speed cooking time. Our taste panel rated this bistro-style meal a hall-of-famer!

4-ingredient

10-minute

When figs are in season, they cook quickly, so choose firm, ripe ones to stand up to the intense heat of the grill. Grill marks on the figs dress them up for a pretty presentation.

Grilled Lamb Chops with Honey Figs
Prep: 4 minutes • Cook: 10 minutes

8 (4-ounce) lean lamb loin chops, trimmed
¼ teaspoon salt
¼ teaspoon freshly ground black pepper
2 tablespoons honey
1 tablespoon olive oil

1 tablespoon chopped fresh rosemary
8 fresh figs, halved
Cooking spray
Rosemary sprigs (optional)

1. Preheat grill.
2. Sprinkle lamb evenly with salt and pepper. Combine honey, oil, and rosemary; brush half of honey mixture over lamb chops. Brush remaining honey mixture over figs.
3. Place lamb and figs on grill rack coated with cooking spray. Grill lamb 4 to 5 minutes on each side or until desired degree of doneness. Grill figs 1 minute on each side or until lightly browned and tender. Garnish with rosemary sprigs, if desired. Yield: 4 servings (serving size: 2 lamb chops and 4 fig halves).

CALORIES 432; FAT 13.7g (sat 5.3g, mono 6.9g, poly 1.5g); PROTEIN 48.8g; CARB 28.1g; FIBER 3g; CHOL 181mg; IRON 4.5mg; SODIUM 249mg; CALC 72mg

serve with
Couscous with Goat Cheese and Pine Nuts
Prep: 2 minutes • Cook: 3 minutes • Other: 5 minutes

1 cup water
3 tablespoons minced green onions
½ teaspoon salt

⅔ cup uncooked whole-wheat couscous
2 tablespoons pine nuts, toasted
2 tablespoons crumbled goat cheese

1. Combine first 3 ingredients in a small saucepan; bring to a boil. Stir in couscous. Remove from heat; cover and let stand 5 minutes. Add pine nuts; fluff with a fork. Sprinkle each serving with goat cheese. Yield: 4 servings (serving size: about ⅔ cup couscous and 1½ teaspoons cheese).

CALORIES 110; FAT 3.9g (sat 0.8g, mono 1.1g, poly 1.9g); PROTEIN 3.8g; CARB 15.9g; FIBER 2.7g; CHOL 3mg; IRON 0.9mg; SODIUM 307mg; CALC 14mg

This lemony Italian classic is elegant and simple. Thinly sliced veal is dredged in flour, briefly pan-fried, and finished with a silky sauce. You can substitute pounded chicken breasts for veal.

Veal Piccata

Prep: 6 minutes • Cook: 12 minutes

1 pound veal scallopini	4 teaspoons olive oil
½ teaspoon freshly ground black pepper	¾ cup fat-free, lower-sodium chicken broth
¼ teaspoon salt	3 tablespoons fresh lemon juice
1.5 ounces all-purpose flour (about ⅓ cup)	1 tablespoon capers, drained

1. Sprinkle veal with pepper and salt; dredge in flour.

2. Heat 2 teaspoons oil in a large nonstick skillet over medium-high heat. Add half of veal to pan; cook 2 minutes on each side or until browned. Transfer to a plate; keep warm. Repeat procedure with remaining oil and veal. Stir in broth and lemon juice, scraping pan to loosen browned bits.

3. Bring mixture to a boil; reduce heat. Add veal and capers to broth mixture. Simmer, uncovered, 2 to 3 minutes or until liquid is slightly thick. Yield: 4 servings (serving size: about 4 ounces veal and 2 tablespoons sauce).

CALORIES 366; FAT 24.7g (sat 6.9g, mono 12.7g, poly 4.9g); PROTEIN 22.8g; CARB 11.1g; FIBER 0.9g; CHOL 76mg; IRON 1.7mg; SODIUM 641mg; CALC 69mg

serve with
Spinach-Tomato Orzo

Prep: 2 minutes • Cook: 7 minutes

¾ cup uncooked orzo (rice-shaped pasta)	¼ teaspoon salt
2 teaspoons olive oil	¼ teaspoon freshly ground black pepper
1 cup grape tomatoes	2 tablespoons crumbled feta cheese
2 cups packed baby spinach	

1. Cook orzo according to package directions, omitting salt and fat. Drain pasta; place in a medium bowl.

2. While orzo cooks, heat oil in a large nonstick skillet over medium-high heat. Add tomatoes; cook 5 minutes or until skins begin to burst. Add spinach, salt, and pepper, stirring until spinach wilts. Add orzo; toss well. Sprinkle with feta cheese. Yield: 4 servings (serving size: about ½ cup).

CALORIES 162; FAT 3.8g (sat 1.3g, mono 2g, poly 0.4g); PROTEIN 5.2g; CARB 26.1g; FIBER 2g; CHOL 4mg; IRON 0.4mg; SODIUM 209mg; CALC 41mg

fix it faster

To make it even faster, consider substituting couscous for the orzo and omitting the feta. Couscous, a staple of North Africa, is actually a pasta. The round pellets are made from semolina flour. Couscous cooks in a jiffy—5 minutes steamed in a boiling flavorful broth or stock. Then fluff it and serve it.

Schnitzel is German for cutlet. Thinly pounded, breaded, and fried, this dish of thin pork chops is traditionally served with spaetzle, tiny noodlelike dumplings. Panko keeps the pork light and crispy with a satisfying crunch.

Pork Schnitzel
Prep: 8 minutes • Cook: 9 minutes

4 (4-ounce) boneless loin pork chops
½ teaspoon salt
½ teaspoon freshly ground black pepper
1.1 ounces all-purpose flour (about ¼ cup)
1 large egg, lightly beaten

1 cup panko (Japanese breadcrumbs)
Cooking spray
3 teaspoons canola oil, divided
4 lemon wedges
Chopped fresh parsley (optional)

1. Place pork between 2 sheets of heavy-duty plastic wrap; pound to ⅛-inch thickness using a meat mallet or small heavy skillet. Cut each piece in half.
2. Sprinkle pork evenly with salt and pepper. Dredge pork in flour; dip in egg. Dredge in panko.
3. Heat a large nonstick skillet over medium-high heat. Coat pan with cooking spray. Add 1½ teaspoons oil to pan; add half of pork. Cook 2 minutes on each side or until desired degree of doneness. Repeat procedure with remaining 1½ teaspoons oil and remaining pork. Serve with lemon wedges, and, if desired, sprinkle with parsley. Yield: 4 servings (serving size: 2 pieces of pork and 1 lemon wedge).

CALORIES 348; FAT 17.9g (sat 5.8g, mono 9.1g, poly 2.9g); PROTEIN 27.2g; CARB 17.1g; FIBER 1g; CHOL 107mg; IRON 1.4mg; SODIUM 385mg; CALC 32mg

serve with
Sautéed Brussels Sprouts and Red Cabbage with Bacon
Prep: 1 minute • Cook: 12 minutes

2 slices center-cut bacon
2 cups shredded Brussels sprouts
2 cups thinly sliced red cabbage
1 cup refrigerated prechopped onion

1 tablespoon brown sugar
2 tablespoons cider vinegar
¼ teaspoon salt
¼ teaspoon freshly ground black pepper

1. Cook bacon in a large nonstick skillet over medium heat until crisp. Remove bacon from pan; crumble. Add Brussels sprouts, cabbage, and onion to drippings in pan; sauté 4 minutes or until tender.
2. Stir in brown sugar and next 3 ingredients. Sauté 2 minutes or until liquid almost evaporates; stir in bacon. Yield: 4 servings (serving size: ¾ cup).

CALORIES 74; FAT 0.9g (sat 0.3g, mono 0.3g, poly 0.3g); PROTEIN 3.6g; CARB 14.5g; FIBER 3.3g; CHOL 3mg; IRON 1.2mg; SODIUM 215mg; CALC 52mg

Grilled Peach Barbecue Pork Chops
Prep: 4 minutes • Cook: 9 minutes

3 large ripe peaches
¼ cup barbecue sauce (such as Sticky Fingers Memphis Original)
1 tablespoon cider vinegar
1 tablespoon honey

4 (6-ounce) bone-in center-cut loin pork chops (about ¾ inch thick), trimmed
¼ teaspoon salt
¼ teaspoon freshly ground black pepper
Cooking spray

1. Preheat grill.
2. Peel, halve, and remove pits from peaches. Coarsely chop 1 peach. Place chopped peach, barbecue sauce, vinegar, and honey in a blender or food processor; process until smooth. Reserve ½ cup of sauce mixture.
3. Sprinkle pork evenly with salt and pepper. Place pork on grill rack coated with cooking spray. Brush ¼ cup sauce on tops of pork. Grill pork 4 minutes. Turn pork over; brush with ¼ cup sauce. Add peach halves to grill rack, cut sides down; grill 4 minutes or until pork reaches desired degree of doneness and peaches are tender. Remove pork and peach halves from grill; cut each peach half into 3 wedges. Serve pork and peach wedges with reserved sauce. Yield: 4 servings (serving size: 1 pork chop, 3 peach wedges, and 2 tablespoons sauce).

CALORIES 256; FAT 7.5g (sat 3g, mono 3.6g, poly 0.9g); PROTEIN 26.9g; CARB 20.2g; FIBER 1.8g; CHOL 74mg; IRON 1.3mg; SODIUM 320mg; CALC 28mg

serve with
Grilled Corn with Jalapeño-Herb "Butter"
Prep: 1 minute • Cook: 10 minutes

4 ears shucked corn
Cooking spray
2 tablespoons yogurt-based spread (such as Brummel & Brown)
1½ tablespoons minced seeded jalapeño pepper (about 1 medium pepper)

1 tablespoon chopped fresh cilantro
1 teaspoon grated lime rind
¼ teaspoon freshly ground black pepper

1. Preheat grill.
2. Place corn on grill rack coated with cooking spray. Grill 10 minutes or until corn is tender, turning occasionally.
3. While corn cooks, combine spread and next 4 ingredients in a small bowl. Spread about 1 tablespoon Jalapeño-Herb "Butter" over each ear of corn. Yield: 4 servings (serving size: 1 ear of corn).

CALORIES 102; FAT 3.6g (sat 0.7g, mono 0.9g, poly 1.9g); PROTEIN 3g; CARB 17.5g; FIBER 2.6g; CHOL 0mg; IRON 0.5mg; SODIUM 59mg; CALC 4mg

Chile paste is a fiery sauce made of dried crushed red pepper seasoned with garlic. Use a light hand when adding this ingredient. This sauce thickens almost immediately when added to the hot skillet; turn the chops over in it until they are nicely glazed.

Sweet and Spicy Chili Pork Chops

Prep: 1 minute • Cook: 10 minutes

Cooking spray
4 (4-ounce) boneless center-cut loin pork chops
1 tablespoon brown sugar
2 tablespoons lower-sodium soy sauce
2 tablespoons chile paste with garlic (such as sambal oelek)
1 tablespoon hoisin sauce
2 teaspoons rice vinegar
¼ cup diagonally sliced green onions

1. Heat a large nonstick skillet over medium-high heat. Coat pan with cooking spray. Add pork; cook 3 to 4 minutes on each side. Remove pan from heat; let pork stand 30 seconds.
2. While pork cooks, combine brown sugar and next 4 ingredients in a small bowl. Add sauce to pork, scraping pan to loosen browned bits. Turn pork over in sauce to coat. Sprinkle with green onions. Yield: 4 servings (serving size: 1 pork chop, about 2½ tablespoons sauce, and 1 tablespoon green onions).

CALORIES 251; FAT 13.8g (sat 5.5g, mono 6.5g, poly 1.8g); PROTEIN 23.9g; CARB 7.8g; FIBER 0.3g; CHOL 62mg; IRON 1.1mg; SODIUM 594mg; CALC 33mg

serve with
Crunchy Asian Vegetable Salad

Prep: 10 minutes

1½ cups thinly sliced red cabbage
1 cup sugar snap peas, halved crosswise
1 cup matchstick-cut peeled cucumber (1 small cucumber)
½ cup matchstick-cut carrots
⅓ cup light sesame-ginger dressing (such as Newman's Own)
¼ cup fresh cilantro leaves
2 tablespoons toasted sesame seeds

1. Place first 6 ingredients in a medium bowl, tossing to coat. Divide salad among 4 plates; sprinkle evenly with sesame seeds. Yield: 4 servings (serving size: about 1 cup salad mixture and 1½ teaspoons sesame seeds).

CALORIES 78; FAT 3g (sat 0.6g, mono 1g, poly 1.2g); PROTEIN 2.2g; CARB 10.8g; FIBER 2.5g; CHOL 0mg; IRON 1mg; SODIUM 294mg; CALC 41mg

A double shot of pepper—black and red—adds kick to this grilled dish. If you want less heat on the pork, use only 1 tablespoon of the ground pepper blend.

Fiery Grilled Pork Tenderloin
Prep: 4 minutes • Cook: 20 minutes • Other: 5 minutes

1   (1-pound) pork tenderloin
2   teaspoons olive oil
1½ tablespoons ground black and red pepper blend (such as McCormick Hot Shot!)
1   tablespoon dark brown sugar
½   teaspoon garlic powder
¼   teaspoon salt
Cooking spray

1. Preheat grill.
2. Pat pork dry with paper towels. Rub oil over pork.
3. Combine pepper blend and next 3 ingredients; rub over pork. Place pork on grill rack coated with cooking spray. Grill 20 minutes or until a thermometer registers 160° (slightly pink), turning once. Remove pork from grill; let stand 5 minutes. Cut pork diagonally into ½-inch slices. Yield: 4 servings (serving size: 3 ounces).

CALORIES 170; FAT 6.1g (sat 1.7g, mono 3.5g, poly 0.8g); PROTEIN 23.9g; CARB 3.6g; FIBER 0g; CHOL 74mg; IRON 1.5mg; SODIUM 204mg; CALC 9mg

serve with
Grilled Summer Squash with Garlic and Lime
Prep: 4 minutes • Cook: 10 minutes

2   teaspoons olive oil
4   large garlic cloves, pressed
3   small yellow squash, cut in half lengthwise
3   small zucchini, cut in half lengthwise
¼   teaspoon salt
¼   teaspoon freshly ground black pepper
Cooking spray
4   lime wedges

1. Preheat grill.
2. Combine oil and garlic in a small bowl; brush over squash. Sprinkle squash and zucchini halves with salt and pepper.
3. Place squash halves on grill rack coated with cooking spray. Grill 5 to 6 minutes on each side or until almost tender.
4. Place squash halves on serving platter; squeeze lime wedges over squash. Yield: 4 servings (serving size: 3 squash halves).

CALORIES 54; FAT 2.6g (sat 0.4g, mono 1.7g, poly 0.4g); PROTEIN 2.4g; CARB 7.4g; FIBER 2.1g; CHOL 0mg; IRON 0.7mg; SODIUM 157mg; CALC 33mg

4-ingredient

Put your microwave to use as a shortcut to our version of steakhouse roasted sweet potatoes, dripping with sweet cinnamon butter. Serve these gems with pan-fried, sage-scented pork medallions blanketed in a sweet-tangy maple glaze.

Sage Pork Medallions with Maple Glaze
Prep: 5 minutes • Cook: 9 minutes

1 (1-pound) pork tenderloin, trimmed	¼ cup maple syrup
Cooking spray	2 tablespoons apple cider vinegar
1½ tablespoons minced fresh sage	2 teaspoons country-style Dijon mustard
1 teaspoon freshly ground black pepper	Sage sprigs (optional)
2 teaspoons olive oil	

1. Pat pork dry with paper towels. Coat pork with cooking spray. Combine sage and pepper; rub mixture onto pork. Cut pork into ¾-inch-thick slices.
2. Heat oil in a large nonstick skillet over medium-high heat. Add pork; cook 3 to 4 minutes on each side or just until desired degree of doneness. Remove pork from pan. Keep warm.
3. Stir maple syrup, vinegar, and mustard into drippings, scraping pan to loosen browned bits. Cook over medium heat 3 to 4 minutes or until slightly reduced.
4. Arrange pork on a platter; drizzle with sauce. Garnish with sage sprigs, if desired. Yield: 4 servings (serving size: 3 ounces pork and about 1 tablespoon sauce).

CALORIES 203; FAT 6.7g (sat 1.6g, mono 3.4g, poly 1.6g); PROTEIN 19.6g; CARB 16.5g; FIBER 0.1g; CHOL 53mg; IRON 1.6mg; SODIUM 737mg; CALC 36mg

serve with
Sweet Potatoes with Brown Sugar–Cinnamon Butter
Prep: 4 minutes • Cook: 10 minutes

2 sweet potatoes (about 1 pound)	2 tablespoons brown sugar
¼ cup light butter, softened	½ teaspoon ground cinnamon

1. Scrub potatoes (do not dry); wrap each individually in wax paper. Place potatoes on a microwave-safe plate. Microwave at HIGH 10 minutes or until very tender.
2. While potatoes cook, combine butter, sugar, and cinnamon in a small bowl.
3. Cut potatoes in half lengthwise. Dollop butter mixture evenly in centers of potato halves. Serve immediately. Yield: 4 servings (serving size: 1 potato half and about 1 tablespoon butter mixture).

CALORIES 189; FAT 7.2g (sat 4.6g, mono 2.2g, poly 0.3g); PROTEIN 2.2g; CARB 29.8g; FIBER 3.6g; CHOL 14mg; IRON 1.1mg; SODIUM 124mg; CALC 50mg

Ham and Roasted Asparagus Crepes with Gruyère Cheese Sauce

Prep: 2 minutes • Cook: 11 minutes

Cooking spray
1 (8-ounce) package presliced mushrooms
¼ teaspoon salt, divided
¼ teaspoon freshly ground black pepper, divided
¾ pound asparagus spears
1 cup prechopped ham

2 teaspoons vegetable oil
4 refrigerated ready-to-use crepes (such as Melissa's)
1 tablespoon water
Gruyère Cheese Sauce
2 tablespoons chopped fresh chives (optional)

1. Preheat oven to 450°. Heat a large nonstick skillet over medium-high heat. Coat pan with cooking spray. Add mushrooms, ⅛ teaspoon salt, and ⅛ teaspoon pepper. Cook 5 minutes without stirring; stir well, and cook 2 minutes or just until the mushrooms are browned around edges.
2. While mushrooms cook, snap off tough ends of asparagus. Combine asparagus, ham, oil, remaining ⅛ teaspoon salt, and remaining ⅛ teaspoon pepper in bottom of a broiler pan or roasting pan coated with cooking spray. Bake at 450° for 10 minutes; do not stir.
3. While asparagus mixture cooks, place crepes on a microwave-safe plate. Cover with a damp paper towel. Microwave at HIGH 20 seconds or until warm.
4. Stir asparagus mixture and 1 tablespoon water into mushrooms, scraping pan to loosen browned bits.
5. Prepare Gruyère Cheese Sauce. Place 1 crepe on each of 4 plates. Spoon ham filling evenly down centers of crepes; fold sides and ends over. Spoon Gruyère Cheese Sauce evenly over crepes. Garnish with chopped chives, if desired. Serve immediately. Yield: 4 servings (serving size: 1 crepe and about ¼ cup sauce).

CALORIES 249; FAT 12.1g (sat 5.7g, mono 4.1g, poly 2.1g); PROTEIN 16.6g; CARB 17.6g; FIBER 3.4g; CHOL 47mg; IRON 2.7mg; SODIUM 708mg; CALC 186mg

Gruyère Cheese Sauce

Prep: 1 minute • Cook: 7 minutes

1 cup fat-free, lower-sodium chicken broth
¼ cup (2 ounces) ⅓-less-fat cream cheese, softened
1 tablespoon all-purpose flour

1½ tablespoons water
½ teaspoon dry mustard
½ cup (2 ounces) shredded light Gruyère cheese

1. Heat broth in a 2-quart saucepan over medium-high heat. Add cream cheese, stirring with a whisk until smooth. Combine flour, 1½ tablespoons water, and mustard, stirring with a whisk until smooth; add to cream cheese mixture, stirring with a whisk until blended. Cook over medium heat, stirring constantly with a whisk, 4 minutes or until slightly thick. Add Gruyère cheese, stirring until cheese melts. Yield: 4 servings (serving size: about ¼ cup).

CALORIES 107; FAT 7.9g (sat 4.8g, mono 2.3g, poly 0.6g); PROTEIN 6.3g; CARB 2.4g; FIBER 0.1g; CHOL 26mg; IRON 0.1mg; SODIUM 249mg; CALC 155mg

Serve these eggs and tiny peas baked in ruffled ham cups as an elegant breakfast or light dinner. Dijon Creamed Mushrooms can be served on the side or as a decadent topping. Enjoy this for a blissful beginning to your day or as a happy ending.

Baked Eggs in Crispy Ham Cups with Petite Peas
Prep: 3 minutes • Cook: 18 minutes

4   (1-ounce) deli smoked ham slices
Cooking spray
¼ cup frozen petite green peas
4   large eggs
2   teaspoons half-and-half
¼ teaspoon salt
¼ teaspoon black pepper
2   (2-ounce) light multigrain English muffins (such as Thomas'), split
Dijon Creamed Mushrooms (optional)

1. Preheat oven to 400°.
2. Place 1 ham slice into each of 4 muffin cups coated with cooking spray, allowing ham to extend over edges of cups. Place 1 tablespoon peas in each cup. Crack 1 egg into each cup. Top each egg with ½ teaspoon half-and-half. Sprinkle eggs evenly with salt and pepper.
3. Bake at 400° for 18 minutes or until eggs are almost set.
4. Place a muffin half on each of 4 plates. Spoon Dijon Creamed Mushrooms over muffin halves, if desired, and top with a ham cup. Yield: 4 servings (serving size: 1 ham cup and 1 muffin half).

CALORIES 157; FAT 5.6g (sat 1.5g, mono 2.6g, poly 1.5g); PROTEIN 14.8g; CARB 14.5g; FIBER 4.4g; CHOL 197mg; IRON 2mg; SODIUM 670mg; CALC 91mg

serve with
Dijon Creamed Mushrooms
Prep: 2 minutes • Cook: 7 minutes

Cooking spray
3   (8-ounce) packages presliced mushrooms
½ teaspoon salt
¼ teaspoon freshly ground black pepper
¼ cup light sour cream
1   tablespoon Dijon mustard
2   teaspoons chopped fresh tarragon

1. Heat a medium skillet over medium-high heat. Coat pan with cooking spray. Add mushrooms, salt, and pepper. Sauté 5 minutes or until mushrooms are tender and liquid is released. Stir in sour cream, mustard, and tarragon. Yield: 4 servings (serving size: ¾ cup).

CALORIES 60; FAT 1.6g (sat 0.9g, mono 0.2g, poly 0.5g); PROTEIN 5.8g; CARB 8.5g; FIBER 1.7g; CHOL 5mg; IRON 0.9mg; SODIUM 404mg; CALC 8mg

4-ingredient

Quick and peppery, puttanesca sauce is a parade of flavors: salty (from the anchovy paste), spicy (from the dried crushed red pepper), and fragrant (from the garlic). It's so rich and flavorful, it's hard to believe it's light. Serve with crusty bread to round out your meal.

Pasta Puttanesca
Prep: 6 minutes • Cook: 5 minutes

8 ounces angel hair pasta
Puttanesca Sauce
8 ounces turkey Italian sausage links (such as Jennie-O)

Cooking spray
3 tablespoons torn basil leaves

1. Cook pasta according to package directions, omitting salt and fat. Drain.
2. While pasta cooks, prepare Puttanesca Sauce. Remove casings from sausage. Heat a large nonstick skillet over medium-high heat. Heavily coat pan with cooking spray. Add sausage; cook 4 minutes or until browned, stirring to crumble. Drain, if necessary. Add Puttanesca Sauce and pasta to pan, tossing to coat.
3. Place pasta evenly on each of 4 plates. Top pasta evenly with basil. Yield: 6 servings (serving size: 1¼ cups pasta and 1½ teaspoons basil).

CALORIES 243; FAT 7.7g (sat 1.6g, mono 3.4g, poly 2.5g); PROTEIN 12.7g; CARB 30.3g; FIBER 2.9g; CHOL 47mg; IRON 2mg; SODIUM 767mg; CALC 78mg

Puttanesca Sauce
Prep: 2 minutes • Cook: 5 minutes

1 (24-ounce) jar fire-roasted tomato-and-garlic pasta sauce (such as Classico)
⅓ cup coarsely chopped pitted kalamata olives

1 teaspoon anchovy paste
½ teaspoon crushed red pepper

1. Combine all ingredients in a medium saucepan. Bring to a boil over medium-high heat, stirring often. Reduce heat, and simmer 3 minutes. Yield: 6 servings (serving size: about ½ cup).

CALORIES 78; FAT 3.1g (sat 0.3g, mono 1.8g, poly 0.8g); PROTEIN 2.1g; CARB 9.9g; FIBER 1.9g; CHOL 3mg; IRON 0.7mg; SODIUM 532mg; CALC 58mg

poultry

Orecchiette with Chicken, Bacon, and Tomato Ragù, 263
Chicken Mole Enchiladas Supreme, 265
Chicken Paella, 266
Moroccan Chicken Kebabs, 269
Stir-Fried Lemon Chicken, 270
Chicken with Creamy Tomato Topping, 272
Tomatillo Chicken, 275
Chicken Milanese, 276
Tandoori Chicken, 279
Prosciutto-Wrapped Chicken, 281
Pan-Seared Chicken Cutlets with Tarragon-Mustard Cream Sauce, 282
Roasted Chicken with Shallots, Grapes, and Thyme, 284
Chicken Pasta Primavera, 287
Chicken Cacciatore, 288
Margarita Chicken Thighs, 291
Apricot-Glazed Grilled Chicken Thighs, 292
Braised Chicken with Saffron and Olives, 294
Chicken with 40 Cloves of Garlic and Creamy Thyme Sauce, 297
Pomegranate-Glazed Duck Breast, 299
Orange-Glazed Turkey with Cranberry Rice, 300

Orecchiette with Chicken, Bacon, and Tomato Ragù

Prep: 2 minutes • Cook: 12 minutes

1½ cups (5 ounces) uncooked orecchiette ("little ears" pasta)
2 slices center-cut bacon
1 cup refrigerated prechopped onion
1 (28-ounce) can no-salt-added whole tomatoes in puree (such as Dei Fratelli)

2 cups shredded cooked chicken
¼ cup fresh basil leaves
½ teaspoon salt
¼ teaspoon freshly ground black pepper
¼ cup (1 ounce) shaved Pecorino-Romano cheese

1. Cook pasta according to package directions, omitting salt and fat; drain.
2. While pasta cooks, cook bacon in a large nonstick skillet over medium heat 5 minutes or until crisp. Remove bacon from pan; crumble. Add onion to drippings in pan; sauté over medium-high heat 3 minutes or until tender.
3. Snip tomatoes in can with kitchen shears until chopped. Add tomatoes to onion. Cook 2 minutes or until sauce thickens, stirring occasionally. Stir in bacon, chicken, and next 3 ingredients. Cook 2 minutes or until thoroughly heated. Stir in pasta. Divide mixture evenly among 4 shallow bowls. Top evenly with cheese. Yield: 4 servings (serving size: 1½ cups pasta mixture and 1 tablespoon cheese).

CALORIES 336; FAT 5.4g (sat 2g, mono 2g, poly 1.3g); PROTEIN 30.2g; CARB 40.9g; FIBER 5.3g; CHOL 67mg; IRON 3.8mg; SODIUM 510mg; CALC 151mg

serve with
Broccolini with Spicy Walnut Butter

Prep: 1 minute • Cook: 11 minutes

2 bunches Broccolini, trimmed (12 ounces)
2 tablespoons yogurt-based spread (such as Brummel & Brown)
2 tablespoons chopped walnuts, toasted

1 teaspoon grated lemon rind
¼ teaspoon crushed red pepper
Cooking spray

1. Pour water into a large nonstick skillet to a depth of 1 inch. Bring to a boil. Add Broccolini; cover and cook 4 minutes or until almost tender, turning after 2 minutes. Drain.
2. While Broccolini cooks, combine yogurt-based spread and next 3 ingredients in a small bowl.
3. Wipe pan dry, and return to medium-high heat; coat pan with cooking spray. Add Broccolini and "butter" to pan. Cook 2 minutes or until Broccolini is crisp-tender. Yield: 4 servings (serving size: ¼ of Broccolini).

CALORIES 82; FAT 4.9g (sat 0.7g, mono 1g, poly 3.2g); PROTEIN 3.6g; CARB 6.6g; FIBER 1.3g; CHOL 0mg; IRON 0.8mg; SODIUM 70mg; CALC 64mg

A Mexican-inspired sauce, mole is a dark, reddish-brown blend of cooked onion, garlic, chiles, and a hint of bittersweet chocolate. The chocolate adds texture and richness, not sweetness. For more fire, use smoky chipotle chiles.

Chicken Mole Enchiladas Supreme

Prep: 2 minutes • Cook: 13 minutes

2 tablespoons bottled mole sauce (such as Dona Maria), stirred
1 cup fat-free, lower-sodium chicken broth
2 cups chopped smoked chicken
6 (6-inch) carb balance flour tortillas (such as Mission)

Cooking spray
2 cups bagged shredded lettuce
1½ cups refrigerated prechopped tomato
¼ cup (1 ounce) crumbled queso fresca
6 tablespoons chopped green onions (3 small)

1. Preheat oven to 425°.
2. Place mole sauce in a medium saucepan. Gradually add chicken broth, stirring with a whisk until smooth. Cook over medium-high heat 4 minutes or until thoroughly heated, stirring often.
3. While sauce cooks, place chicken in a microwave-safe bowl. Cover bowl with plastic wrap; vent. Microwave at HIGH 1 to 2 minutes or until thoroughly heated.
4. Place ⅓ cup chicken down center of each tortilla. Spoon 1 tablespoon sauce over chicken on each tortilla; fold 2 sides toward center, and place, folded side down, in an 11 x 7–inch baking dish coated with cooking spray. Pour remaining sauce over enchiladas.
5. Bake, uncovered, at 425° for 9 minutes.
6. Place 1 enchilada on each of 6 plates, and top each with ⅓ cup lettuce, ¼ cup tomato, 2 teaspoons cheese, and 1 tablespoon green onions. Yield: 6 servings (serving size: 1 enchilada).

CALORIES 201; FAT 6.6g (sat 1.4g, mono 3.2g, poly 1.8g); PROTEIN 15.3g; CARB 17.5g; FIBER 9.4g; CHOL 29mg; IRON 1.5mg; SODIUM 957mg; CALC 112mg

serve with
Green Tea Mojitos

Prep: 5 minutes

½ cup fresh mint leaves
2 (16-ounce) bottles green tea with honey (such as Lipton Pure Leaf)
1½ cups light rum (such as Bacardi), chilled

⅓ cup fresh lime juice (3 limes)
1 cup club soda, chilled
Crushed ice

1. Rub mint leaves between fingers to release oils; place in a pitcher. Stir in green tea, rum, and lime juice.
2. Add club soda; serve immediately in tall glasses over crushed ice. Yield: 6 servings (serving size: about ¾ cup).

CALORIES 176; FAT 0g (sat 0g, mono 0g, poly 0g); PROTEIN 0.1g; CARB 12.1g; FIBER 0.2g; CHOL 0mg; IRON 0.1mg; SODIUM 9.2mg; CALC 9mg

Chicken Paella

Prep: 1 minute • Cook: 4 minutes

Olive oil-flavored cooking spray
1 (8.8-ounce) package microwavable precooked Spanish-style rice (such as Uncle Ben's Ready Rice)
2 cups chopped cooked chicken
¼ cup coarsely chopped pimiento-stuffed olives
2 tablespoons water
½ teaspoon smoked paprika
1 (2-ounce) jar diced pimiento, drained

1. Heat a large nonstick skillet over medium-high heat. Coat pan with cooking spray. Add rice and next 4 ingredients; sauté 3 to 4 minutes or until thoroughly heated. Stir in pimiento just before serving. Yield: 4 servings (serving size: about 1 cup).

CALORIES 225; FAT 5.3g (sat 0.9g, mono 2.8g, poly 1.5g); PROTEIN 23.6g; CARB 19.4g; FIBER 0.8g; CHOL 60mg; IRON 1.1mg; SODIUM 626mg; CALC 32mg

serve with
Spanish Peas

Prep: 1 minute • Cook: 5 minutes

1 (10-ounce) package frozen peas
Olive oil-flavored cooking spray
⅓ cup diced Spanish chorizo (1 ounce)
2 large garlic cloves, chopped
¼ cup finely chopped bottled roasted red bell pepper

1. Place peas in a sieve. Rinse under cold water until thawed; drain well. Press peas between layers of paper towels to remove excess moisture.
2. Heat a large nonstick skillet over medium-high heat. Coat pan with cooking spray. Add chorizo to pan; sauté 3 minutes or until crisp. Add garlic, and sauté 30 seconds. Add peas; cook 1 minute or until thoroughly heated. Remove pan from heat; stir in bell pepper. Yield: 4 servings (serving size: ½ cup).

CALORIES 82; FAT 2.2g (sat 0.7g, mono 0.9g, poly 0.4g); PROTEIN 5.2g; CARB 10.7g; FIBER 3g; CHOL 0mg; IRON 1.1mg; SODIUM 106mg; CALC 18mg

ingredient spotlight

Spanish chorizo is a cured, ready-to-eat smoked pork sausage not to be confused with Mexican chorizo, which is made from fresh pork and must be cooked before using. The Spanish variety gets its fire from dried smoked red peppers and its deep, reddish-brown color from the peppers and paprika.

Inspired by the classic Spanish dish brimming with seafood and sausage, this version of paella mimics the real thing—it's just simpler to prepare and a little easier on the budget.

10-minute

Moroccan cooking often combines meat with dried fruits and spices.

Moroccan Chicken Kebabs
Prep: 5 minutes • Cook: 10 minutes

½ cup apricot preserves
1 teaspoon ground cumin
1 teaspoon ground cinnamon
½ teaspoon ground coriander
½ teaspoon salt

4 (6-ounce) skinless, boneless chicken breast halves, cut into 1½-inch pieces
4 metal skewers
Cooking spray

1. Preheat grill.
2. Combine first 5 ingredients in a large bowl. Place chicken pieces in bowl, turning to coat. Thread chicken onto skewers.
3. Coat chicken with cooking spray; place on grill rack coated with cooking spray. Grill 5 minutes on each side or until done. Yield: 4 servings (serving size: 1 kebab).

CALORIES 283; FAT 4.2g (sat 1.3g, mono 1.6g, poly 1.1g); PROTEIN 34.7g; CARB 26.4g; FIBER 0.6g; CHOL 94mg; IRON 1.7mg; SODIUM 390mg; CALC 36mg

serve with
Whole-Wheat Couscous with Ginger and Currants
Prep: 6 minutes • Cook: 4 minutes • Other: 5 minutes

¾ cup water
1 tablespoon extra-virgin olive oil
¼ teaspoon salt
⅔ cup uncooked whole-wheat couscous

½ cup currants
2 teaspoons grated peeled fresh ginger
1 tablespoon chopped fresh mint

1. Bring first 3 ingredients to a boil in a medium saucepan. Stir in couscous, currants, and ginger. Remove from heat; cover and let stand 5 minutes. Add mint, and fluff with a fork. Yield: 4 servings (serving size: about ½ cup).

CALORIES 151; FAT 3.8g (sat 0.5g, mono 2.6g, poly 0.7g); PROTEIN 3.2g; CARB 28.7g; FIBER 3.4g; CHOL 0mg; IRON 1.2mg; SODIUM 146mg; CALC 28mg

quick flip

Swap the exotic locale of Morocco for the flavor of the Mediterranean. Substitute mango chutney for the apricot preserves and 1 tablespoon of an all-in-one Mediterranean-spiced sea salt for the cumin, cinnamon, coriander, and salt.

Stir-Fried Lemon Chicken

Prep: 2 minutes • Cook: 10 minutes

1 pound skinless, boneless chicken breast, cut into bite-sized pieces
½ teaspoon freshly ground black pepper
¼ teaspoon salt
Cooking spray
4 garlic cloves, minced
¾ cup matchstick-cut carrots
2 tablespoons water
1 (8.8-ounce) package microwavable precooked jasmine rice (such as Uncle Ben's Ready Rice)
1 tablespoon grated lemon rind

1. Sprinkle chicken with pepper and salt. Heat a large nonstick skillet over medium-high heat. Coat pan with cooking spray. Add chicken; stir-fry 5 minutes or until done. Add garlic; stir-fry 1 minute. Transfer chicken to a serving plate; cover and keep warm.
2. Recoat pan with cooking spray. Add carrots to pan; stir-fry 2 minutes or just until tender, adding 2 tablespoons water to prevent sticking. Add rice and lemon rind; stir-fry 1 minute. Add chicken; stir-fry 1 minute. Serve immediately. Yield: 4 servings (serving size: about ¾ cup).

CALORIES 263; FAT 4g (sat 0.9g, mono 1.8g, poly 1.3g); PROTEIN 25.9g; CARB 29.6g; FIBER 1.1g; CHOL 63mg; IRON 1.8mg; SODIUM 206mg; CALC 35mg

serve with
Sugared Asparagus

Prep: 1 minute • Cook: 3 minutes

1 pound asparagus spears, trimmed
Cooking spray
1 tablespoon sugar
¼ teaspoon freshly ground black pepper

1. Preheat grill.
2. Place asparagus on a jelly-roll pan. Coat asparagus with cooking spray; sprinkle with sugar and pepper. Toss gently to coat.
3. Place asparagus on grill rack coated with cooking spray. Grill 3 minutes or until crisp-tender, turning occasionally. Yield: 4 servings (serving size: ¼ of asparagus).

CALORIES 41; FAT 0.1g (sat 0g, mono 0g, poly 0.1g); PROTEIN 2.5g; CARB 7.6g; FIBER 2.4g; CHOL 0mg; IRON 2.4mg; SODIUM 2mg; CALC 28mg

fix it faster

Grab the grill pan for a quick, easy, and delicious twist to the grilled asparagus. A sprinkle of sugar sweetens these beauties and adds just a hint of caramelization. The kiss of sugar elevates the taste of the asparagus to star status.

This fresh and simple chicken stir-fry is best served right from the skillet. Make sure all the ingredients are prepped ahead and ready to go. Stir-frying is a brisk cooking method. It's easy eating and even easier cleanup.

Chicken with Creamy Tomato Topping
Prep: 2 minutes • Cook: 16 minutes

4   (6-ounce) skinless, boneless chicken breast halves
½   teaspoon freshly ground black pepper
¼   teaspoon salt
Cooking spray

2   cups grape tomatoes, halved
¼   cup refrigerated reduced-fat pesto (such as Bertoli)
2   tablespoons fat-free cream cheese, softened

1. Sprinkle chicken with pepper and salt. Heat a large nonstick skillet over medium-high heat. Coat pan with cooking spray. Add chicken, and cook 5 minutes on each side or until done. Transfer to a serving dish, and keep warm.
2. Add tomatoes to hot pan; sauté 4 minutes or until tomatoes soften and begin to release their juices. Add pesto and cream cheese, stirring until smooth.
3. Cut chicken crosswise into ½-inch-thick medallions; place medallions from 1 chicken breast half on each of 4 plates. Spoon sauce evenly over medallions. Serve immediately. Yield: 4 servings (serving size: 1 chicken breast half and ¼ cup tomato topping).

CALORIES 264; FAT 8.8g (sat 2.4g, mono 4.6g, poly 1.8g); PROTEIN 37.6g; CARB 5.8g; FIBER 1.6g; CHOL 98mg; IRON 1.2mg; SODIUM 405mg; CALC 93mg

serve with
Lemon-Parmesan Barley
Prep: 1 minute • Cook: 15 minutes • Other: 5 minutes

1½ cups water
1   tablespoon extra-virgin olive oil
¼   teaspoon freshly ground black pepper
¾   cup uncooked quick-cooking barley (such as Quaker)

¼   cup (1 ounce) shaved fresh Parmesan cheese
1   tablespoon grated lemon rind
1   tablespoon chopped fresh parsley

1. Combine first 3 ingredients in a medium saucepan; bring to a boil. Stir in barley; cover, reduce heat, and simmer 13 minutes or until tender and liquid evaporates.
2. Remove pan from heat; stir in cheese, lemon rind, and parsley. Cover and let stand 5 minutes. Fluff with a fork before serving. Yield: 4 servings (serving size: about ½ cup).

CALORIES 152; FAT 5.8g (sat 1.7g, mono 3.1g, poly 0.9g); PROTEIN 5.6g; CARB 21.5g; FIBER 3g; CHOL 6mg; IRON 0.6mg; SODIUM 109mg; CALC 82mg

fix it faster

Trim cook time by about 10 minutes by trading speedy couscous for the barley. All it takes is 5 minutes to cook and a fork to fluff this side.

Refrigerated prepared pesto brings a vibrant finish to this creamy tomato sauce. The pairing of tomatoes and basil is heaven-sent; adding cream cheese makes it divine.

4-ingredient

Tomatillos or green tomatoes cook up quickly for a fresh take on tomato sauce. This small round fruit imparts a lemony, apple, herb flavor. Be sure to remove the papery husks from the tomatillos, and wash them well to remove the sticky residue.

4-ingredient

Tomatillo Chicken
Prep: 3 minutes • Cook: 15 minutes

2 teaspoons ground cumin
½ teaspoon salt
½ teaspoon freshly ground black pepper
4 (6-ounce) skinless, boneless chicken breast
   halves
Cooking spray

1 tablespoon olive oil
1½ cups chopped tomatillos (about
   4 tomatillos)
2 tablespoons minced seeded jalapeño
   pepper (1 pepper)
Lime wedges (optional)

1. Combine first 3 ingredients in a small bowl; rub mixture over chicken.
2. Place a large nonstick skillet over medium-high heat. Coat pan with cooking spray. Add chicken; cook 6 minutes on each side or until done. Remove chicken from pan, and keep warm.
3. Add oil to pan. Stir in tomatillos and jalapeño pepper. Cook, stirring constantly, 3 minutes or until tender and saucy. Place a chicken breast half on each of 4 plates. Spoon sauce evenly over chicken. Garnish with lime wedges, if desired. Yield: 4 servings (serving size: 1 chicken breast half and ¼ cup sauce).

CALORIES 235; FAT 8.1g (sat 1.9g, mono 4.4g, poly 1.7g); PROTEIN 35g; CARB 3.7g; FIBER 1.5g; CHOL 94mg; IRON 1.9mg; SODIUM 375mg; CALC 30mg

serve with
Coconut-Lime Rice
Prep: 2 minutes • Cook: 17 minutes • Other: 5 minutes

⅔ cup light coconut milk
⅔ cup water
¼ teaspoon salt
1 (4.4-ounce) package whole-grain white
   long-grain rice (such as Uncle Ben's)

2 tablespoons chopped fresh cilantro
1 teaspoon grated lime rind

1. Combine first 4 ingredients in a medium saucepan. Bring to a boil; cover, reduce heat, and simmer 10 minutes. Keep pan covered, and remove from heat. Let stand 5 minutes or until liquid is absorbed. Uncover; stir in cilantro and lime rind. Fluff with a fork, and serve immediately. Yield: 4 servings (serving size: ½ cup).

CALORIES 133; FAT 2.6g (sat 2.2g, mono 0.2g, poly 0.2g); PROTEIN 3.8g; CARB 24.6g; FIBER 0.6g; CHOL 0mg; IRON 1.2mg; SODIUM 566mg; CALC 23mg

fix it faster

To beat the clock with this recipe, use ready-to-serve tomatillo salsa or salsa verde instead of chopping tomatillos and mincing and seeding jalapeño pepper. Look for these prepared sauces on the ethnic foods aisle of your supermarket.

A simple, chunky, fresh tomato sauce adds the magical finish to this chicken cooked Milanese-style. That means the food is breaded and fried. Incredibly light, crispy Italian-seasoned panko breadcrumbs add the crunchy layer of flavor to this chicken. Be sure the oil is hot before pan-frying for best results.

Chicken Milanese
Prep: 9 minutes • Cook: 19 minutes

Fresh Milanese Sauce
1½ tablespoons olive oil
½ cup Italian-seasoned panko
  (Japanese breadcrumbs)

¼ cup (1 ounce) grated fresh Parmesan cheese
4 (6-ounce) skinless, boneless chicken breast
  halves
Olive oil-flavored cooking spray

1. Prepare Fresh Milanese Sauce; keep warm.
2. Heat a large nonstick skillet over medium heat until hot; add olive oil.
3. While pan heats, combine panko and cheese in a shallow dish; coat both sides of chicken with cooking spray, and dredge in panko mixture.
4. Cook chicken in hot oil over medium heat 7 minutes on each side or until done. Place 1 chicken breast half on each of 4 plates. Spoon Fresh Milanese Sauce evenly over chicken. Yield: 4 servings (serving size: 1 chicken breast half and 6 tablespoons tomato sauce).

CALORIES 347; FAT 13.8g (sat 3.3g, mono 8.1g, poly 2.2g); PROTEIN 39.2g; CARB 12.4g; FIBER 2.3g; CHOL 99mg; IRON 1.2mg; SODIUM 427mg; CALC 141mg

Fresh Milanese Sauce
Prep: 5 minutes • Cook: 5 minutes

2 teaspoons olive oil
2 cups grape tomatoes, halved lengthwise
1 large shallot, chopped
¼ teaspoon salt

¼ teaspoon freshly ground black pepper
½ cup fresh basil leaves
¼ cup dry red wine

1. Heat a large nonstick skillet over medium-high heat until hot; add oil. Stir in tomatoes and next 3 ingredients. Cook 4 minutes or until shallots are tender, stirring often.
2. While tomato mixture cooks, coarsely chop basil.
3. Stir wine into tomato mixture. Cook 30 seconds. Remove pan from heat, and stir in basil. Yield: 4 servings (serving size: 6 tablespoons).

CALORIES 53; FAT 2.3g (sat 0.3g, mono 1.7g, poly 0.3g); PROTEIN 0.8g; CARB 4.9g; FIBER 1.3g; CHOL 0mg; IRON 0.3mg; SODIUM 150mg; CALC 23mg

A tandoor is a brick and clay pot that's used throughout India. In this ovenlike cooker, food is cooked at an intense heat level over direct heat. Food prepared by this method is also labeled tandoori.

Tandoori Chicken

Prep: 8 minutes • Cook: 10 minutes • Other: 8 hours

Tandoori Marinade
  4 (6-ounce) skinless, boneless chicken breast halves
Cooking spray

1 (8.8-ounce) package microwavable precooked basmati rice (such as Uncle Ben's Ready Rice)
Lime wedges
Fresh cilantro leaves (optional)

1. Prepare Tandoori Marinade; set aside ½ cup.
2. Combine chicken and remaining marinade in a large heavy-duty zip-top plastic bag. Seal bag; marinate in refrigerator 8 hours.
3. Preheat grill.
4. Remove chicken from marinade, discarding marinade. Place chicken on grill rack coated with cooking spray. Grill 5 to 6 minutes on each side or until chicken is done.
5. While chicken cooks, microwave rice according to package directions. Place 1 chicken breast half on each of 4 plates. Spoon 2 tablespoons reserved marinade over each chicken breast half. Serve with rice, lime wedges, and, if desired, cilantro. Yield: 4 servings (serving size: 1 chicken breast half, about 6 tablespoons rice, and 2 tablespoons sauce).

CALORIES 324; FAT 5.5g (sat 1.6g, mono 2.2g, poly 1.5g); PROTEIN 39.7g; CARB 28.1g; FIBER 1.4g; CHOL 95mg; IRON 2.3mg; SODIUM 415mg; CALC 123mg

Tandoori Marinade

Prep: 7 minutes

1 (6-ounce) carton plain fat-free yogurt
3 tablespoons fresh lime juice
1 tablespoon minced peeled fresh ginger
3 garlic cloves, pressed
½ teaspoon salt

½ teaspoon ground coriander
½ teaspoon ground cumin
½ teaspoon paprika
½ teaspoon freshly ground black pepper
¼ teaspoon ground turmeric

1. Combine all ingredients in a small bowl. Yield: 4 servings (serving size: 3 tablespoons).

CALORIES 33; FAT 0.1g (sat 0g, mono 0.1g, poly 0g); PROTEIN 2.6g; CARB 5.7g; FIBER 0.4g; CHOL 1mg; IRON 0.3mg; SODIUM 326mg; CALC 95mg

4-ingredient

Paper-thin prosciutto slices envelop chicken breasts topped with delicate sage leaves, and lend an earthy saltiness to this entrée. For best results, prepare these a day ahead, and store in the refrigerator. Chilling makes them easier to cook.

Prosciutto-Wrapped Chicken
Prep: 5 minutes • Cook: 10 minutes

4 (6-ounce) skinless, boneless chicken breast halves
4 fresh sage leaves
4 (⅔-ounce) slices prosciutto
1 tablespoon olive oil

1.1 ounces all-purpose flour (about ¼ cup)
½ teaspoon salt
½ teaspoon freshly ground black pepper
Sage leaves (optional)

1. Pat chicken breast halves dry with paper towels. Place 1 sage leaf on top of each breast. Wrap each with a slice of prosciutto.
2. Heat oil in a large nonstick skillet over medium-high heat. While oil heats, combine flour, salt, and pepper in a shallow dish. Dredge chicken in flour mixture, and add to hot oil. Cook chicken 5 minutes on each side or until done. Garnish with sage leaves, if desired. Yield: 4 servings (serving size: 1 chicken breast half).

CALORIES 288; FAT 9.6g (sat 2.7g, mono 4.9g, poly 1.8g); PROTEIN 40.7g; CARB 7.7g; FIBER 0.6g; CHOL 109mg; IRON 1.8mg; SODIUM 879mg; CALC 32mg

serve with
Lemon-Caper Spinach
Prep: 2 minutes • Cook: 6 minutes

1 tablespoon butter
1 lemon

2 (6-ounce) packages baby spinach
2 tablespoons capers, drained

1. Melt butter in a large nonstick skillet over medium heat.
2. While butter melts, grate rind and squeeze juice from lemon to measure 1 teaspoon rind and 2 tablespoons juice.
3. Gradually add spinach to butter; cook 5 minutes, turning with tongs until spinach wilts. Stir in lemon rind, lemon juice, and capers; toss well. Yield: 4 servings (serving size: about ½ cup).

CALORIES 48; FAT 2.9g (sat 1.9g, mono 0.8g, poly 0.1g); PROTEIN 2.2g; CARB 4g; FIBER 2.2g; CHOL 8mg; IRON 2.8mg; SODIUM 162mg; CALC 84mg

Pan-Seared Chicken Cutlets with Tarragon-Mustard Cream Sauce

Prep: 3 minutes • Cook: 14 minutes

3 tablespoons all-purpose flour
¼ teaspoon salt
¼ teaspoon black pepper
4 (4-ounce) chicken breast cutlets (1 pound)
2 teaspoons olive oil

Cooking spray
¾ cup fat-free, lower-sodium chicken broth
¼ cup half-and-half
2 teaspoons stone-ground mustard
1 tablespoon chopped fresh tarragon

1. Combine first 3 ingredients in a heavy-duty zip-top plastic bag; add chicken. Seal bag; shake to coat chicken.
2. Heat oil in a large nonstick skillet over medium-high heat; coat pan and chicken with cooking spray. Add chicken to pan; cook 3 minutes on each side or until browned.
3. Combine broth and next 3 ingredients, stirring with a whisk. Add to pan; bring to a boil. Reduce heat, and simmer 6 minutes or until chicken is done and sauce is slightly thick. Yield: 4 servings (serving size: 1 chicken cutlet and 2 tablespoons sauce).

CALORIES 186; FAT 6.8g (sat 2.2g, mono 3.4g, poly 1.1g); PROTEIN 24.2g; CARB 5.5g; FIBER 0.2g; CHOL 68mg; IRON 1.1mg; SODIUM 342mg; CALC 31mg

serve with
Orange Roasted Carrots

Prep: 3 minutes • Cook: 18 minutes

1 (12-ounce) package carrot sticks (about 3 cups)
Cooking spray
¼ teaspoon salt

¼ teaspoon freshly ground black pepper
1 tablespoon olive oil
1 tablespoon honey
2 teaspoons grated orange rind

1. Preheat oven to 500°.
2. Cut larger carrot sticks in half lengthwise. Arrange carrots on a jelly-roll pan coated with cooking spray. Coat carrots with cooking spray, and sprinkle with salt and pepper. Toss well.
3. Bake at 500° for 10 minutes.
4. Combine oil, honey, and orange rind; add to carrots, and toss well. Bake an additional 8 minutes or until carrots are browned and tender. Yield: 4 servings (serving size: ½ cup).

CALORIES 82; FAT 3.4g (sat 0.5g, mono 2.5g, poly 0.4g); PROTEIN 1.1g; CARB 12.7g; FIBER 2.2g; CHOL 0mg; IRON 0.4mg; SODIUM 146mg; CALC 23mg

Tarragon is a flavorful herb popular in French cooking. It shows up in eggs, sauces, vegetables, fish, and chicken dishes. It's mostly known as the herb that flavors béarnaise sauce, a silky butter sauce.

Savor this beautiful browned chicken dish that boasts sweet red grapes roasted to coax out their sweetness.

Roasted Chicken with Shallots, Grapes, and Thyme
Prep: 4 minutes • Cook: 33 minutes

2 teaspoons olive oil, divided	2 cups seedless red grapes
4 (8-ounce) skinless, bone-in chicken leg quarters	1 tablespoon fresh thyme leaves
½ teaspoon freshly ground black pepper	4 large shallots, peeled and quartered
¼ teaspoon salt	Thyme sprigs (optional)

1. Preheat oven to 425°.
2. Heat 1 teaspoon oil in a 12-inch cast-iron skillet or other ovenproof skillet over medium-high heat. Sprinkle chicken with pepper and salt. Add chicken to pan; cook 4 minutes on each side or until browned. Remove pan from heat.
3. While chicken cooks, combine remaining 1 teaspoon oil, grapes, thyme, and shallots. Spoon grape mixture around chicken in pan. Bake, uncovered, at 425° for 22 to 25 minutes or until chicken is done.
4. Place 1 chicken quarter on each of 4 plates. Spoon grape mixture evenly over chicken. Garnish with thyme sprigs, if desired. Yield: 4 servings (serving size: 1 chicken quarter and about ½ cup shallot mixture).

CALORIES 293; FAT 8.7g (sat 2.3g, mono 4.1g, poly 2.2g); PROTEIN 35.4g; CARB 17.5g; FIBER 1.2g; CHOL 136mg; IRON 2.4mg; SODIUM 297mg; CALC 37mg

serve with
Mushroom–Whole-Grain Rice Pilaf
Prep: 2 minutes • Cook: 5 minutes

1 (8.5-ounce) package microwavable seven-whole-grain rice mixture (such as Seeds of Change)	1 cup sliced fresh mushrooms
	2 garlic cloves, minced
1 teaspoon olive oil	2 tablespoons coarsely chopped pecans, toasted

1. Microwave rice according to package directions.
2. While rice cooks, heat oil in a large nonstick skillet over medium-high heat. Add mushrooms and garlic; sauté 4 minutes or until mushrooms are browned and tender, stirring in pecans during the last minute. Stir in hot rice. Yield: 4 servings (serving size: ½ cup).

CALORIES 139; FAT 5.6g (sat 0.6g, mono 3.2g, poly 1.7g); PROTEIN 4.2g; CARB 21.6g; FIBER 3.9g; CHOL 0mg; IRON 0.2mg; SODIUM 1mg; CALC 6mg

4-ingredient

Zesty Italian seasoning, brightly colored vegetables, and nutty-flavored Parmigiano-Reggiano cheese perfume this Italian classic.

Chicken Pasta Primavera

Prep: 1 minute • Cook: 9 minutes

6 ounces uncooked whole-wheat fusilli (short twisted spaghetti)
¾ pound frozen chicken thigh strips, thawed
1 teaspoon salt-free Italian medley seasoning blend (such as Mrs. Dash)
1 tablespoon olive oil, divided
1 cup refrigerated tricolor bell pepper strips

1 (12-ounce) package fresh-cut vegetable stir-fry with broccoli, carrot, red cabbage, and snow peas (such as Eat Smart)
¼ cup dry white wine
⅓ cup (1.3 ounces) grated Parmigiano-Reggiano cheese
½ teaspoon freshly ground black pepper
¼ teaspoon salt
3 tablespoons chopped fresh basil

1. Cook pasta according to package directions, omitting salt and fat; drain.
2. While pasta cooks, sprinkle chicken with Italian seasoning blend. Heat a large nonstick skillet over medium-high heat until hot; add 2 teaspoons oil. Add chicken to pan; sauté 4 minutes or until chicken is done and is lightly browned.
3. Remove chicken from pan. Add remaining 1 teaspoon oil to pan. Add bell pepper and vegetable stir-fry. Stir-fry over medium-high heat 3 minutes or just until vegetables are almost tender. Stir in wine. Stir in hot pasta. Add cheese, black pepper, salt, and chicken; toss well. Divide pasta mixture evenly among 4 plates, and sprinkle evenly with basil. Yield: 4 servings (serving size: 1¾ cups pasta mixture and about 1½ teaspoons basil).

CALORIES 385; FAT 14.1g (sat 3.6g, mono 6.8g, poly 3.6g); PROTEIN 23.1g; CARB 40.2g; FIBER 6.3g; CHOL 56mg; IRON 3.4mg; SODIUM 325mg; CALC 98mg

serve with
Mâche Salad with Dijon Dressing

Prep: 4 minutes • Cook: 4 minutes

3 tablespoons rice vinegar
1 tablespoon honey
2 teaspoons extra-virgin olive oil
2 teaspoons Dijon mustard

1 (3.5-ounce) package mâche (about 6 cups)
2 tablespoons coarsely chopped walnuts, toasted

1. Combine first 4 ingredients in a large bowl; add mâche, and toss gently to coat. Divide salad evenly among 4 plates; sprinkle evenly with walnuts. Yield: 4 servings (serving size: 1½ cups salad and 1½ teaspoons walnuts).

CALORIES 68; FAT 4.7g (sat 0.6g, mono 2g, poly 2.1g); PROTEIN 1.1g; CARB 6.4g; FIBER 0.8g; CHOL 0mg; IRON 0.6mg; SODIUM 61mg; CALC 28mg

Chicken Cacciatore
Prep: 2 minutes • Cook: 21 minutes

1 tablespoon canola oil
8 skinless, boneless chicken thighs (1½ pounds)
Cooking spray
½ teaspoon freshly ground black pepper
¼ teaspoon salt
1 tablespoon canola oil

2 cups tomato-and-basil pasta sauce (such as Classico)
¼ cup dry white wine
1 (16-ounce) package frozen bell pepper stir-fry (such as Birds Eye)

1. Heat oil in a large nonstick skillet over medium-high heat. Coat chicken with cooking spray; sprinkle with pepper and salt.
2. Cook chicken in hot oil 4 minutes on each side or until browned. Stir in pasta sauce, wine, and bell pepper stir-fry. Bring to a boil; cover, reduce heat, and simmer 10 minutes or until chicken is done. Yield: 4 servings (serving size: 2 chicken thighs and about 1 cup sauce mixture).

CALORIES 371; FAT 17.3g (sat 4.6g, mono 8.1g, poly 4.6g); PROTEIN 33.8g; CARB 17.7g; FIBER 3.4g; CHOL 112mg; IRON 2.4mg; SODIUM 742mg; CALC 96mg

serve with
Herbed Mushroom Spaghetti
Prep: 1 minute • Cook: 8 minutes

4 ounces uncooked multigrain thin spaghetti (such as Barilla Plus)
2 teaspoons olive oil
1 (8-ounce) package sliced cremini mushrooms

2 tablespoons chopped fresh herbs
¼ teaspoon freshly ground black pepper
⅛ teaspoon salt
2 tablespoons grated fresh Parmesan cheese

1. Cook pasta according to package directions, omitting fat and salt; drain in a colander over a bowl, reserving 2 tablespoons cooking liquid. Return pasta to pan.
2. While pasta cooks, heat oil in a large nonstick skillet over medium-high heat. Add mushrooms; sauté 6 minutes or until tender. Stir in herbs, pepper, and salt. Then add mushroom mixture to cooked pasta; toss well. Sprinkle with Parmesan cheese. Yield: 4 servings (serving size: ¾ cup).

CALORIES 158; FAT 4.3g (sat 0.8g, mono 2.5g, poly 1g); PROTEIN 8g; CARB 21.8g; FIBER 2.5g; CHOL 3mg; IRON 0.3mg; SODIUM 152mg; CALC 63mg

fix it faster

Save time by not having to chop fresh herbs. Substitute 2¼ teaspoons Italian herb seasoning grind (such as McCormick) for the chopped herbs and freshly ground black pepper.

This "hunter-style" dish is a hearty stew of braised tomatoes, vegetables, and chicken. Serve it over a side of spaghetti along with crusty bread—a must-have for soaking up the serious sauce.

4-ingredient

This simple, flavorful, versatile marinade starts with frozen margarita mix. Not only does it work with chicken, pork chops, and pork tenderloin, but it's also a great match for shrimp before grilling. Just be sure to reduce marinating time to one hour for shrimp.

Margarita Chicken Thighs

Prep: 5 minutes • Cook: 12 minutes • Other: 8 hours

½ cup frozen margarita mix (such as Bacardi), thawed
1½ tablespoons salt-free fiesta lime seasoning (such as Mrs. Dash)

2 tablespoons tequila
1 teaspoon olive oil
12 (3-ounce) skinless, boneless chicken thighs
Cooking spray

1. Place first 4 ingredients in a heavy-duty zip-top plastic bag. Seal bag; shake until blended. Add chicken to marinade; seal bag. Marinate in refrigerator 8 hours.
2. Preheat grill.
3. Remove chicken from marinade, discarding marinade. Place chicken on grill rack coated with cooking spray. Grill chicken 6 minutes on each side or until done. Yield: 6 servings (serving size: 2 chicken thighs).

CALORIES 293; FAT 13.5g (sat 4.4g, mono 6.3g, poly 2.8g); PROTEIN 30.5g; CARB 8.3g; FIBER 0g; CHOL 112mg; IRON 1.5mg; SODIUM 103mg; CALC 14mg

serve with
Calico Spanish Rice

Prep: 1 minute • Cook: 7 minutes

Cooking spray
1 cup refrigerated prechopped tricolor bell pepper
¾ cup frozen baby gold and white corn (such as Birds Eye)

1 (8.8-ounce) package microwavable precooked long-grain rice (such as Uncle Ben's Ready Rice)
1 (8.8-ounce) package microwaveable precooked Spanish-style rice (such as Uncle Ben's Ready Rice)

1. Heat a large nonstick skillet over medium-high heat. Coat pan with cooking spray. Add bell pepper and corn; sauté 5 minutes or until tender.
2. Microwave rice according to package directions. Add rice to bell pepper mixture; toss well. Yield: 6 servings (serving size: ⅔ cup).

CALORIES 228; FAT 1.6g (sat 0.4g, mono 0.5g, poly 0.7g); PROTEIN 6.3g; CARB 46.8g; FIBER 1.9g; CHOL 0mg; IRON 1.9mg; SODIUM 728mg; CALC 43mg

Two types of pepper—black and red—ignite these grilled chicken thighs. The apricot glaze is a saucy surprise flavor. Accompany the chicken with grilled summer squash and coleslaw.

Apricot-Glazed Grilled Chicken Thighs

Prep: 3 minutes • Cook: 16 minutes

3 tablespoons apricot preserves
2 tablespoons red wine vinegar
1½ tablespoons olive oil
1 garlic clove, minced
½ teaspoon salt, divided

8 skinless, boneless chicken thighs (1½ pounds)
¼ teaspoon freshly ground black pepper
⅛ teaspoon ground red pepper
Cooking spray

1. Preheat grill.
2. Combine first 4 ingredients and ¼ teaspoon salt in a small bowl, stirring well.
3. Sprinkle chicken with remaining ¼ teaspoon salt and peppers; coat with cooking spray. Place chicken on grill rack coated with cooking spray. Grill 6 minutes on each side. Brush with half of apricot mixture; grill 2 minutes. Turn chicken over; brush with remaining apricot mixture. Grill 2 minutes or until chicken is done. Yield: 4 servings (serving size: 2 chicken thighs).

CALORIES 289; FAT 12g (sat 2.4g, mono 5.8g, poly 2.2g); PROTEIN 33.6g; CARB 10.1g; FIBER 0.1g; CHOL 141mg; IRON 1.9mg; SODIUM 444mg; CALC 23mg

ingredient spotlight

Red wine vinegar is made by allowing fermentation to continue while wine turns sour, and then straining and bottling. Artisanal varieties (unlike commercial products) are aged in wooden barrels for up to two years before bottling, imparting some of the same flavors found in red wine, including fruit flavors and wood flavors. This vinegar should be a pantry staple because it adds flavor while contributing no sodium and few or no calories. Because such small amounts are used in most recipes, red wine vinegar has essentially no impact on nutrition.

Braised Chicken with Saffron and Olives

Prep: 1 minute • Cook: 11 minutes

1½ pounds skinless, boneless chicken thighs
(about 8 thighs)
Cooking spray
¾ teaspoon paprika
½ teaspoon freshly ground black pepper
¼ teaspoon salt
2 teaspoons olive oil
2 cups refrigerated prechopped tricolor
bell pepper

¾ cup fat-free, lower-sodium chicken broth
1 tablespoon fresh thyme leaves
¾ teaspoon saffron threads
3 garlic cloves, minced
⅓ cup halved small green olives
Thyme sprigs or leaves (optional)

1. Coat chicken with cooking spray. Combine paprika, black pepper, and salt; sprinkle evenly over chicken.
2. Heat oil in a large nonstick skillet over medium-high heat. Add chicken; cook 3 minutes on each side or until lightly browned. Remove from pan; keep warm.
3. Add bell pepper to pan. Stir in broth and next 3 ingredients, scraping pan to loosen browned bits. Return chicken to pan. Cover, reduce heat to medium, and cook 3 minutes or just until chicken is done and sauce is slightly thick. Stir in olives; cook 1 minute. Garnish with thyme sprigs, if desired. Yield: 4 servings (serving size: 2 chicken thighs and ⅓ cup vegetable mixture).

CALORIES 309; FAT 16.5g (sat 4.2g, mono 8.2g, poly 4g); PROTEIN 32.6g; CARB 5g; FIBER 1g; CHOL 113mg; IRON 2.3mg; SODIUM 543mg; CALC 22mg

serve with
Sugared Almond Basmati Rice

Prep: 1 minute • Cook: 6 minutes

1 tablespoon light butter
2 tablespoons brown sugar
2 tablespoons sliced almonds
1 (8.8-ounce) package microwavable
precooked basmati rice (such as
Uncle Ben's Ready Rice)

⅛ teaspoon salt
1 teaspoon grated lemon rind

1. Melt butter in a medium nonstick skillet over medium heat. Add brown sugar and almonds; cook 3 minutes or until almonds are lightly browned, stirring often.
2. While almonds cook, microwave rice according to package directions.
3. Stir salt into almond mixture. Stir in rice and lemon rind. Cook 1 minute or until thoroughly heated. Yield: 4 servings (serving size: about ½ cup).

CALORIES 163; FAT 4.7g (sat 1.2g, mono 2.2g, poly 1.1g); PROTEIN 3.6g; CARB 28g; FIBER 0.9g; CHOL 4mg; IRON 1.1mg; SODIUM 97mg; CALC 27mg

Meaty chicken thighs are layered in flavor and brightness thanks to a colorful medley of bell peppers and deep-red saffron. The chicken simmers in a broth-based stew. And it all comes together quickly—in under 15 minutes.

No fear, just fun and flavor in this dish with the attention-grabbing title. As the garlic-infused chicken roasts, the garlic cloves and seasonings mellow into a to-die-for aroma.

Chicken with 40 Cloves of Garlic and Creamy Thyme Sauce

Prep: 7 minutes • Cook: 1 hour and 20 minutes • Other: 5 minutes

1 cup frozen seasoning blend
1 teaspoon dried thyme, divided
1 (6-ounce) jar peeled garlic cloves (about 40 cloves), divided
1 (3½-pound) whole chicken
½ teaspoon freshly ground black pepper
¼ teaspoon salt
Olive oil-flavored cooking spray
Creamy Thyme Sauce
Thyme sprigs (optional)

1. Preheat oven to 375°.
2. Combine seasoning blend, ½ teaspoon thyme, and 5 garlic cloves; place in cavity of chicken. Place chicken, breast side up, on a rack in a roasting pan. Sprinkle chicken with pepper, salt, and remaining ½ teaspoon thyme. Coat chicken with cooking spray. Place remaining garlic cloves in pan.
3. Tie ends of legs together with twine. Lift wing tips up and over back; tuck under chicken.
4. Bake at 375° for 40 minutes.
5. Increase oven temperature to 450°, and bake an additional 20 minutes or until a thermometer registers 170°. Transfer chicken to a platter; cover with foil, and let rest 5 minutes before carving. Remove garlic from pan with a slotted spoon, reserving 5 cloves. Place remaining garlic cloves around chicken on platter.
6. Prepare Creamy Thyme Sauce using reserved garlic cloves.
7. Remove and discard skin from chicken; carve chicken. Garnish with thyme sprigs, if desired. Serve with garlic cloves and Creamy Thyme Sauce. Yield: 4 servings (serving size: 3 ounces chicken and 6 tablespoons sauce).

CALORIES 335; FAT 6.1g (sat 1.8g, mono 2.4g, poly 1.8g); PROTEIN 44.9g; CARB 22.3g; FIBER 1.5g; CHOL 132mg; IRON 3.3mg; SODIUM 755mg; CALC 109mg

Creamy Thyme Sauce

Prep: 1 minute • Cook: 20 minutes

1½ cups fat-free, lower-sodium chicken broth
¼ cup white wine
1 teaspoon chopped fresh thyme
¼ teaspoon salt
5 reserved roasted garlic cloves from Chicken with 40 Cloves of Garlic
2 tablespoons all-purpose flour
3 tablespoons water

1. Place first 5 ingredients a medium saucepan. Bring to a boil; cover, reduce heat, and simmer 10 minutes.
2. While broth mixture cooks, combine flour and 3 tablespoons water in a small bowl, stirring with a whisk until smooth; stir into broth mixture. Simmer 5 minutes or until thick, whisking often. Remove and discard garlic. Yield: 4 servings (serving size: 6 tablespoons).

CALORIES 35; FAT 0.3g (sat 0g, mono 0.2g, poly 0.1g); PROTEIN 1g; CARB 6.4g; FIBER 0.2g; CHOL 0mg; IRON 0.4mg; SODIUM 442mg; CALC 10mg

Duck, with its dark, succulent flesh, calls for a bold-flavored sauce, and this pomegranate molasses fills the bill. It's a thick syrup made by reducing pomegranate juice and imparts a rich depth of flavor to meats. Look for it on the ethnic foods aisle of your supermarket or in specialty markets.

Pomegranate-Glazed Duck Breast

Prep: 2 minutes • Cook: 11 minutes

4 (6-ounce) boneless duck breast halves, skinned
¼ teaspoon salt
2 tablespoons sliced almonds
Cooking spray

¼ cup water
2 tablespoons pomegranate molasses
1 tablespoon honey
½ teaspoon ground cinnamon
Pomegranate seeds (optional)

1. Sprinkle duck evenly with salt. Heat a large nonstick skillet over medium-high heat. Add almonds; cook, stirring constantly, 2 minutes or until toasted. Remove almonds from pan. Coat pan with cooking spray. Add duck; cook 4 minutes on each side or until desired degree of doneness. Remove from pan, and keep warm.
2. Stir in ¼ cup water and next 3 ingredients, scraping pan to loosen browned bits. Cook, stirring constantly, 1 minute or until slightly thick. Remove pan from heat.
3. Add duck and almonds to sauce, turning to coat. Cut duck across grain into thin slices. Drizzle with sauce; sprinkle with pomegranate seeds, if desired. Yield: 4 servings (serving size: 1 duck breast and about 1 tablespoon sauce).

CALORIES 312; FAT 9.5g (sat 3.2g, mono 4.4g, poly 1.8g); PROTEIN 34.7g; CARB 19g; FIBER 0.7g; CHOL 131mg; IRON 9.1mg; SODIUM 243mg; CALC 50mg

serve with
Red Onion and Orange Salad

Prep: 4 minutes

1 tablespoon chopped fresh mint
1 tablespoon extra-virgin olive oil
¼ teaspoon salt
1 cup vertically sliced red onion

2 navel oranges, cut crosswise into thin slices
½ cup (2 ounces) crumbled goat cheese

1. Combine first 3 ingredients in a medium bowl. Add onion and orange slices, turning orange slices in dressing to coat. Divide salad among 4 plates; sprinkle evenly with cheese. Yield: 4 servings (serving size: ¾ cup salad and 2 tablespoons cheese).

CALORIES 109; FAT 6.6g (sat 2.6g, mono 3.2g, poly 0.6g); PROTEIN 3.5g; CARB 10.4g; FIBER 1.8g; CHOL 7mg; IRON 0.4mg; SODIUM 200mg; CALC 53mg

quick flip

For a little more tang in the salad, try substituting feta for the goat cheese. This white crumbly Greek cheese adds plenty of zip to appetizers, salads, and sides.

Celebrate the festive flavors and seasonal fruit of Thanksgiving any time of year. Orange-scented dried cranberries stud quick-cooking rice that accompanies pan-fried turkey cutlets and broccoli.

Orange-Glazed Turkey with Cranberry Rice

Prep: 8 minutes • Cook: 7 minutes

1 (8.8-ounce) package microwavable precooked brown rice (such as Uncle Ben's Ready Rice)
½ cup orange-flavored dried sweetened cranberries (such as Craisins)
2 tablespoons chopped pecans, toasted
⅛ teaspoon salt
1½ pounds turkey cutlets (about 12 cutlets)
¼ teaspoon salt, divided
Butter-flavored cooking spray
⅓ cup low-sugar orange marmalade

1. Prepare rice in microwave according to package directions. Place cranberries in a medium bowl. Pour hot rice over cranberries; let stand 1 minute. Stir pecans and ⅛ teaspoon salt into rice mixture; cover and keep warm.
2. Sprinkle turkey cutlets evenly with ⅛ teaspoon salt. Heat a large nonstick skillet over medium-high heat. Coat pan with cooking spray.
3. Add cutlets to pan, salted sides down. Cook 1 minute; coat cutlets with cooking spray, and sprinkle with remaining ⅛ teaspoon salt. Turn cutlets; cook 1 minute. Transfer turkey to a platter. Turn off heat; add marmalade to hot pan, and stir 30 seconds. Return turkey and accumulated juices to pan, turning to coat cutlets.
4. Spoon rice mixture onto 4 plates. Top rice mixture with turkey cutlets; spoon sauce over cutlets. Yield: 4 servings (serving size: about 3 cutlets, about ½ cup rice, and ½ tablespoon sauce).

CALORIES 357; FAT 3.9g (sat 0.5g, mono 1.9g, poly 1.1g); PROTEIN 44.2g; CARB 35.2g; FIBER 2.0g; CHOL 68mg; IRON 2.3mg; SODIUM 370mg; CALC 12mg

quick flip

Skinless, boneless turkey cutlets, also known as turkey scallopini, are ideal for this recipe. However, chicken cutlets or veal cutlets make a great substitution, too. Any of these three ingredients is perfect for sautéed dishes. Flip it for your convenience or personal taste.

desserts

Apricot-Pistachio Chocolates, 304

Loaded Bittersweet Chocolate Bark, 307

Chocolate-Pecan Butter Crunch Candy, 309

Orange-Sicle Tartlets, 310

Mississippi Mud Baby Cakes, 312

Pumpkin-Gingersnap Bars, 315

Chocolate-Covered Strawberry Ice Cream Sandwiches, 316

Chocolate Chip Collision Ice Cream Sandwiches, 319

Peanut Butter Granola Apple Rings, 321

Ginger-Berry Granita, 322

S'mores Shake Shots, 325

Honey-Laced Blueberry Parfaits, 326

Strawberry-Meringue Desserts, 328

Frozen Tiramisu Trifles, 331

Candy Bar–Caramel Cheesecake Dessert, 333

Peaches-n-Cream Parfaits, 334

Affogato, 337

Vanilla Bean–Coconut Pudding, 338

Pudding with Roasted Fruit Compote and Cinnamon Twists, 341

Chocolate Espresso Panna Cotta, 343

Prickly Pear–Mango Sundaes, 344

Strawberries with Fresh Mango-Mint Sauce, 346

Chocolate-Hazelnut Panini Sundaes, 349

Apple Granola Crisp, 350

Fresh Strawberry Tart, 353

Antioxidant-rich apricots and health-boosting bittersweet chocolate accented with pistachios and a hit of salt make this a surprise medley of flavors. Apricots and pistachios are popular ingredients in Mediterranean cuisine.

Apricot-Pistachio Chocolates
Prep: 5 minutes • Cook: 2 minutes • Other: 10 minutes

6 ounces bittersweet chocolate, chopped
¼ cup chopped pistachios

¼ cup chopped dried apricots
½ teaspoon coarse sea salt

1. Place chocolate in a small microwave-safe bowl. Microwave at HIGH 1 minute or until melted, stirring after 30 seconds. Spoon chocolate by tablespoonfuls onto wax paper–lined baking sheets. Sprinkle evenly with pistachios, apricots, and sea salt. Refrigerate 10 minutes or until firm. Yield: 10 servings (serving size: 1 piece).

CALORIES 114; FAT 8.7g (sat 3.8g, mono 3.8g, poly 1g); PROTEIN 2g; CARB 11.9g; FIBER 1.8g; CHOL 0mg; IRON 0.7mg; SODIUM 115mg; CALC 6mg

Cranberries will also partner deliciously with chocolate and pistachios. Their sweetness plays well against the coarse sea salt finish.

 is the "quick flip" badge.

4-ingredient

Three types of chocolate make these decadent yet light nibbles a powerhouse of fun and flavor. Just remember, though, moderation with chocolate is key.

Loaded Bittersweet Chocolate Bark
Prep: 2 minutes • Cook: 2 minutes • Other: 30 minutes

1 (11.5-ounce) package bittersweet chocolate chips (such as Ghirardelli)
1 cup thin salted pretzel sticks, broken
Cooking spray
⅓ cup finely chopped white chocolate
¼ cup crushed low-fat granola without raisins (such as Kellogg's)
1 (6-ounce) package dark chocolate-coated dried plum bites (such as Sunsweet), coarsely chopped

1. Place chocolate chips in a microwave-safe bowl; microwave at HIGH 2 minutes or until melted, stirring after 1 minute. Stir in pretzel pieces.
2. Coat a 13 x 9–inch baking dish with cooking spray; line pan with wax paper. Spread chocolate-pretzel mixture onto prepared dish. Sprinkle white chocolate, granola, and plum bites evenly over top, pressing into chocolate-pretzel mixture. Refrigerate candy 30 minutes or until firm.
3. Invert candy onto a cutting board; peel off wax paper. Cut into 16 pieces. Yield: 1½ pounds (serving size: 1 piece).

CALORIES 181; FAT 8.9g (sat 5.3g, mono 2.9g, poly 0.6g); PROTEIN 1.8g; CARB 27.4g; FIBER 1.1g; CHOL 0mg; IRON 0.7mg; SODIUM 116mg; CALC 15mg

Savor this barklike candy for its ease of preparation and rich taste. And it's light! It's a go-to holiday recipe for gift giving or an everyday indulgence.

Chocolate-Pecan Butter Crunch Candy
Prep: 5 minutes • Cook: 15 minutes • Other: 1 hour and 3 minutes

68 reduced-fat round buttery crackers (such as Ritz, 2 sleeves)
½ cup light butter
½ cup firmly packed brown sugar
1½ cups milk chocolate chips
½ cup chopped pecans

1. Preheat oven to 350°.

2. Place crackers, slightly overlapping, on a jelly-roll pan lined with parchment paper. Bring butter and brown sugar to a boil in a medium saucepan over medium-high heat. Reduce heat to medium; cook, stirring occasionally, 5 minutes. Pour mixture evenly over crackers.

3. Bake at 350° for 10 minutes. Turn off oven. Sprinkle crackers with chocolate chips; let stand in oven, with door closed, 3 minutes or until chocolate melts. Spread melted chocolate evenly over crackers; sprinkle with pecans.

4. Carefully slide parchment paper with candy onto a cool pan. Refrigerate candy 1 hour or until chocolate is firm. Peel paper from candy, and break candy into 16 pieces. Yield: 16 servings (serving size: 1 piece).

CALORIES 228; FAT 12.6g (sat 5.3g, mono 5.2g, poly 2g); PROTEIN 2.6g; CARB 25.9g; FIBER 0.9g; CHOL 11mg; IRON 1.3mg; SODIUM 172mg; CALC 58mg

These citrusy tartlets take you back to that dreamy summertime ice cream pop treat. We just swapped the stick with a tartlet shell to capture the creamy goodness.

Orange-Sicle Tartlets
Prep: 9 minutes • Other: 3 hours

1 large navel orange
6 tablespoons fresh lemon juice (about 2 lemons)
1 (14-ounce) can fat-free sweetened condensed milk
2 (1.9-ounce) packages frozen miniature phyllo shells
5 tablespoons frozen fat-free whipped topping, thawed
Orange rind strips (optional)

1. Grate rind and squeeze juice from orange to measure 1 tablespoon rind and ¼ cup juice.
2. Combine orange rind, lemon juice, and condensed milk in a medium bowl, stirring with a whisk. Stir in orange juice. Cover and chill in refrigerator 3 hours.
3. Spoon filling evenly into phyllo shells. Top each with 1 teaspoon whipped topping, and garnish with orange rind strips, if desired. Yield: 15 servings (serving size: 2 tartlets).

CALORIES 55; FAT 1.8g (sat 0g, mono 1g, poly 0.3g); PROTEIN 0.6g; CARB 9.2g; FIBER 0.2g; CHOL 1mg; IRON 0.3mg; SODIUM 29mg; CALC 20mg

Mississippi Mud Baby Cakes boast a bonanza of flavor. They may be small, but they live up to the gooey dessert's reputation.

Mississippi Mud Baby Cakes

Prep: 10 minutes • Cook: 20 minutes • Other: 10 minutes

Cooking spray
1 (13.7-ounce) package fat-free brownie mix (such as No Pudge)
1 (6-ounce) carton French vanilla low-fat yogurt (such as Yoplait Light Thick and Creamy)
3 tablespoons finely chopped pecans
¾ cup miniature marshmallows (72 marshmallows)
24 chocolate kisses (such as Hershey's Meltaway Milk Chocolates)

1. Preheat oven to 350°.
2. Place 24 paper muffin cup liners in miniature muffin cups; coat with cooking spray.
3. Prepare brownie mix according to package directions, using French vanilla yogurt. Spoon batter evenly into prepared muffin cups. Sprinkle evenly with pecans.
4. Bake at 350° for 19 minutes. Remove cakes from oven. Place 3 marshmallows on top of each baby cake; place 1 chocolate kiss in center of marshmallows. Bake an additional 1 minute. Gently swirl melted chocolate kiss to "frost" each cake and hold marshmallows in place. Cool in pans on wire racks 10 minutes; remove from pans. Cool completely on wire racks. Yield: 24 servings (serving size: 1 baby cake).

CALORIES 100; FAT 2.2g (sat 1g, mono 0.9g, poly 0.3g); PROTEIN 2g; CARB 19g; FIBER 0.2g; CHOL 2mg; IRON 0.8mg; SODIUM 69mg; CALC 47mg

The peppery, spicy bite of ginger is tamed by the creamy, fluffy pumpkin layer in these bars. Cinnamon-sugar adds another layer of flavor to the thin cookie-crust base.

Pumpkin-Gingersnap Bars

Prep: 9 minutes • Cook: 26 minutes

1½ cups crushed gingersnap cookies (about
  26 cookies)
 3 tablespoons light butter, melted
 3 tablespoons bottled cinnamon-sugar, divided

Cooking spray
Pumpkin Filling
 1 cup frozen fat-free whipped
  topping, thawed

1. Preheat oven to 350°.
2. Combine crushed cookies, butter, and 2 tablespoons cinnamon-sugar in a small bowl. Press mixture evenly into a 13 x 9–inch baking pan coated with cooking spray. Bake at 350° for 6 minutes or until set.
3. While crust bakes, prepare Pumpkin Filling. Spread filling evenly over crust. Bake an additional 20 to 22 minutes or until a wooden pick inserted in center comes out almost clean. Cool completely on a wire rack, and then cut into bars. Serve with a dollop of whipped topping, and sprinkle evenly with remaining 1 tablespoon cinnamon-sugar. Yield: 15 servings (serving size: 1 bar and about 1 tablespoon topping).

CALORIES 202; FAT 4.9g (sat 1.4g, mono 2.3g, poly 1g); PROTEIN 2.8g; CARB 32.9g; FIBER 1.4g; CHOL 3mg; IRON 1.9mg; SODIUM 211mg; CALC 52mg

Pumpkin Filling

Prep: 6 minutes

4.5 ounces all-purpose flour (about 1 cup)
 1 cup reduced-calorie sugar for baking
  blend (such as Splenda)
 1 teaspoon baking powder
 ½ teaspoon pumpkin pie spice

 ¼ teaspoon salt
 1 cup canned pumpkin
 ½ cup egg substitute
 2 tablespoons canola oil

1. Weigh or lightly spoon flour into a dry measuring cup; level with a knife. Combine flour and next 4 ingredients in a medium bowl. Combine pumpkin, egg substitute, and oil in a small bowl, stirring with a whisk. Add pumpkin mixture to dry ingredients, stirring until blended. Yield: 2¼ cups.

CALORIES 124; FAT 2.3g (sat 0.2g, mono 1.2g, poly 0.7g); PROTEIN 2.1g; CARB 20.7g; FIBER 0.7g; CHOL 0.1mg; IRON 0.8mg; SODIUM 117mg; CALC 33mg

ingredient spotlight

Light butter adds the essence of butter flavor but subtracts 50% of the fat and calories per serving found in regular butter. It's the next best thing to real butter.

Chewy devil's food cookies encase strawberry preserves and ice cream for a double shot of decadence. Keep these guilt-free sandwich treats on hand in your freezer for a quick dessert.

Chocolate-Covered Strawberry Ice Cream Sandwiches
Prep: 6 minutes • Other: 2 hours

12 devil's food cookie cakes (such as SnackWell's)
2 tablespoons sugar-free hot fudge topping (such as Smucker's)

2 tablespoons sugar-free strawberry preserves
¾ cup strawberry light ice cream (such as Edy's)

1. Place cookies, flat sides up, on a baking sheet. Top each of 6 cookies with 1 teaspoon fudge topping. Top each of remaining 6 cookies with 1 teaspoon preserves and 2 tablespoons ice cream. Place fudge-topped cookies on top of ice cream, topping sides down, pressing gently.

2. Wrap each sandwich in wax paper, and freeze at least 2 hours or until firm. Yield: 6 servings (serving size: 1 ice cream sandwich).

CALORIES 145; FAT 0.8g (sat 0.5g, mono 0.3g, poly 0g); PROTEIN 2.9g; CARB 33.9g; FIBER 0.2g; CHOL 4mg; IRON 1mg; SODIUM 68mg; CALC 38mg

4-ingredient

A three-way collision of chocolate defines these confections: A yogurt and chocolate morsels mix is sandwiched between chewy, chocolaty, brownielike cookies. Make these bite-sized treats ahead, and freeze them to have on hand when a chocolate craving hits.

Chocolate Chip Collision Ice Cream Sandwiches

Prep: 10 minutes • Cook: 9 minutes • Other: 25 minutes

1¾ cups chocolate and vanilla low-fat frozen yogurt (such as Ben & Jerry's Half Baked FroYo)
¼ cup semisweet chocolate minichips
¼ cup finely chopped toasted pecans

1 (13.7-ounce) package fat-free brownie mix (such as No Pudge)
1 (6-ounce) carton vanilla fat-free yogurt
Cooking spray

1. Preheat oven to 400°.
2. Combine first 3 ingredients in a small bowl. Cover and freeze 20 minutes.
3. Combine brownie mix and vanilla yogurt according to package directions. Drop dough by tablespoonfuls onto parchment paper–lined baking sheets coated with cooking spray to yield 30 cookies.
4. Bake at 400° for 9 minutes. Cool 5 minutes on baking sheets. Remove cookies to wire racks to cool completely.
5. Spread 1 heaping tablespoon ice cream mixture over flat side of each of 15 cookies. Top with remaining cookies, flat sides down, pressing gently. Serve immediately, or wrap each sandwich tightly in plastic wrap, and freeze until firm. Yield: 15 servings (serving size: 1 ice cream sandwich).

CALORIES 173; FAT 3g (sat 1g, mono 1.4g, poly 0.6g); PROTEIN 3.9g; CARB 34g; FIBER 0.6g; CHOL 5mg; IRON 1.4mg; SODIUM 124mg; CALC 106mg

4-ingredient

Vitamin- and fiber-rich, these crisp apples get extra crunch from a pecan-studded granola topping. We used a Granny Smith apple for crispness and a Braeburn apple for more color, but choose your favorite, depending on your sweet cravings.

Peanut Butter Granola Apple Rings

Prep: 7 minutes • Cook: 31 minutes • Other: 10 minutes

1 cup Cinnamon-Pecan Granola
¼ cup natural-style peanut butter (such as Smucker's)
1 tablespoon honey

2 red or green apples, cored and each cut into 6 rings

1. Prepare Cinnamon-Pecan Granola. Place 1 cup granola in a small dish.
2. Combine peanut butter and honey in a small bowl, stirring until smooth. Spread mixture evenly on 1 side of each apple slice. Sprinkle evenly with granola. Yield: 6 servings (serving size: 2 apple rings).

CALORIES 179; FAT 10.1g (sat 1.1g, mono 5.5g, poly 3.4g); PROTEIN 4.3g; CARB 20.4g; FIBER 2.5g; CHOL 0mg; IRON 0.8mg; SODIUM 29mg; CALC 20mg

Cinnamon-Pecan Granola

Prep: 2 minutes • Cook: 31 minutes • Other: 10 minutes

¼ cup brown sugar
1 tablespoon water
2 teaspoons canola oil
½ teaspoon ground cinnamon

1 cup uncooked old-fashioned rolled oats
½ cup chopped pecans
Cooking spray

1. Preheat oven to 300°.
2. Combine brown sugar and 1 tablespoon water in a medium microwave-safe bowl. Microwave at HIGH 30 seconds or until sugar is dissolved. Stir in oil and cinnamon. Add oats and pecans, stirring until coated. Spread oat mixture on a large rimmed baking sheet coated with cooking spray.
3. Bake at 300° for 30 minutes or until browned, stirring twice. Spread mixture in a single layer on wax paper to cool completely. Store in an airtight container. Yield: 12 servings (serving size: about 3 tablespoons).

CALORIES 85; FAT 4.8g (sat 0.4g, mono 2.6g, poly 1.6g); PROTEIN 1.6g; CARB 9.7g; FIBER 1.2g; CHOL 0mg; IRON 0.6mg; SODIUM 2mg; CALC 12mg

Juicy, plump blueberries, convenient frozen strawberries, and fresh ginger make this icy treat satisfying, healthful, and delicious. The make-ahead frozen concoction is a cool ending to a summer meal.

Ginger-Berry Granita
Prep: 5 minutes • Other: 8 hours

1 (10-ounce) package frozen strawberry halves in light syrup, thawed
1 cup blueberries

2 teaspoons grated peeled fresh ginger
2 cups sugar-free ginger ale
Mint leaves (optional)

1. Place first 3 ingredients in a blender; process 30 seconds or until pureed, stopping as necessary to scrape sides. Stir in ginger ale; pour mixture into an 8-inch square pan. Cover and freeze 8 hours or until firm.
2. Remove mixture from freezer; scrape entire mixture with a fork until fluffy. Garnish with mint leaves, if desired. Yield: 16 servings (serving size: about ½ cup).

CALORIES 15; FAT 0g (sat 0g, mono 0g, poly 0g); PROTEIN 0.2g; CARB 3.7g; FIBER 0.4g; CHOL 0mg; IRON 0.1mg; SODIUM 10mg; CALC 1mg

ingredient spotlight

Ginger's warm, slightly woody flavor makes it one of the world's favorite spices. Virtually all of the plant possesses ginger's signature spicy fragrance, although cooks look solely to the pungent root for their purposes. Fresh ginger, with its gnarled root and papery brown skin, is available in almost every grocery's produce department. Chopped or grated, fresh ginger gives subtle sweetness to many dishes.

S'mores in a glass captured our attention! This campfire classic reinvents itself to be served in shot glasses as tiny layered parfait treats with big flavor.

S'mores Shake Shots
Prep: 8 minutes • Cook: 2 minutes

4 regular-size marshmallows
1½ cups chocolate light ice cream (such as Edy's)
½ cup 1% low-fat chocolate milk
2 reduced-fat graham cracker sheets, divided

1. Preheat broiler.
2. Place marshmallows on a small rimmed baking sheet lined with parchment paper. Broil 2 minutes or until toasted.
3. While marshmallows toast, place ice cream, milk, and 1 graham cracker sheet in a blender; process until smooth.
4. Crumble 1 graham cracker (one-fourth of remaining sheet) into each of 4 large shot glasses. Divide ice cream mixture among glasses. Top with toasted marshmallows. Yield: 4 servings (serving size: 6 tablespoons shake mixture and 1 marshmallow).

CALORIES 153; FAT 3.3g (sat 1.7g, mono 1.2g, poly 0.4g); PROTEIN 3.8g; CARB 26.9g; FIBER 1g; CHOL 16mg; IRON 0.3mg; SODIUM 110mg; CALC 117mg

Sweet, juicy blueberries nestle in pillow-soft layers of yogurt and airy angel food cake. Blueberries are high in fiber and low in fat and are the most antioxidant-rich of all fruits.

Honey-Laced Blueberry Parfaits
Prep: 8 minutes

1 (6-ounce) carton French vanilla low-fat yogurt (such as Yoplait Light Thick and Creamy)
1 (6-ounce) carton blueberry low-fat yogurt (such as Yoplait Light Thick and Creamy Blueberry Pie)
1½ cups frozen fat-free whipped topping, thawed

3 cups (1-inch) cubed angel food cake
2 cups blueberries
1 tablespoon honey
½ cup honey-almond flax cereal (such as Kashi GoLean Crunch!), coarsely crushed

1. Combine yogurts in a bowl; gently fold in whipped topping.
2. Layer about ⅓ cup angel food cake, ¼ cup blueberries, and ⅓ cup yogurt mixture in each of 4 dessert glasses. Repeat procedure once. Drizzle honey evenly over parfaits. Top evenly with cereal. Serve immediately. Yield: 4 servings (serving size: 1 parfait).

CALORIES 359; FAT 2.6g (sat 1.1g, mono 0.8g, poly 0.6g); PROTEIN 9.7g; CARB 71.1g; FIBER 3.3g; CHOL 10mg; IRON 2.3mg; SODIUM 379mg; CALC 288mg

10-minute

Create a little magic by stirring light sour cream and orange zest into prepared pudding. It gives these desserts a creamy, made-from-scratch taste.

Strawberry-Meringue Desserts
Prep: 12 minutes

3 (3.75-ounce) cups refrigerated sugar-free vanilla pudding cups (such as Jell-O)
½ cup light sour cream
1 tablespoon grated orange rind

2 cups sliced fresh strawberries
4 chocolate chip meringue cookies, coarsely crumbled (such as Miss Meringue)
4 teaspoons shaved bittersweet chocolate

1. Combine first 3 ingredients in a small bowl. Layer pudding mixture, strawberries, and meringue cookies evenly in 4 parfait glasses or other dessert dishes. Top each serving with 1 teaspoon bittersweet chocolate shavings. Yield: 4 servings (serving size: 1 parfait).

CALORIES 202; FAT 6g (sat 3.4g, mono 1.7g, poly 0.8g); PROTEIN 2.7g; CARB 36.3g; FIBER 2.1g; CHOL 10mg; IRON 0.4mg; SODIUM 149mg; CALC 45mg

A good tiramisu starts with a strong coffee flavor. Here, we have two jolts to perk up the flavor—from the liqueur and ice cream. Serve this quick version of the famed coffee pick-me-up right away, or freeze it for later. If frozen, let the desserts stand 10 minutes before serving.

Frozen Tiramisu Trifles
Prep: 11 minutes

2 tablespoons Kahlúa (coffee-flavored liqueur)
2 tablespoons water
16 cakelike ladyfingers
⅓ cup (3 ounces) ⅓-less-fat cream cheese, softened
2 tablespoons powdered sugar

1 teaspoon vanilla extract
2 cups frozen fat-free whipped topping, thawed
1½ cups coffee light ice cream, softened (such as Edy's)
Bittersweet chocolate shavings (optional)

1. Combine liqueur and 2 tablespoons water in a small bowl. Brush ladyfingers evenly with liqueur mixture. Set aside.
2. Place cream cheese and sugar in a bowl; beat with a mixer at medium speed until blended. Beat in vanilla. Fold whipped topping into cream cheese mixture; set aside.
3. Place 2 ladyfingers in each of 4 bowls. Top each serving with 3 tablespoons ice cream and ¼ cup cream cheese mixture. Repeat layers once with remaining ladyfingers, ice cream, and cream cheese mixture. Sprinkle each serving with chocolate shavings, if desired. Serve immediately, or freeze until ready to serve. Yield: 4 servings (serving size: 1 trifle).

CALORIES 433; FAT 13.8g (sat 7.6g, mono 4.2g, poly 2g); PROTEIN 10.8g; CARB 62.2g; FIBER 0.4g; CHOL 224mg; IRON 0.3mg; SODIUM 160mg; CALC 90mg

10-minute

Cheesecake in five minutes? And only five ingredients? Just scoop this simple free-form cheesecake and candy mixture into your favorite little dessert dishes for an indulgent treat.

Candy Bar–Caramel Cheesecake Dessert
Prep: 5 minutes

1½ cups refrigerated ready-to-eat cheesecake filling
4 (0.55-ounce) chocolate-covered peanut butter cup candies, chilled and chopped
1 cup frozen fat-free whipped topping, thawed

Caramel Drizzle
⅓ cup coarsely crushed chocolate teddy bear–shaped graham cookies (such as Teddy Grahams, about 30 cookies)

1. Combine cheesecake filling and chopped candies. Gently fold in whipped topping. Spoon evenly into 8 small dessert dishes. Prepare Caramel Drizzle. Top each dessert with about 1 teaspoon Caramel Drizzle, and sprinkle with about 1 tablespoon cookie crumbs. Yield: 8 servings (serving size: 1 dessert).

CALORIES 246; FAT 14.6g (sat 7.7g, mono 2.4g, poly 3.7g); PROTEIN 3.6g; CARB 25g; FIBER 0.6g; CHOL 43mg; IRON 0.3mg; SODIUM 251mg; CALC 70mg

Caramel Drizzle
Prep: 1 minute • Cook: 1 minute

⅓ cup sugar-free caramel topping (such as Smucker's)

1 tablespoon creamy peanut butter

1. Combine caramel and peanut butter in a small microwave-safe bowl. Microwave at HIGH 20 to 30 seconds or until warm. Stir until smooth. Yield: 8 servings (serving size: 1¼ teaspoons).

CALORIES 42; FAT 1g (sat 0.2g, mono 0.5g, poly 0.3g); PROTEIN 0.5g; CARB 8.4g; FIBER 0.1g; CHOL 0mg; IRON 0mg; SODIUM 31mg; CALC 1mg

ingredient spotlight

Ready-to-eat cheesecake filling doesn't require time to set. Use it for cheesecakes, puddings, or parfaits. It's all pleasure, no guilt.

What's better than eating a juicy, ripe peach?
Peaches at their peak in a parfait, for starters. Use tall
stemmed glasses to showcase the delicious layering of
creamy yogurt and fresh peaches.

Peaches-n-Cream Parfaits
Prep: 10 minutes

½ cup vanilla fat-free yogurt
½ cup light sour cream
4 cups coarsely chopped peeled peaches

¼ cup firmly packed light brown sugar
Chopped fresh mint (optional)

1. Combine yogurt and sour cream.
2. Spoon ½ cup peaches into each of 4 glasses; sprinkle with 1½ teaspoons brown sugar, and top with 2 tablespoons yogurt mixture. Repeat layers with remaining peaches, brown sugar, and yogurt mixture. Sprinkle each with chopped fresh mint, if desired. Yield: 4 servings (serving size: 1 parfait).

CALORIES 181; FAT 2.4g (sat 1.5g, mono 0.5g, poly 0.3g); PROTEIN 4.1g; CARB 38.7g; FIBER 2.5g; CHOL 11mg; IRON 0.7mg; SODIUM 58mg; CALC 78mg

Juicy, ripe strawberries easily sub for peaches in these parfaits. If fresh strawberries aren't in peak season, use frozen ones.

Affogato is an Italian coffee-flavored beverage or dessert, usually gelato, drowned in espresso. This is a light version of the traditional treat. No espresso? Strong brewed or instant coffee works fine. In Italian, affogato means "drowned."

Affogato
Prep: 3 minutes

2 cups vanilla fat-free ice cream

2 cups espresso, chilled
¼ cup frozen fat-free whipped topping, thawed
1 teaspoon unsweetened cocoa

1. Scoop ½ cup ice cream into each of 4 tall glasses. Pour ½ cup espresso into each glass. Top each with 1 tablespoon whipped topping and sprinkle each with ¼ teaspoon cocoa. Serve immediately. Yield: 4 servings.

CALORIES 119; FAT 0.3g (sat 0.1g, mono 0g, poly 0.1g); PROTEIN 3.1g; CARB 26.1g; FIBER 0.2g; CHOL 0mg; IRON 0.2mg; SODIUM 64mg; CALC 83mg

Tofu takes on the flavor of coconut in this luscious dessert. Start with silky tofu and coconut milk for a light take on pudding. A fragrant vanilla bean adds deep flavor. Be sure to use heart-wise coconut milk, a blend of coconut and water, and skip the heart-stopping cream of coconut.

Vanilla Bean–Coconut Pudding
Prep: 8 minutes • Cook: 2 minutes • Other: 8 hours and 23 minutes

1 (12-ounce) package soft silken tofu (such as Mori-Nu)	⅛ teaspoon salt
1 cup coconut milk	1 vanilla bean, split
¼ cup sugar	¼ cup unsweetened organic coconut flakes, toasted

1. Place tofu on several layers of paper towels; top with several more layers of paper towels. Top with a cast-iron skillet or other heavy pan. Let stand 20 minutes.
2. While tofu drains, combine coconut milk and next 3 ingredients in a small saucepan; bring just to a simmer over medium-high heat. Remove pan from heat, and let stand 20 minutes. Remove and discard vanilla bean.
3. Place milk mixture and tofu in a food processor; process 2 minutes or until mixture is smooth, scraping sides of bowl twice. Spoon mixture evenly into 4 (4-ounce) ramekins or dessert dishes. Cover and refrigerate 8 hours or until thoroughly chilled.
4. Sprinkle puddings evenly with toasted coconut just before serving. Yield: 4 servings (serving size: 1 pudding and 1 tablespoon coconut).

CALORIES 242; FAT 17.9g (sat 14.2g, mono 1.4g, poly 2.2g); PROTEIN 5.5g; CARB 17.4g; FIBER 1.3g; CHOL 0mg; IRON 2.7mg; SODIUM 82mg; CALC 35mg

You can prepare the pudding, fruit compote, and twists ahead. Store remaining five biscuits in a zip-top plastic bag.

Pudding with Roasted Fruit Compote and Cinnamon Twists
Prep: 6 minutes • Cook: 20 minutes

Roasted Fruit Compote
  2 tablespoons bottled cinnamon-sugar
  1 (7.5-ounce) can refrigerated buttermilk biscuits (such as Pillsbury)

Butter-flavored cooking spray
  2 (3.75-ounce) refrigerated sugar-free vanilla pudding cups (such as Jell-O)
  ¼ cup fat-free sour cream

1. Prepare Roasted Fruit Compote.
2. While fruit roasts, place cinnamon-sugar on a plate. Roll out 5 biscuits into 10-inch-long strips. Coat 1 side of each strip with cooking spray, and press into cinnamon-sugar. Gently twist each strip, with cinnamon-sugar to the outside, into a 6-inch-long breadstick shape, and place on a baking sheet coated with cooking spray. Store remaining five biscuits in a zip-top bag for another use.
3. During last 10 minutes of fruit compote cook time, place twists in oven, and bake at 450° for 10 minutes or until browned.
4. While twists bake, combine pudding and sour cream in a small bowl. Divide mixture evenly among 5 dishes. Just before serving, top each pudding with ½ cup compote. Serve with twists. Yield: 5 servings (serving size: about ⅓ cup pudding mixture, ½ cup compote, and 1 twist).

CALORIES 275; FAT 2.8g (sat 0.8g, mono 1.4g, poly 0.5g); PROTEIN 5.5g; CARB 58.5g; FIBER 4.1g; CHOL 2mg; IRON 1.7mg; SODIUM 435mg; CALC 81mg

Roasted Fruit Compote
Prep: 6 minutes • Cook: 20 minutes

1¼ cups coarsely chopped peeled ripe red pear (1 pear)
  8 fresh Mission figs, halved
  3 apricots, quartered and pitted

Cooking spray
  2 tablespoons riesling or other slightly sweet white wine
  ½ (6-inch) vanilla bean, split

1. Preheat oven to 450°.
2. Combine fruits on a large rimmed baking sheet coated with cooking spray. Bake at 450° for 20 minutes or until fruit is tender, stirring once. Gently stir in wine; bake an additional 5 minutes.
3. Transfer fruit to a medium bowl. Scrape seeds from vanilla bean; gently stir seeds into fruit. Serve warm or chilled. Yield: 5 servings (serving size: ½ cup).

CALORIES 94; FAT 0.4g (sat 0.1g, mono 0.1g, poly 0.1g); PROTEIN 1g; CARB 22.9g; FIBER 3.8g; CHOL 0mg; IRON 0.4mg; SODIUM 1mg; CALC 34mg

Panna cotta is an Italian eggless custard or "cooked cream." A hint of espresso enhances the chocolate flavor in these silky-smooth, decadent delights.

Chocolate Espresso Panna Cotta
Prep: 6 minutes • Cook: 2 minutes • Other: 8 hours

1 envelope unflavored gelatin
2 cups 1% low-fat milk, divided
¼ cup sugar
6 ounces bittersweet chocolate, divided

2 teaspoons instant espresso granules
5 tablespoons frozen reduced-calorie whipped topping, thawed (optional)

1. Sprinkle gelatin over ½ cup milk in a small saucepan; let stand 1 to 2 minutes. Add sugar to milk mixture. Cook, stirring constantly, over medium heat 2 minutes or until gelatin and sugar dissolve; remove from heat. Shave 1 ounce chocolate, and set aside. Chop 5 ounces chocolate; stir chopped chocolate and espresso granules into milk mixture, stirring until chocolate melts.
2. Gradually stir in remaining 1½ cups milk. Pour ½ cup espresso mixture into each of 5 (6-ounce) custard cups. Cover and chill 8 hours.
3. To unmold, dip bottoms of custard cups in warm water for about 20 seconds. Place a small dessert plate, upside down, on top of each custard cup; invert onto plates. Top each with 1 tablespoon whipped topping, if desired, and sprinkle evenly with 1 ounce shaved chocolate. Yield: 5 servings (serving size: 1 panna cotta and about 1 teaspoon shaved chocolate).

CALORIES 315; FAT 15.6g (sat 7.9g, mono 6.7g, poly 0.9g); PROTEIN 7g; CARB 47.1g; FIBER 2.4g; CHOL 4mg; IRON 1mg; SODIUM 133mg; CALC 121mg

Prickly pear is close in flavor to kiwifruit, strawberries, watermelon, honeydew, figs, banana, and citrus fruits. And, if that's not enough, it boasts a bright crimson color. Substitute raspberry sorbet if prickly pear isn't available.

Prickly Pear–Mango Sundaes

Prep: 9 minutes • Cook: 8 minutes • Other: 5 minutes

4 Sugary Lime Tortilla Bowls
2 cups prickly pear sorbet (such as Ciao Bella)
1 cup chopped fresh mango (about 1 mango)

Frozen reduced-calorie whipped topping, thawed (optional)
Mint sprigs (optional)

1. Prepare Sugary Lime Tortilla Bowls.
2. Scoop ½ cup sorbet into each tortilla bowl. Top with ¼ cup mango. Garnish with whipped topping and mint sprigs, if desired. Yield: 4 servings (serving size: 1 sundae).

CALORIES 242; FAT 1.3g (sat 0g, mono 0.9g, poly 0.3g); PROTEIN 3.2g; CARB 54.9g; FIBER 3.7g; CHOL 0mg; IRON 1.7mg; SODIUM 213mg; CALC 74mg

Sugary Lime Tortilla Bowls

Prep: 4 minutes • Cook: 8 minutes • Other: 5 minutes

4 (6½-inch) flour tortillas
Butter-flavored cooking spray
2 tablespoons turbinado sugar

1 teaspoon crystallized lime (such as True Lime, 5 packets)

1. Preheat oven to 450°.
2. Fit 1 tortilla in each of 4 (10-ounce) custard cups coated with cooking spray. Coat tortillas with cooking spray, and sprinkle with sugar and lime.
3. Bake at 450° for 8 to 10 minutes or until browned and crisp. Let cool in cups 5 minutes or until tortillas retain their shape. Yield: 4 servings (serving size: 1 tortilla bowl).

CALORIES 115; FAT 1.2g (sat 0g, mono 0.9g, poly 0.3g); PROTEIN 2g; CARB 22.9g; FIBER 2g; CHOL 0mg; IRON 1.3mg; SODIUM 212mg; CALC 70mg

fix it faster

A mango takes some skill to peel and chop. If you're short on time or would rather practice your knife skills later, use jarred mango slices.

4-ingredient

Strawberries and mango bring a happy ending to mealtime. Mint freshens and enhances the fruity sauce that tops the ice cream mounds.

Strawberries with Fresh Mango-Mint Sauce

Prep: 11 minutes • Cook: 5 minutes

Fresh Mango-Mint Sauce
2 cups sliced strawberries

1⅓ cups vanilla low-fat ice cream
8 teaspoons chopped toasted pistachios

1. Prepare Fresh Mango-Mint Sauce.
2. Spoon ½ cup strawberries into each of 4 dessert dishes; top each with ⅓ cup ice cream, ¼ cup Fresh Mango-Mint Sauce, and 2 teaspoons pistachios. Yield: 4 servings.

CALORIES 186; FAT 4.9g (sat 1.7g, mono 2.1g, poly 1g); PROTEIN 4g; CARB 34.3g; FIBER 3.2g; CHOL 12mg; IRON 0.7mg; SODIUM 34mg; CALC 96mg

Fresh Mango-Mint Sauce

Prep: 6 minutes

1 cup chopped peeled mango (1 medium mango)

2 tablespoons agave nectar
2 tablespoons chopped fresh mint leaves

1. Place mango and nectar in a food processor; process until smooth. Stir in mint. Yield: 4 servings (serving size: ¼ cup).

CALORIES 57; FAT 0.1g (sat 0g, mono 0.1g, poly 0g); PROTEIN 0.2g; CARB 15.1g; FIBER 0.8g; CHOL 0mg; IRON 0.1mg; SODIUM 1mg; CALC 6mg

quick flip

Pistachios have a delicate flavor. Substitute macadamia nuts for a heartier, buttery-rich flavor. Because macadamia nuts contain more fat than pistachios, use half as much per serving.

4-ingredient

These petite Italian dessert sandwiches make a delicious closing statement. Serve them hot off the press drizzled with chocolate-hazelnut spread. They won over our taste panel and received the highest rating.

Chocolate-Hazelnut Panini Sundaes

Prep: 2 minutes • Cook: 2 minutes

4 (⅝-ounce) slices very thin white bread (such as Pepperidge Farm)
¼ cup chocolate-hazelnut spread (such as Nutella), divided
1 tablespoon chopped toasted hazelnuts

Butter-flavored cooking spray
1 cup vanilla light ice cream (such as Edy's)
2 teaspoons chopped toasted hazelnuts (optional)

1. Preheat panini grill.
2. Trim crusts from bread slices. Spread 2 tablespoons chocolate-hazelnut spread evenly over 2 bread slices. Sprinkle evenly with nuts. Top with remaining 2 bread slices. Coat both sides of sandwiches with cooking spray. Place sandwiches on panini grill; cook 1½ minutes or until golden. Cut each sandwich diagonally in half.
3. Place 1 panini triangle on each of 4 small dessert plates. Top each triangle with ¼ cup ice cream.
4. Place 2 tablespoons chocolate-hazelnut spread in a microwave-safe bowl. Microwave at HIGH 25 seconds or until warm; drizzle 1½ teaspoons over each scoop of ice cream. Garnish with ½ teaspoon hazelnuts, if desired. Serve immediately. Yield: 4 servings (serving size: 1 sundae).

CALORIES 198; FAT 8.9g (sat 2.8g, mono 4.3g, poly 1.7g); PROTEIN 4.6g; CARB 26.8g; FIBER 1g; CHOL 10mg; IRON 0.8mg; SODIUM 113mg; CALC 65mg

Sweet-tart Granny Smith apples hold up well when heated and keep their shape in this warm and comforting apple crisp. If you prefer a sweeter apple, try Golden Delicious, Rome Beauty, or York.

Apple-Granola Crisp

Prep: 8 minutes • Cook: 7 minutes

4 cups sliced Granny Smith apple (about 3 large apples)
1 tablespoon brown sugar
1 tablespoon cornstarch
1 tablespoon lemon juice

½ teaspoon vanilla extract
Butter-flavored cooking spray
1¼ cups low-fat granola with raisins
1 cup vanilla light ice cream

1. Combine first 5 ingredients in a large bowl; toss well. Spoon mixture into an 11 x 7–inch baking dish coated with cooking spray. Cover with heavy-duty plastic wrap; microwave at HIGH 5 minutes or until apple is tender; stir after 3 minutes.
2. Stir apple mixture, and top apple mixture with granola. Coat generously with cooking spray. Microwave, uncovered, at HIGH 2 minutes. Serve with ice cream. Yield: 4 servings (serving size: 1 cup apple mixture and ¼ cup ice cream).

CALORIES 247; FAT 3.6g (sat 0.3g, mono 1.1g, poly 0.6g); PROTEIN 4.4g; CARB 51.9g; FIBER 3.4g; CHOL 10mg; IRON 1mg; SODIUM 99mg; CALC 80mg

fix it faster

One (16-ounce) package of presliced apples makes this apple crisp recipe even quicker. You'll find already-sliced apples prepackaged in the produce department of your supermarket.

This elegant tart could be the star in a French pastry shop's dessert case. It combines a creamy, citrusy custard crowned with juicy berries, all atop a flaky crust.

Fresh Strawberry Tart
Prep: 13 minutes • Cook: 21 minutes • Other: 25 minutes

½ (14.1-ounce) package refrigerated pie dough
 (such as Pillsbury)
Lemon Custard

6 cups hulled small strawberries
2 tablespoons red raspberry jelly

1. Preheat oven to 450°.
2. Roll pie dough into a 12-inch circle. Fit dough into a 10-inch round removable-bottom tart pan, and pierce dough with a fork; bake at 450° for 10 minutes or until golden. Cool completely on a wire rack.
3. While crust bakes, prepare Lemon Custard.
4. Spread custard into bottom of prepared crust. Arrange strawberries, hulled sides down, over custard.
5. Place jelly in a small microwave-safe bowl. Microwave at HIGH 30 seconds or until melted. Gently brush jelly over strawberries. Chill tart until ready to serve. Yield: 8 servings (serving size: 1 wedge).

CALORIES 227; FAT 7.9g (sat 2.9g, mono 3.6g, poly 1.3g); PROTEIN 3.1g; CARB 36.6g; FIBER 2.4g; CHOL 30mg; IRON 0.6mg; SODIUM 128mg; CALC 78mg

Lemon Custard
Prep: 2 minutes • Cook: 9 minutes • Other: 5 minutes

1½ cups 1% low-fat milk, divided
⅓ cup sugar
2 tablespoons cornstarch

1 large egg yolk
2 teaspoons grated lemon rind

1. Bring 1¼ cups milk to a boil in a medium saucepan over medium heat, stirring frequently. Remove pan from heat.
2. While milk comes to a boil, combine sugar and cornstarch in a medium bowl. Add remaining ¼ cup milk and egg yolk to cornstarch mixture, stirring with a whisk until smooth.
3. Gradually stir half of hot milk into egg yolk mixture, stirring constantly with a whisk. Stir egg yolk mixture into remaining hot milk in pan; cook, stirring constantly with a whisk, over medium-high heat 3 minutes or until thick. Stir in lemon rind. Spoon custard into another medium bowl. Place bowl in a larger bowl filled with ice water. Cool 5 minutes or until thoroughly chilled, stirring frequently. Yield: 8 servings (serving size: about 3 tablespoons).

CALORIES 66; FAT 1g (sat 0.5g, mono 0.4g, poly 0.1g); PROTEIN 1.9g; CARB 12.5g; FIBER 0.1g; CHOL 27mg; IRON 0.1mg; SODIUM 24mg; CALC 60mg

seasonal produce guide

When you use fresh fruits and vegetables in your recipes, you don't have to do much to make them taste good. Sometimes just pulling them out of your market basket and rinsing them is all you need to do. From summer's garden-fresh corn to winter's juicy citrus fruits, there are plenty of colorful, delightful, and, above all, delicious items to choose from throughout the year.

Choosing the season's best foods for taste and freshness is reason enough to cook seasonally. But here's another: Fresh, in-season produce maximizes nutrients and adds variety to your meals, too. Take vitamin C–packed strawberries, for instance. They're in season—and most nutritious—in springtime. They're an excellent source of potassium and fiber, and they also offer folate, a B vitamin known for its role in reducing the risk of birth defects. And don't forget about autumn's famed crisp, crunchy apples. They're a good source of fiber, which helps lower cholesterol and control blood sugar.

Cooking with in-season fruits and vegetables can also save you money. Out-of-season produce is costly and generally lacks flavor. Our recommendation is to skip it and choose fruits and vegetables that are in season. When produce is at its peak, there's an abundance of it—and you can find it at a bargain. In the summer, enjoy tomatoes, cucumbers, fresh herbs, bell peppers, and more. During autumn and winter, look to winter squashes; dark, leafy greens; citrus fruits; and sweet potatoes. And in spring, try berries, asparagus, artichokes, and fresh peas.

Let *Cooking Light* be your guide to exploring and enjoying new varieties and flavors of fresh produce all year long.

Spring

Whether shopping at your local farmers' market or the produce section of your favorite supermarket, take advantage of the bounty of spring with the fresh flavors of quintessential favorites such as asparagus, green peas, spring onions, strawberries, and more.

Fruits
Bananas
Blood oranges
Coconuts
Grapefruit
Kiwifruit
Lemons
Limes
Mangoes
Navel oranges
Papayas
Passion fruit
Pineapples
Strawberries
Tangerines
Valencia oranges

Vegetables
Artichokes
Arugula
Asparagus
Avocados
Baby leeks
Beets
Belgian endive
Broccoli
Cauliflower
Dandelion greens
Fava beans
Green onions
Green peas
Kale
Lettuce
Mushrooms
Radishes
Red potatoes
Rhubarb
Snap beans
Snow peas
Spinach
Sugar snap peas
Sweet onions
Swiss chard

Herbs
Chives
Dill
Garlic chives
Lemongrass
Mint
Parsley
Thyme

Summer

Unlike any other season, summer is marked by the arrival of fresh corn, juicy peaches, vine-ripened tomatoes, and sweet watermelons. It's so easy, enjoyable, and affordable to indulge your cravings for fresh fruits and vegetables this time of year.

Fruits
Blackberries
Blueberries
Boysenberries
Cantaloupes
Casaba melons
Cherries
Crenshaw melons
Grapes
Guava
Honeydew melons
Mangoes
Nectarines
Papayas
Peaches
Plums
Raspberries
Strawberries
Watermelons

Vegetables
Avocados
Beets
Bell peppers
Cabbage
Carrots
Celery
Chile peppers
Collards
Corn
Cucumbers
Eggplant
Green beans
Jicama
Lima beans
Okra
Pattypan squash
Peas
Radicchio
Radishes
Summer squash
Tomatoes
Zucchini

Herbs
Basil
Bay leaves
Borage
Chives
Cilantro
Dill
Lavender
Lemon verbena
Marjoram
Mint
Oregano
Rosemary
Sage
Summer savory
Tarragon
Thyme

Autumn

Autumn's bumper crop of fruits and vegetables offers a range of intense flavors and substantial textures. Groceries and farmers' markets are full of apples, figs, pears, pumpkins, sweet potatoes, and winter squash.

Fruits
Apples
Cranberries
Figs
Grapes
Pears
Persimmons
Pomegranates
Quinces

Vegetables
Belgian endive
Bell peppers
Broccoli
Brussels sprouts
Cabbage
Cauliflower
Eggplant
Escarole
Fennel
Frisée
Leeks
Mushrooms
Parsnips
Pumpkins
Red potatoes
Rutabagas
Shallots
Sweet potatoes
Winter squash
Yukon gold potatoes

Herbs
Basil
Bay leaves
Parsley
Rosemary
Sage
Tarragon
Thyme

Winter

Let the recipes of winter warm you with hardy root vegetables, tangy cranberries, robust greens, and citrus fruits.

Fruits
Apples
Blood oranges
Cranberries
Grapefruit
Kiwifruit
Kumquats
Lemons
Limes
Mandarin oranges
Navel oranges
Pears
Persimmons
Pomegranates
Pomelos
Satsuma oranges
Tangelos
Tangerines
Quinces

Vegetables
Baby turnips
Beets
Belgian endive
Brussels sprouts
Celeriac (celery root)
Chile peppers
Cipollini onions
Dried beans
Escarole
Fennel
Frisée
Jerusalem artichokes
Kale
Leeks
Mushrooms
Onions
Parsnips
Potatoes
Rutabagas
Sweet potatoes
Swiss chard
Turnips
Watercress
Winter squash

Herbs
Bay leaves
Chives
Parsley
Peppermint
Rosemary
Sage
Thyme

time-saving tools & gadgets

Here are some tools and gadgets our Test Kitchens crew and editors recommend for getting dinner on the table superfast. Armed with these handy equipment must-haves, you can cut down on your time in the kitchen and actually spend more time with the ones you love.

Blender
A blender is a necessity when making quick frozen beverages, sensational smoothies, and slushy drinks. If you make frozen beverages often, choose a blender with an ice-crushing mode.

Chef's Knife
The chef's knife is the workhorse of the *Cooking Light* Test Kitchens. It's ideal for chopping herbs, onions, garlic, fruits, and vegetables, and for cutting boneless meats, slicing and dicing, and general cutting tasks.

Citrus Press
For the best flavor, fresh citrus juice can't be beat. A citrus press is a quick and easy way to get a lot of juice from your fruit. To get the most juice, bring your fruit to room temperature before pressing it.

Food Processor
A food processor is a handy piece of equipment that can save time. Use the shredder blade to quickly shred vegetables such as potatoes and carrots.

Garlic Press
A garlic press is a real time-saver. It crushes garlic right into your pan or bowl. You don't even have to peel the clove.

Graters
Graters, whether handheld or box, are kitchen tools that speed up preparation time. Use the smaller holes for grating hard cheese or chocolate. For ingredients such as cheddar cheese or carrots, the largest holes work best.

Grill Pan
A grill pan is a good alternative to a gas or charcoal grill. Meat and fish turn out juicy, with no need for added fat, and you save time by not having to heat up a traditional grill.

Kitchen Shears
Keep kitchen shears on hand to mince small amounts of herbs, chop canned tomatoes, trim fat from meat and skin from poultry, and make slits in bread dough.

Microplane Grater
When it comes to finely grating foods, nothing works better or faster than a Microplane grater. It works great on everything from hard cheese and citrus fruits to chocolate.

Measuring Cups and Spoons
While every kitchen needs these tools, we recommend at least two sets of each in a variety of sizes. With multiples, you'll save time by not having to rinse in the middle of a recipe.

Panini Press
A panini press is great for making hot sandwiches quickly. You can find one at most kitchen stores.

Peeler
A peeler removes the skin from vegetables and fruits, as well as the gnarled roots of fresh ginger. Select one with a comfortable grip and an eyer to remove potato eyes and other blemishes. It also makes quick work of shaving Parmesan cheese and curling chocolate.

Peppermill
Give your food a bit of pungent flavor with a quick turn of a peppermill for a sprinkle of cracked or freshly ground black pepper. It's a gotta-have kitchen gadget for quick cooking.

Pitter
An easy-to-use pitter is the perfect tool to easily remove olive and cherry pits.

Pizza Cutter
Everyone needs a pizza cutter for cutting pizza. But it also works great for cutting toast, focaccia, and even pancakes or waffles.

Vegetable Steamer
Steaming vegetables helps them retain their water-soluble vitamins. It's a quick and easy process, especially when you use a collapsible metal vegetable steamer. Using this tool will assist you in getting vegetable sides on your table in a flash.

Nutritional Analysis

How to Use It and Why

Glance at the end of any *Cooking Light* recipe, and you'll see how committed we are to helping you make the best of today's light cooking. With chefs, registered dietitians, home economists, and a computer system that analyzes every ingredient we use, *Cooking Light* gives you authoritative dietary detail like no other magazine. We go to such lengths so you can see how our recipes fit into your healthful eating plan. If you're trying to lose weight, the calorie and fat figures will probably help most. But if you're keeping a close eye on the sodium, cholesterol, and saturated fat in your diet, we provide those numbers, too. And because many women don't get enough iron or calcium, we can help there, as well. Finally, there's a fiber analysis for those of us who don't get enough roughage.

Here's a helpful guide to put our nutritional analysis numbers into perspective. Remember, one size doesn't fit all, so take your lifestyle, age, and circumstances into consideration when determining your nutrition needs. For example, pregnant or breast-feeding women need more protein, calories, and calcium. And women older than 50 need 1,200mg of calcium daily, 200mg more than the amount recommended for younger women.

In Our Nutritional Analysis, We Use These Abbreviations

sat	saturated fat	**CHOL**	cholesterol
mono	monounsaturated fat	**CALC**	calcium
poly	polyunsaturated fat	**g**	gram
CARB	carbohydrates	**mg**	milligram

Daily Nutrition Guide

	Women ages 25 to 50	Women over 50	Men over 24
Calories	2,000	2,000 or less	2,700
Protein	50g	50g or less	63g
Fat	65g or less	65g or less	88g or less
Saturated Fat	20g or less	20g or less	27g or less
Carbohydrates	304g	304g	410g
Fiber	25g to 35g	25g to 35g	25g to 35g
Cholesterol	300mg or less	300mg or less	300mg or less
Iron	18 mg	8mg	8mg
Sodium	2,300mg or less	1,500mg or less	2,300mg or less
Calcium	1,000mg	1,200mg	1,000mg

The nutritional values used in our calculations either come from The Food Processor, Version 8.9 (ESHA Research), or are provided by food manufacturers.

Metric Equivalents

The information in the following charts is provided to help cooks outside the United States successfully use the recipes in this book. All equivalents are approximate.

Cooking/Oven Temperatures

	Fahrenheit	Celsius	Gas Mark
Freeze Water	32° F	0° C	
Room Temperature	68° F	20° C	
Boil Water	212° F	100° C	
Bake	325° F	160° C	3
	350° F	180° C	4
	375° F	190° C	5
	400° F	200° C	6
	425° F	220° C	7
	450° F	230° C	8
Broil			Grill

Liquid Ingredients by Volume

¼ tsp				=	1 ml
½ tsp				=	2 ml
1 tsp				=	5 ml
3 tsp = 1 tbl		= ½ fl oz	=	15 ml
	2 tbls = ⅛ cup	= 1 fl oz	=	30 ml
	4 tbls = ¼ cup	= 2 fl oz	=	60 ml
	5⅓ tbls = ⅓ cup	= 3 fl oz	=	80 ml
	8 tbls = ½ cup	= 4 fl oz	=	120 ml
	10⅔ tbls = ⅔ cup	= 5 fl oz	=	160 ml
	12 tbls = ¾ cup	= 6 fl oz	=	180 ml
	16 tbls = 1 cup	= 8 fl oz	=	240 ml
	1 pt = 2 cups	= 16 fl oz	=	480 ml
	1 qt = 4 cups	= 32 fl oz	=	960 ml
		33 fl oz	= 1000 ml	= 1l

Dry Ingredients by Weight

(To convert ounces to grams, multiply the number of ounces by 30.)

1 oz	=	¹⁄₁₆ lb	=	30 g
4 oz	=	¼ lb	=	120 g
8 oz	=	½ lb	=	240 g
12 oz	=	¾ lb	=	360 g
16 oz	=	1 lb	=	480 g

Length

(To convert inches to centimeters, multiply the number of inches by 2.5.)

1 in	=		2.5 cm	
6 in	=	½ ft	= 15 cm	
12 in	=	1 ft	= 30 cm	
36 in	=	3 ft = 1yd	= 90 cm	
40 in	=		100 cm	= 1m

Equivalents for Different Types of Ingredients

Standard Cup	Fine Powder (ex. flour)	Grain (ex. rice)	Granular (ex. sugar)	Liquid Solids (ex. butter)	Liquid (ex. milk)
1	140 g	150 g	190 g	200 g	240 ml
¾	105 g	113 g	143 g	150 g	180 ml
⅔	93 g	100 g	125 g	133 g	160 ml
½	70 g	75 g	95 g	100 g	120 ml
⅓	47 g	50 g	63 g	67 g	80 ml
¼	35 g	38 g	48 g	50 g	60 ml
⅛	18 g	19 g	24 g	25 g	30 ml

index

Apples, 350
Crisp, Apple-Granola, 350
Dressing, Creamy Apple, 118
Quesadillas, Apple and Olive, 150
Rings, Peanut Butter Granola Apple, 321
Apricot-Pistachio Chocolates, 304
Artichoke Frittata, Lemon-, 165
Artichokes with Wild Rice, Shrimp and, 212
Arugula Pesto, Fig-, 156
Asparagus, 163
Grilled Asparagus with Shallot-Dijon Vinaigrette, 181
Omelet, Asparagus and Basil, 163
Sugared Asparagus, 270
Avocado with Lime-Cilantro Cream, Grilled, 209

Bacon
BLTs with Pimiento Cheese, 69
Peppered Rosemary Bacon, 28
Vinaigrette, Maple-Bacon, 117
Beans. *See* **Soups and Stews, Bean or Lentil; specific beans**
Beef. *See also* **Soups and Stews, Beef**
Ground
Beef and Pepperoni Pizza, 224
Blue Cheeseburger, 63
Dolmathes, 221
Shepherd's Pie, 222
Steak
"Black and Blue" Steak Salad, 114
Chili-Lime Flank Steak, 228
Flank Steak Sandwiches with Carrot Slaw, 64
Grecian Steaks, 238
Jamaican-Spiced Hanger Steak with Banana-Mango Chutney, 233
Steak Soft Tacos with Grilled Onion, 231
Stir-Fry, Beef and Bok Choy, 227
Tenderloin, Apricot-Glazed Beef, 234
Tenderloin with Mushroom Gravy, Beef, 237
Veal Piccata, 243
Beet Risotto with Walnuts and Goat Cheese, Roasted, 136
Berries. *See also* **specific berries**
Granita, Ginger-Berry, 322
Romanoff, Balsamic Berries, 114
Beverages
Cranberry-Apple Spritzer, 150
Green Tea Mojitos, 265
Mango Lassi, 202

Mint Limeade, 88
Pineapple Agua Fresca, 144
S'mores Shake Shots, 325
Strawberry Milk Shakes, Mini, 141
Watermelon-Limeade Sparkler, 113
Black Beans
Jalapeño Black Beans and Corn, 166
Topping, Black Bean, 149
Tropical Black Beans, 147
Blueberries
Dressing, Blueberry-Thyme, 129
Parfaits, Honey-Laced Blueberry, 326
Salad, Blueberry Citrus, 165
Blue Cheese, 130, 238
Cheeseburger, Blue, 63
Salad, "Black and Blue" Steak, 114
Bok Choy Stir-Fry, Beef and, 227
Breads, 69, 103
Biscuits, Chive Cheese, 37
Grissini, Basil-Asiago, 21
Pitas, Goat Cheese and Olive, 25
Spirals, Cornmeal-Herb, 34
Toasts
Crushed Heirloom Tomato and Shrimp Bruschetta, 56
Fontina-Pesto Toasts, 22
Garlic-Pepper Toasts, 95
Rustic Tomato-Garlic Toasts, 40
Broccoli
Roasted Broccoli with Garlic and Pine Nuts, 187
Salad, Curried Chicken and Broccoli, 120
Sauté, Broccoli, 31
Soup, Broccoli-Cheese, 31
Broccolini with Spicy Walnut Butter, 263
Brussels Sprouts and Red Cabbage with Bacon, Sautéed, 244
Burritos, Spicy Vegetable, 144

Cabbage with Bacon, Sautéed Brussels Sprouts and Red, 244
Candies
Apricot-Pistachio Chocolates, 304
Chocolate-Pecan Butter Crunch Candy, 309
Loaded Bittersweet Chocolate Bark, 307
Carrots
Orange Roasted Carrots, 282
Quiches, Mini Carrot, 48
Slaw, Carrot, 64
Soup, Garbanzo-Carrot, 16
Toss, Carrot-Red Onion, 61
Cheese. *See also* **specific cheeses**
Grissini, Basil-Asiago, 21
Pitas, Goat Cheese and Olive, 25
Pizza, Goat Cheese–Mushroom Naan, 154

Sauce, Ham and Roasted Asparagus Crepes with Gruyère Cheese, 254
Vinaigrette, Olive-Parmesan, 96

Chicken, 122. *See also* **Salads, Chicken; Sandwiches, Chicken; Soups and Stews, Chicken**
Braised Chicken with Saffron and Olives, 294
Cacciatore, Chicken, 288
Cutlets with Tarragon-Mustard Cream Sauce, Pan-Seared Chicken, 282
Dijon Chicken, 123
Enchiladas Supreme, Chicken Mole, 265
40 Cloves of Garlic and Creamy Thyme Sauce, Chicken with, 297
Kebabs, Moroccan Chicken, 269
Milanese, Chicken, 276
Orecchiette with Chicken, Bacon, and Tomato Ragù, 263
Paella, Chicken, 266
Pasta Primavera, Chicken, 287
Prosciutto-Wrapped Chicken, 281
Roasted Chicken with Shallots, Grapes, and Thyme, 284
Sausages with Caraway Slaw, Grilled Chicken, 91
Stir-Fried Lemon Chicken, 270
Tandoori Chicken, 279
Thighs, Apricot-Glazed Grilled Chicken, 292
Thighs, Margarita Chicken, 291
Tomatillo Chicken, 275
Tomato Topping, Chicken with Creamy, 272

Chickpeas
Hummus, Macadamia, 70
Salad, Chickpea, 26
Salad, Chickpea, Feta, and Orzo, 101
Soup, Garbanzo-Carrot, 16

Chile peppers. *See* **Peppers, Jalapeño**

Chili. *See under* **Soups and Stews**

Chocolate. *See also* **Candies**
Baby Cakes, Mississippi Mud, 312
Ice Cream Sandwiches, Chocolate Chip Collision, 319
Ice Cream Sandwiches, Chocolate-Covered Strawberry, 316
Panna Cotta, Chocolate Espresso, 343
Sundaes, Chocolate-Hazelnut Panini, 349

Chowder. *See under* **Soups and Stews**

Coconut
Pudding, Vanilla Bean–Coconut, 338
Rice, Coconut, 147
Rice, Coconut-Lime, 275

Condiments. *See also* **Mayonnaise; Pesto; Toppings**
Banana-Mango Chutney, Jamaican-Spiced Hanger Steak with, 233
Cilantro Cream, 231
Dill Sour Cream, 15
Lime-Cilantro Cream, Grilled Avocado with, 209

Corn
Chowder with Chicken, Coconut Corn, 48
Grilled Corn with Jalapeño-Herb "Butter," 246
Summer Succotash, 143

Couscous, 243, 272
Couscous with Goat Cheese and Pine Nuts, 241
Greek Couscous, 138
Whole-Wheat Couscous with Ginger and Currants, 269
Zucchini and Tomato Couscous, 188

Cranberries
Cranberry-Apple Spritzer, 150
Salad, Turkey-Cranberry, 133

Crepes with Gruyère Cheese Sauce, Ham and Roasted Asparagus, 254

Cucumber-Thyme Relish, 101

Cucumber Tuna Salad, 58

Desserts. *See also* **Candies**
Baby Cakes, Mississippi Mud, 312
Bars, Pumpkin-Gingersnap, 315
Cheesecake Dessert, Candy Bar–Caramel, 333
Crisp, Apple-Granola, 350
Custard, Lemon, 353

Frozen
Affogato, 337
Granita, Ginger-Berry, 322
Ice Cream Sandwiches, Chocolate Chip Collision, 319
Ice Cream Sandwiches, Chocolate-Covered Strawberry, 316
Milk Shakes, Mini Strawberry, 141
Shake Shots, S'mores, 325
Sundaes, Chocolate-Hazelnut Panini, 349
Sundaes, Prickly Pear–Mango, 344
Tiramisu Trifles, Frozen, 331
Panna Cotta, Chocolate Espresso, 343
Parfaits, Honey-Laced Blueberry, 326
Parfaits, Peaches-n-Cream, 334
Peanut Butter Granola Apple Rings, 321
Pudding, Vanilla Bean–Coconut, 338
Pudding with Roasted Fruit Compote and Cinnamon Twists, 341
Strawberries with Fresh Mango-Mint Sauce, 346
Strawberry-Meringue Desserts, 328
Tart, Fresh Strawberry, 353
Tartlets, Orange-Sicle, 310
Tortilla Bowls, Sugary Lime, 344

Dips and Spreads
Lemon-Feta Spread, 76
Macadamia Hummus, 70

Dolmathes, 221

Duck Breast, Pomegranate-Glazed, 299

Edamame Salad with Wasabi Vinaigrette, Chicken, 127
Eggplant with Feta and Greek Couscous, Grilled, 138
Eggs
    Baked Eggs in Crispy Ham Cups with Petite Peas, 256
    Frittata, Lemon-Artichoke, 165
    Frittata, Southwest Rice, 166
    Omelet, Asparagus and Basil, 163
    Quiches, Mini Carrot, 48
Enchiladas Supreme, Chicken Mole, 265

Fennel-Orange Salad, Grilled Shrimp with, 107
Feta Cheese, 299
    Dressing, Greek Feta, 108
    Sandwiches, Feta-Olive, 16
    Spread, Greek Chicken Sandwich with Lemon-Feta, 76
Fig and Arugula Pizzas with Goat Cheese, 156
Fig-Arugula Pesto, 156
Fish, 197. *See also* **Salmon; Tuna**
    Flounder with Fried Rosemary and Garlic, Pan-Seared, 178
    Grouper Sandwiches with Chile Mayo, Grilled, 52
    Halibut with Bacon and Balsamic Tomatoes, 181
    Mahimahi with Grilled Pineapple Relish, 183
    Sole, Baked Lemon, 188
    Tilapia, Parmesan-Broiled, 191
    Tostadas, Baja Fish, 192
    Trout with Bourbon-Pecan Butter Sauce, Cornmeal-Crusted, 197
    Trout with Onion Jam and Bacon, 194
Fontina Cheese
    Mushroom Macaroni and Cheese, 169
    Sandwiches, Italian Grilled Cheese, 87
    Toasts, Fontina-Pesto, 22
Frittata, Lemon-Artichoke, 165
Frittata, Southwest Rice, 166
Fruit, seasonal guide, 354-357
Fruit Compote, Roasted, 341

Garlic, 216
    Chicken with 40 Cloves of Garlic and Creamy Thyme Sauce, 297
    Pizza, Garlic-Mashed Potato, 153
Ginger-Berry, Granita, 322
Ginger Dressing, Spicy, 111
Glaze, Sage Pork Medallions with Maple, 253
Glazed Salmon, Sweet and Smoky, 184
Grains. *See also* **Rice**
    Barley, Lemon-Parmesan, 272
    Barley Soup, Beef and, 34
    Quinoa Salad, Tarragon-Chicken, 118
Granola, Cinnamon-Pecan, 321

Granola Crisp, Apple-, 350
Grits, Jalapeño, 234

Ham
    Baked Eggs in Crispy Ham Cups with Petite Peas, 256
    Crepes with Gruyère Cheese Sauce, Ham and Roasted Asparagus, 254
    Prosciutto-Wrapped Chicken, 281
    Sandwiches, Waffled Hawaiian, 70

Lamb
    Chops with Honey Figs, Grilled Lamb, 241
    Soup with Gremolata, White Bean and Lamb, 39
    Wraps with Tzatziki Sauce, Lamb, 66
Lemon
    Barley, Lemon-Parmesan, 272
    Custard, Lemon, 353
    Sole, Baked Lemon, 188
    Spinach, Lemon-Caper, 281
    Spread, Greek Chicken Sandwich with Lemon-Feta, 76
Lemongrass Chicken Lettuce Wraps, 79
Lemongrass Vinaigrette, 79
Lettuce, 123
    Butter Lettuce-Orange Salad with Sweet and Sour Dressing, 154
    Wedge with Spicy Miso Dressing, Lettuce, 43
    Wraps, Lemongrass Chicken Lettuce, 79
Lime
    Cream, Grilled Avocado with Lime-Cilantro, 209
    Mint Limeade, 88
    Rice, Coconut-Lime, 275
    Watermelon-Limeade Sparkler, 113

Mango, 344
    Lassi, Mango, 202
    Sauce, Strawberries with Fresh Mango-Mint, 346
    Sundaes, Prickly Pear-Mango, 344
Maple-Bacon Vinaigrette, 117
Maple Glaze, Sage Pork Medallions with, 253
Marinades and Rubs
    Jamaican Rub, 233
    Smoked Paprika Rub, 55
    Tandoori Marinade, 279
Mayonnaise
    Basil Mayo, 82
    Chile Mayo, 52
    Pesto Mayo, 81
    Smoked Paprika Aioli, 85
Metric equivalents, 361

Mushrooms
Dijon Creamed Mushrooms, 256
Macaroni and Cheese, Mushroom, 169
Pilaf, Mushroom–Whole-Grain Rice, 284
Pizza, Goat Cheese–Mushroom Naan, 154
Sherry-Roasted Wild Mushrooms, 169
Spaghetti, Herbed Mushroom, 288

Mustard
Dijon Chicken, 123
Dijon Creamed Mushrooms, 256
Dijon Dressing, Mâche Salad with, 287
Shallot-Dijon Vinaigrette, Grilled Asparagus with, 181
Tarragon-Mustard Cream Sauce, Pan-Seared Chicken
        Cutlets with, 282

Noodles, **205.** *See also* **Pasta**
Green Onion Soba Noodles, 205
Salad, Asian Soba Noodle, 124
Nutrition analysis, 360
Nuts, 133, 346
Almond Basmati Rice, Sugared, 294
Bourbon-Pecan Butter Sauce, Cornmeal-Crusted Trout
        with, 197
Cinnamon-Pecan Granola, 321
Macadamia Hummus, 70
Walnut Butter, Broccolini with Spicy, 263

Olives
Pitas, Goat Cheese and Olive, 25
Sandwiches, Feta-Olive, 16
Vinaigrette, Olive-Parmesan, 96
Omelet, Asparagus and Basil, 163
Onion
Green Onion Soba Noodles, 205
Salad, Red Onion and Orange, 299
Toss, Carrot-Red Onion, 61
Orange
Carrots, Orange Roasted, 282
Salad
    Blueberry Citrus Salad, 165
    Butter Lettuce–Orange Salad with Sweet and Sour
        Dressing, 154
    Grilled Shrimp with Fennel-Orange Salad, 107
    Red Onion and Orange Salad, 299
Sauce, Orange Stir-Fry, 227
Tartlets, Orange-Sicle, 310
Vinaigrette, Orange, 124
Vinaigrette, Watercress Salad with Balsamic Orange, 215

Paella, Chicken, 266
Paprika Aioli, Smoked, 85
Paprika Rub, Smoked, 55
Pasta, 101. *See also* **Couscous; Noodles**
Chicken Pasta Primavera, 287
Macaroni and Cheese, Mushroom, 169
Orecchiette with Chicken, Bacon, and Tomato Ragù, 263
Orzo, Spinach-Tomato, 243
Orzo Salad, Chickpea, Feta, and, 101
Pappardelle with Roasted Zucchini, Mascarpone, and
        Pine Nuts, 170
Pasta Puttanesca, 259
Penne, Fresh Tomato Sauce with, 172
Penne with Roasted Ratatouille, 172
Ravioli with Butternut Squash Cream Sauce, Baked, 175
Salad, Mediterranean Pasta, 96
Spaghetti, Herbed Mushroom, 288
Peaches
Grilled Peach Barbecue Pork Chops, 246
Parfaits, Peaches-n-Cream, 334
Peas
Chile-Ginger Sugar Snaps, 200
Petite Green Peas with Mint Butter, 184
Spanish Peas, 266
Peppers
Bell Pepper Soup, Creamy Roasted Red, 25
Jalapeño
    Black Beans and Corn, Jalapeño, 166
    Grilled Corn with Jalapeño-Herb "Butter," 246
    Grits, Jalapeño, 234
Pesto
Fig-Arugula Pesto, 156
Fontina-Pesto Toasts, 22
Pesto Mayo, 81
Pineapple
Agua Fresca, Pineapple, 144
Relish, Grilled Pineapple, 183
Tropical Shrimp Salad, 111
Pizza
Beef and Pepperoni Pizza, 224
Fig and Arugula Pizzas with Goat Cheese, 156
Garlic-Mashed Potato Pizza, 153
Goat Cheese-Mushroom Naan Pizza, 154
Pork. *See also* **Bacon; Ham; Sausage**
Chops, Grilled Peach Barbecue Pork, 246
Chops, Sweet and Spicy Chili Pork, 249
Medallions with Maple Glaze, Sage Pork, 253
Schnitzel, Pork, 244
Tenderloin, Fiery Grilled Pork, 250
Tenderloin Salad with Maple-Bacon Vinaigrette, Grilled
        Pork, 117

Potatoes. *See also* **Sweet Potatoes**
Fries, Lemon-Pepper, 238
Fries, Two-Potato Peppered, 75
Lavender Potatoes, 191
Mashed Potatoes, Lemony, 178
Pizza, Garlic-Mashed Potato, 153
Smashed Potatoes, Garlicky, 237
Soup, Baked Potato, 28
Poultry. *See* **Chicken; Turkey**
Prickly Pear-Mango Sundaes, 344

Quesadillas, Apple and Olive, 150
Quesadilla with Tropical Salsa, Shrimp, 206

Rice, 136
Cajun Rice, 12
Calico Spanish Rice, 291
Coconut-Lime Rice, 275
Coconut Rice, 147
Cranberry Rice, Orange-Glazed Turkey with, 300
Fried Rice, Shrimp, 211
Frittata, Southwest Rice, 166
Pilaf, Mushroom-Whole-Grain Rice, 284
Risotto Milanese with Mussels, 199
Risotto with Walnuts and Goat Cheese, Roasted Beet, 136
Sugared Almond Basmati Rice, 294

Salad Dressings
Apple Dressing, Creamy, 118
Blueberry-Thyme Dressing, 129
Buttermilk Dressing, 104
Curry-Yogurt Dressing, 120
Dijon Dressing, Mâche Salad with, 287
Dill Dressing, Chopped Salad with Creamy, 72
Feta Dressing, Greek, 108
Ginger Dressing, Spicy, 111
Miso Dressing, Lettuce Wedge with Spicy, 43
Sweet and Sour Dressing, Butter Lettuce-Orange Salad with, 154
Vinaigrette
Balsamic Orange Vinaigrette, Watercress Salad with, 215
Classic Vinaigrette Salad, 224
Lemongrass Vinaigrette, 79
Maple-Bacon Vinaigrette, 117
Olive-Parmesan Vinaigrette, 96
Orange Vinaigrette, 124
Shallot-Dijon Vinaigrette, Grilled Asparagus with, 181
Wasabi Vinaigrette, 127

Salads
Antipasto Salad, 98
Asian Soba Noodle Salad, 124
Asian Vegetable Salad, Crunchy, 249
"Black and Blue" Steak Salad, 114
Blueberry Citrus Salad, 165
Candied Balsamic Tomatoes and Mozzarella Salad, 95
Chicken
Blueberry Spinach Salad with Grilled Chicken, 129
Chicken Caesar, 123
Chicken Edamame Salad with Wasabi Vinaigrette, 127
Curried Chicken and Broccoli Salad, 120
Tarragon-Chicken Quinoa Salad, 118
Chickpea, Feta, and Orzo Salad, 101
Chickpea Salad, 26
Chipotle Taco Salad, 113
Chopped Salad with Creamy Dill Dressing, 72
Green
Butter Lettuce-Orange Salad with Sweet and Sour Dressing, 154
Classic Vinaigrette Salad, 224
Lettuce Wedge with Spicy Miso Dressing, 43
Mâche Salad with Dijon Dressing, 287
Red Onion and Orange Salad, 299
Watercress Salad with Balsamic Orange Vinaigrette, 215
Grilled Pork Tenderloin Salad with Maple-Bacon Vinaigrette, 117
Pasta Salad, Mediterranean, 96
Seafood
Crab Salad with Buttermilk Dressing, 104
Greek Shrimp Salad, 108
Grilled Shrimp with Fennel-Orange Salad, 107
Tropical Shrimp Salad, 111
Tuna-Pita Chip Panzanella, 103
Slaw
Caraway Slaw, 91
Carrot Slaw, 64
Cilantro Slaw, 194
Pico de Gallo Slaw, 192
Turkey-Blue Cheese Salad, 130
Turkey-Cranberry Salad, 133
Watermelon Salad, 87
Salmon
Horseradish-Dill Salmon, 187
Sliders, Smoked Paprika Salmon, 55
Sweet and Smoky Glazed Salmon, 184
Salsa, Shrimp Quesadilla with Tropical, 206
Sandwiches
Cheeseburger, Blue, 63
Chicken
Buffalo Chicken Salad Sandwiches, 75

California Smoked Chicken Sandwiches, 85
Greek Chicken Sandwich with Lemon-Feta Spread, 76
Grilled Chicken Sausages with Caraway Slaw, 91
Lemongrass Chicken Lettuce Wraps, 79
Mega Crostini Chicken Sandwiches, 81
Shaved Chicken, Apple, and Cheddar Sandwiches
with Basil Mayo, 82
Feta-Olive Sandwiches, 16
Flank Steak Sandwiches with Carrot Slaw, 64
Lamb Wraps with Tzatziki Sauce, 66

Pork
BLTs with Pimiento Cheese, 69
Italian Grilled Cheese Sandwiches, 87
Italian Sausage Calzones, 72
Waffled Hawaiian Sandwiches, 70

Seafood
Crushed Heirloom Tomato and Shrimp Bruschetta, 56
Grilled Grouper Sandwiches with Chile Mayo, 52
Havarti-Dill Tuna Melt, 58
Smoked Paprika Salmon Sliders, 55
Turkey and Strawberry Sandwiches, Hot, 88

Sauces. *See also* **Toppings**
Avgolemono Sauce, 221
Bourbon-Pecan Butter Sauce, 197
Butternut Squash Cream Sauce, 175
Cream Sauce, 212
Gruyère Cheese Sauce, 254
Mango-Mint Sauce, Fresh, 346
Milanese Sauce, Fresh, 276
Mint-Yogurt Sauce, 19
Orange Stir-Fry Sauce, 227
Puttanesca Sauce, 259
Thyme Sauce, Creamy, 297
Tomato Sauce with Penne, Fresh, 172
Tzatziki Sauce, 66

Sausage, 266
Calzones, Italian Sausage, 72
Grilled Chicken Sausages with Caraway Slaw, 91

Scallops
Crispy Curry Scallops, 200
Green Curry Scallops with Shiitakes, 202
Sesame-Crusted Scallops with Teriyaki Glaze, 205

Shellfish. *See also* **Scallops; Shrimp**
Crab Salad with Buttermilk Dressing, 104
Mussels, Risotto Milanese with, 199
Mussels with Tomato and Fennel, Steamed, 199

Shrimp. *See also under* **Salads, Seafood**
Bruschetta, Crushed Heirloom Tomato and Shrimp, 56
Fried Rice, Shrimp, 211
Gazpacho with Smoky Shrimp, 10
Gumbo, Quick Shrimp, 12
Jambalaya, Shrimp, 215

Quesadilla with Tropical Salsa, Shrimp, 206
Scampi, Shrimp, 216
Shrimp and Artichokes with Wild Rice, 212
Smoky BBQ Shrimp, 209

Soups and Stews
Baked Potato Soup, 28
Bean or Lentil
Chorizo Rice and Bean Soup, 40
Garbanzo-Carrot Soup, 16
Greek Lentil Soup with Mint-Yogurt Sauce, 19
White Bean and Lamb Soup with Gremolata, 39
Beef
Beef and Barley Soup, 34
Beer-Braised Beef Stew, 37
Easy Vegetable-Beef Soup, 33
Borscht, 15
Broccoli-Cheese Soup, 31
Chicken
Chicken Posole Chili, 44
Chicken Pot Sticker Soup, 43
Chicken Tortilla Soup, 46
Coconut Corn Chowder with Chicken, 48
Gazpacho with Smoky Shrimp, 10
Minestrone, 21
Roasted Red Bell Pepper Soup, Creamy, 25
Roasted Tomato–Basil Soup, 22
Shrimp Gumbo, Quick, 12
Vegetable Soup, Curried, 26

Spinach
Lemon-Caper Spinach, 281
Salad with Grilled Chicken, Blueberry Spinach, 129
Spanakopita, 160
Spinach-Tomato Orzo, 243

Squash. *See* **Summer Squash; Winter Squash**
Stews. *See* **Soups and Stews**
Stir-Fried Lemon Chicken, 270
Stir-Fry, Beef and Bok Choy, 227
Strawberries
Ice Cream Sandwiches, Chocolate-Covered
Strawberry, 316
Milk Shakes, Mini Strawberry, 141
Sandwiches, Hot Turkey and Strawberry, 88
Strawberries with Fresh Mango-Mint Sauce, 346
Strawberry-Meringue Desserts, 328
Tart, Fresh Strawberry, 353
Succotash, Summer, 143
Summer Squash
Grilled Summer Squash with Garlic and
Lime, 250
Pappardelle with Roasted Zucchini, Mascarpone, and
Pine Nuts, 170
Zucchini and Tomato Couscous, 188

Sweet Potatoes
Fries, Chili-Cheese Sweet Potato, 141
Fries, Two-Potato Peppered, 75
Sweet Potatoes with Brown Sugar–Cinnamon Butter, 253

Tacos with Grilled Onion, Steak Soft, 231
Tomatillo Chicken, 275
Tomatoes
Candied Balsamic Tomatoes and Mozzarella Salad, 95
Salt and Pepper Tomatoes, 103
Sauce, Fresh Milanese, 276
Sauce with Penne, Fresh Tomato, 172
Soup, Roasted Tomato–Basil, 22
Spinach-Tomato Orzo, 243
Succotash-Stuffed Tomatoes, 143
Toasts, Rustic Tomato-Garlic, 40
Toppings
Chicken with Creamy Tomato Topping, 272
Crushed Heirloom Tomato and Shrimp Topping, 56
Tomato Topping, 153
Zucchini and Tomato Couscous, 188
Tools and Gadgets, time-saving, 358-359
Toppings. *See also* **Pesto; Sauces; Tomatoes, Toppings**
Banana-Mango Chutney, Jamaican-Spiced Hanger Steak
with, 233
Black Bean Topping, 149
Caramel Drizzle, 333
Cucumber-Thyme Relish, 101
Grilled Pineapple Relish, 183
Tortilla Bowls, Sugary Lime, 344
Tortilla Strips, Spicy, 46
Tostadas, 149
Tostadas, Baja Fish, 192
Tuna, 58
Melt, Havarti-Dill Tuna, 58
Panzanella, Tuna-Pita Chip, 103
Salad, Cucumber Tuna, 58
Turkey, 300
Orange-Glazed Turkey with Cranberry Rice, 300
Salad, Turkey-Blue Cheese, 130
Salad, Turkey-Cranberry, 133
Sandwiches, Hot Turkey and Strawberry, 88

Vegetables. *See also* **specific vegetables**
Burritos, Spicy Vegetable, 144
Chicken Pasta Primavera, 287
Penne with Roasted Ratatouille, 172

Roasted Bell Peppers, Potatoes, and Onion, 228
Roll-ups, Veggie, 61
Salad, Crunchy Asian Vegetable, 249
seasonal guide, 354-357
Soup
Curried Vegetable Soup, 26
Easy Vegetable-Beef Soup, 33
Minestrone, 21
Vegetarian Main Dishes
Apple and Olive Quesadillas, 150
Asparagus and Basil Omelet, 163
Baked Ravioli with Butternut Squash Cream Sauce, 175
Chili-Cheese Sweet Potato Fries, 141
Fig and Arugula Pizzas with Goat Cheese, 156
Garlic-Mashed Potato Pizza, 153
Goat Cheese–Mushroom Naan Pizza, 154
Grilled Eggplant with Feta and Greek Couscous, 138
Lemon-Artichoke Frittata, 165
Mushroom Macaroni and Cheese, 169
Pappardelle with Roasted Zucchini, Mascarpone, and
Pine Nuts, 170
Penne with Roasted Ratatouille, 172
Roasted Beet Risotto with Walnuts and Goat Cheese, 136
Southwest Rice Frittata, 166
Spanakopita, 160
Spicy Vegetable Burritos, 144
Stromboli, 159
Succotash-Stuffed Tomatoes, 143
Tostadas, 149
Tropical Black Beans, 147

Watermelon-Limeade Sparkler, 113
Watermelon Salad, 87
Winter Squash
Baked Ravioli with Butternut Squash Cream Sauce, 175
Pumpkin-Gingersnap Bars, 315
Wraps and roll-ups. *See under* **Sandwiches**

Yogurt
Dressing, Creamy Apple, 118
Dressing, Curry-Yogurt, 120
Lassi, Mango, 202
Sauce, Greek Lentil Soup with Mint-Yogurt, 19
Sauce, Tzatziki, 66

Zucchini. *See also* **Summer squash**